THE WRITER'S COMPANION

D1365442

THE
WRITER'S
COMPANION

The essential guide to being published

BARRY TURNER

MACMILLAN

First published 1996 by Macmillan Reference Books
a division of Macmillan Publishers Limited
25 Eccleston Place, London SW1W 9NF
and Basingstoke

Associated companies throughout the world

ISBN 0 333 62133 6

Copyright © Barry Turner

The right of Barry Turner to be identified as the
author of this work has been asserted by him in accordance
with the Copyright, Designs and Patents Act 1988.

All rights reserved. No reproduction, copy or transmission
of this publication may be made without written permission.
No paragraph of this publication may be reproduced, copied
or transmitted save with written permission or in accordance
with the provisions of the Copyright Act 1956 (as amended).
Any person who does any unauthorized act in relation to
this publication may be liable to criminal prosecution
and civil claims for damages.

1 3 5 7 9 8 6 4 2

A CIP catalogue record for this book is available from
the British Library

Typeset by CentraCet Limited, Cambridge
Printed by Mackays of Chatham plc, Chatham, Kent

Contents

Contents   vii

Preface

ANYONE WHO VENTURES a book on the business of writing has to be ready to justify his presumption. What did *you* do in the media war, Daddy? Well, I've been around, that's for sure. I have worked for newspapers and publishers, edited and marketed, been a television reporter and a radio presenter. I have written books, articles and scripts. I know what it is to climb into the bestseller lists and then to fall almost immediately into the dump bin of cut-priced remainders. My ratio of being hired to being fired is around to two to one which may shock a business executive but is not bad for someone who makes a living from words.

Some years ago I ghosted the biography of the actor John Le Mesurier. He chose for his title *A Jobbing Actor.* I go for that. A jobbing writer is what I am and what I am pleased to be.

This polymorphous career is the springboard for *The Writer's Companion.* It is not simply that I have actually encountered many of the problems that beset writers; more to the point is that *The Writer's Companion* is the book I would liked to have had by my side when I was venturing into the deep end of publishing. It is one of the curiosities of this trade that while there is a surplus of advice on how to write (much of it spurious) we have very little in the way of practical guidance on how to manage our affairs. Learning by mistakes may be effective but it is also time wasting and invariably expensive. The purpose of *The Writer's Companion* is to provide a career backup of essential knowledge that will help writers to exploit their talents to best advantage. Where I am short on knowledge I have called in the relevant experts. Thus Peter Finch lifts the lid on poetry publishing and A.P. Kernon tells how to cope with the overactive tax inspector. Timothy West's hilarious and marvellously instructive spoof of a radio play, *This Gun That I Have in My Right Hand is Loaded*, is reproduced here by generous permission of the author.

Thanks also to Harlequin Mills and Boon for permission to quote extensively from their guide to writing romantic fiction, to the National Union of Journalists for extracts from *Guide to Freelancing*, to the Writers' Guild and Society of Authors for extracts from negotiated agreements with publishers and producers and to all the agents, directors and producers who took the trouble to fill in our questionnaires. Carole Blake of Blake Friedmann Literary Agency has kindly allowed me to quote her entire letter to me on the relationship between agents and authors. All the writers' associations have given unstinting support but special thanks must go to Mark Le Fanu, Kate Pool and Gareth Shannon of The Society of Authors who have responded patiently and wisely to a catalogue of abstruse questions.

Quite apart from the catholic experience mentioned earlier, inspiration has come from ten years of editing *The Writer's Handbook*. Jill Fenner, my right hand on that publication, has exercised the same muscle on *The Writer's Companion*. If, notwithstanding her skill in detecting errors and ambiguities, any imperfections remain, feel free to take it out on me.

The Writer's Companion

INTRODUCTION

WE BEGIN with the book. This may surprise the arm-wavers of communication technology. Other writers' markets must surely have a prior claim to attention. Television, for example, or radio; even computer games. The average citizen devotes eight hours a week to the printed word, while broadcasting commands twenty-two hours. Yet the book remains pre-eminent, and for a number of sound, and not so sound, reasons.

The first inclination of anyone who has ideas to express is to write a book. A newspaper article has an impact on a wide readership for a day; a broadcast has the same limitation. People keep books, re-read them and refer back to them. Librarians fall over themselves to find a particular title. Books outlive their authors.

You can get more into a book, in length and depth, than into any rival medium. Of course, a CD-ROM encompasses vastly more than any single book and it is undoubtedly handy to be able to store the complete twentieth-century poetry or the entire works of Jane Austen on a small disk, but these are still books we are talking about, albeit in another format. Has anyone heard of a CD-ROM of *original* poetry? Maybe it will come but not for a long time yet.

When, recently, a forward rider of the superhighway gave his vision of where the communications revolution is leading us, he chose to do it in a book. The irony was not lost on Nicholas Negroponte, who went to great lengths to rationalize why he had decided to put over his futuristic theses in old-fashioned print. He gave three reasons:

First, there are just not enough digital media in the hands of executives, politicians, parents, and all those who most need to understand this radically new culture. Even where computers are omnipresent, the current interface is primitive – clumsy at best . . . A second reason is my monthly column in *Wired* magazine. The rapid and astonishing success of *Wired* has shown that there is a large audience for information (in print) about digital life-styles and people, not just theory and equipment . . .

The third is a more personal, slightly ascetic reason. Interactive multimedia leave very little to the imagination. Like a Hollywood film, multimedia narrative includes such specific representations that less and less is left to the mind's eye. By contrast, the written word sparks images and evokes metaphors that get much of their meaning from the reader's imagination and experiences. When you read a novel, much of the colour, sound and motion come from you. I think the same kind of personal extension is needed to feel and understand what 'being digital' might mean to your life.

In other words, the humble book is more interactive than the most advanced piece of interactive technology.

The book, to use a current marketing term, is user friendly. As the novelist Nicholson Baker has observed, 'We've come up with a beautifully browsable invention that needs no electricity and exists in a readable form no matter what happens.' Try curling up with a computer. Try reading a computer screen on a long plane journey. One of the more significant facts of modern book selling is the concentration of activity at airports. 'What,' asks Nikki Gerrard, 'are planes but flying reading-rooms?'

Television and cinema pay deference to the book. A producer with a big budget and not much idea how to spend it goes first to the bestseller lists. The peak-time schedules groan under the weight of mini and major drama series inspired by famous authors. Hollywood's highest paid originators of screen stories are the novelists John Grisham and Michael Crichton. The way a producer's mind works, if a book proves to be popular then it is some way to a guarantee that a movie or television series will also find a market. Short of a film of the book he may commission an original screenplay but he will be more nervous as a result. And if the gamble comes off? Why, he will publish a book of the film. It is a badge of respectability they all seek.

Television's subservience to print extends beyond the book to all forms of reading matter. It is rare for current affairs producers to be credited with scoops. They are more inclined to set their agendas by what appears in the newspapers. One of the longest-running programmes on television is *What the Papers Say*. It is hard to imagine an equivalent print feature, *What Television Says*.

Theatre might be thought an exception to the argument. But plays are books. Well into this century plays were invariably published as books to be read before they were performed. Even now, there are playwrights of the stature of John Osborne and Arnold Wesker whose plays probably earn more from print than from performance fees.

The problem with books is that the prestige attaching to them is liable to strain their intellectual pretensions. Would-be literary novelists take note. To be part of an ancient and honourable tradition is not in itself a guarantee of interest and originality. Much of contemporary fiction is tedious and uninspired, a release for the writer who is only too happy to pour out his life (how we like talking about ourselves) but a burden, and an increasingly expensive one at that, for the reader who has more than enough problems of his own without buying someone else's to study on the journey home.

As the critic Roger Lewis observes, 'There are just too many books about ex-college pals meeting up to be miserable; too many whimsies about Irish girls or summers in Tuscan villas.' D.J. Taylor extends the hit list to 'books about bourgeois childhoods, divorce in NW3, about women in Conran dresses fretting over adultery, about – God Save Us All – literary London'.

That these incestuous pursuits receive more attention than they deserve is largely the fault of literary editors who flatter the authors with encouraging reviews. They do this out of kindness of heart. Or because they all went to the same university. Or because they are liable to meet face to face at the next state-of-the-novel seminar. But everyone knows, except possibly the authors themselves, that the market for literary novels is fading fast.

In a recent *Times* article, literary critic Derwent May let the cat out of the bag. 'All reviewers,' he wrote, 'will tell you that apart from a few very good novels and the downmarket rubbish, most of the books they get are well written, with good characterisation and plot and so on and they feel obliged to praise them. But they would never dream of recommending their friends to read them.'

'These,' he adds, 'are the novels that will vanish.'

The trend shows up on every publisher's balance sheet. Libraries are buying less. At the beginning of the decade, libraries subscribed to 45 per cent of all first novels and 30 per cent of all literary fiction. No longer. The squeeze on budgets has led to a severe cutback on what are clearly seen to be, by the number of borrowings, the least popular books. With the disappearance of a base sale, publishers are trying to protect margins by cutting print runs and putting up prices. This is causing a fall in bookshop sales. And so the spiral accelerates with ever smaller print runs chasing ever fewer customers. Eventually, only hard-core buyers, probably other literary novelists, will sustain what is left of the market.

Meanwhile, the rest of the publishing industry is enjoying varying degrees of prosperity. The total market in Britain is worth around £2.3 billion, the world's fourth largest after the USA, Japan and Germany. But in number of titles in relation to population, Britain is way ahead with an annual output of 80,000 plus. Even allowing for specialist products with a restricted sale – training manuals, for example, or obscure reference – the figure is mightily impressive.

Holding to fiction for a moment, the demand for thrillers and romance is enduring, though social and political changes can alter the framework of the market. One has only to think of the decline of the spy story and the near disappearance of some Cold War writers who were big names a few years ago. On the way down they will have noticed, with varying degrees of empathy, the corresponding rise of gay and lesbian novelists, who now occupy whole shelves of prime buying space.

Taking account of every new fiction title, the total represents about 10 per cent of publishing output. The rest is non-fiction, with science, travel, biography, sport, hobbies and reference among the categories which regularly feature in the bestseller list. Children's books do well, not least because the publishers are promoting their wares beyond the conventional bookshops into the supermarkets, where they sell up to two-thirds of their output.

One of the curiosities of non-fiction, and a possible reason why its contribution to the publishing economy is underplayed, is that until the NCR Prize (now the AT & T Non-fiction Award) was inaugurated in 1988, there was not a single major award for non-fiction. Even publishers, but especially those of the old school, are liable to forget that it is non-fiction that keeps a large part of the industry going. Writing in the *Guardian*, Robert McCrum, literary editor of Faber, extols the book as the agent of civilized behaviour.

> . . . in an instant and often highly public culture, the book stands for a mode of thought and behaviour that is deliberative, ruminative and private. A book offers an avenue into a shared past as well as a gateway into a personal future. A book can define who we are to ourselves, and to others.

This over-the-top and faraway philosophy clearly relates to the literary novel, a subject close to McCrum's publishing interests. None the less, it is puzzling that he should have concluded his ruminations with the general message (spelled out in bold), THERE IS NO MONEY IN BOOKS. Back comes the response from his peers. OH YES THERE IS.

A few days after the McCrum article appeared, there was a news story of a retired teacher who died leaving an estate valued at over £1 million. How had he managed to acquire so much? 'He wrote a lot of English text books for schools,' explained his daughter.

Enough said.

The Nuts and Bolts of Authorship
A BEGINNER'S GUIDE

BEING HONEST WITH YOURSELF can save time. What is your book trying to achieve? What is its market? Can we agree that enough people will want to possess this volume – to the tune of £15 or so a time? It is a grievous mistake to bash out 80,000 words in the expectation that a publisher will be unable to resist such obvious dedication and effort. He will only too easily, with a printed rejection slip which comes with a government health warning against self-induced depression and despair.

The fact is that too many weighty manuscripts are sent to publishers who have neither the energy nor the optimism to wade through reams of what just might turn out to be the blockbuster of the century but more probably will not. A synopsis and a sample chapter are all that is needed for a publisher to make a judgement. Preparation is critical. It is possible for a bad book to follow a good synopsis but it is rare for a good book to follow a poor synopsis. The publisher knows this better than anyone.

The synopsis should begin with a line or two of justification. The marketing guys have a way of fastening on to what they like to call a book's unique selling points, or lack of them. It is best to get in early with a memorable by-line – 'The first biography of a leading Arctic explorer based on hitherto unpublished letters and diaries'. It is not enough to claim that a book will appeal to the general reader. Every author likes to think that he is reaching out to the mass audience but in reality each book has a core appeal on which the sales potential will be judged.

To stay with the example of the Arctic explorer, it could be that the name of the subject and the scale of his achievements are such as to command universal appeal. But if the spirit of adventure is blunted by technical proficiency — with diagrams and tables to support a story of scientific dedication — then a rather more specialist readership can be predicted.

Once an author has settled on a snappy justification, the synopsis can be used to describe the book in some detail. It is impossible to specify length — where a single page may suffice for a beginner's guide to beekeeping, a closely argued case for energy conservation might require several thousand words. An idea for a novel has sparked interest on the strength of one paragraph. What is essential is for the synopsis to be a clear and logical description of the book.

It should end with a few pertinent details. What is the intended size of the book? This has an important bearing on production costs and thus on the sales forecast. The best estimate of size is the number of words, with the average book falling within the 70,000–90,000 bracket.

Will there be illustrations? If so, what sort? Library pictures must be paid for, and can be very expensive. Commissioned drawings raise the question of the role and standing of the illustrator in the origination of the book.

What about an index? All too often a non-fiction writer who is new to the game will be so overwhelmed by the prospect of seeing his name in large type, that he will brush aside such petty-fogging questions. Any literate can throw together an index. Wrong. Indexing is a highly professional task and the quality of an index can make or break a reputation for creating what publishers are pleased to call 'user-friendly' books. Douglas Mathews, one-time librarian of the London Library and a professional indexer of long standing, holds that the author is the best person to compile an index. 'But it is understandable that by the time a book is finished an author may well be weary of it and prefer to call for an outside indexer to play midwife.'

When will the manuscript be delivered? Publishers are rightly suspicious of authors who think that it takes five years to create a saleable product. The trouble is that five years can so easily become seven years, which is to move out of range of any feasible sales forecast. Fashion changes, often with bewildering speed. A hot seller next year (linking in to an anniversary, for example, or a current political interest) could easily become a candidate for the remainder shelves if publication is delayed even by a few months. What the publisher needs is a volume that he can put on to the market within two years at most. Allowing for the time it takes to print and promote a book (a minimum of six months), he is looking to an ideal delivery date of a year to eighteen months ahead.

Submissions – synopsis, sample chapter and a covering letter pointing up writing experience and relevant specialist knowledge – should be typewritten (with double spacing for the manuscript) and free of messy corrections. Publishers, being human, are liable to be put off by a grubby piece of manuscript patched together with sellotape. How many others have seen and rejected this sad little offering? But there is no need to go mad on presentation. There are self-styled writing experts who seem to suggest that flashy appearances can help to compensate for literary deficiencies. They are wrong. John Diamond makes the point in a *Spectator* article on the perils of freelancing. Everything he says about unsolicited newspaper features applies equally to book proposals.

I could always spot a correspondence writing school graduate's efforts. It always came with a brisk letter which begged the 'favour of consideration'. It would be Amstrad word-processed and a paragraph would never be allowed to turn a page. At the bottom of each folio would be the word *More* – very professional that – and at the end of the last was the hopefully arrogant annotation 'First British Rights only © Trelawney O'Wells 1990'. Like a school project book whose author hopes that fancy presentation will serve as a decoy from lousy contents, the whole would be fronted – the biggest giveaway of all – by a cover sheet, blank, save for an improbably alliterative title like 'Cats, Craters and Catamites'.

Don't overdo it!

The priority now is to decide on the lucky recipients of your book proposal. The tendency is to go for one of the big publishing houses – Random Century, HarperCollins, Hodder Headline, Macmillan – who together account for some 20 per cent of the titles that appear in the bookshops. But the risk is of disappearing into the mass of unsolicited material that jams the postal system of every large company. Editors refer disparagingly to the 'slush pile', the manuscripts waiting to be read and which may, just may, in the fullness of time, be given a cursory glance before being returned to sender with a less than sensitive rejection slip.

The fact is that the leading houses are none too interested in promoting untried talent. Do not be misled by occasional front-page stories of first-time authors landing million-pound contracts. It can happen. Anything can happen. But the odds on emerging triumphantly from the slush pile are very long indeed. Editors are far too preoccupied commissioning work from their existing authors – particularly the star names – or setting up projects which have long-running appeal, like a series on a particular theme. Without reliable advance knowledge, outsiders are not likely to come up with ideas that slot neatly into the marketing plan. Of course, the big publishers do have their second- and third-rank list of authors, those who are being groomed for stardom. But mostly they have come from agents or other contacts who have a direct line to editorial decision-makers.

All this may seem desperately unfair – even commercially myopic – but it has to be said that publishers have to find some way of coping with the huge quantity of material that turns up for consideration. Faced with the choice of reading the latest submission from a tried and trusted author or his agent or delving into the slush pile on the odd chance of finding a publishable manuscript, what would you, as a hard-pressed editor, decide to do?

Looked at from the point of view of the newcomer, the challenge is to avoid association with the no-hopers. There are ways of doing this, one of which is to skip the conglomerates altogether and instead make a pitch to a smaller company, ideally one that has a track record in publishing related books. Small in this context means an annual turnover of £1 million plus (by way of comparison, HarperCollins brings in over £200 million a year). A publisher in, say, the £1–5 million bracket will invariably be based outside London and may well be run as a family firm – a husband and wife partnership, perhaps, with five or six back-up staff. There are authors who worry that this type of operation is, by definition, weak at marketing. Where is the army of reps visiting the bookshops? What happens to overseas sales? But those in the second league of publishers can easily overcome any marketing disabilities by agency deals for sales at home or abroad, and by linking in to a modern computerized distribution service. Conversely, the strength of the small publisher is in offering authors a personal service – knowing them always by name rather than by book title.

There is another category of publisher – smaller than small. Around 6000 small presses operate in the UK – the beneficiaries of high-tech desktop printing which requires modest capital and a spare room at the back of the house to get started. Many are well-managed businesses with clever and imaginative editors. They do not pay out very much; they cannot possibly afford big advances, but they do offer unrivalled opportunities to get into print – the first vital step for an author who wants to be taken seriously. The problem at this level is that publishing attracts more than its fair share of charlatans, mavericks and entrepreneurs of easy virtue who would not know an honest royalty statement if it came to them in a gift-wrapped package. The dozy-headed idealist who believes that we should all be writing for the glory of a particular cause is every bit as dangerous as the con artist who persuades the author to join him in a two-way profit share deal which inevitably turns out to be a one-way loss. Clearly, great care needs to be taken in deciding which publisher to approach. The best test of the honesty – and competence – of any publisher is to talk to his existing authors. Are they happy in their relationship? Do they feel that they are treated fairly? Are they satisfied with the editorial and marketing skills on offer?

Once a book proposal has been sent off, allow at least a month even for an acknowledgement and up to three months for a considered reply.

Don't be impatient. Writers are often sinned against but they can be unreasonable in their assumption of a quick decision on what, after all, is a risky investment. If, after a decent interval, nothing is heard, a telephone call is justified. But a polite inquiry is more likely to get results than a demand to know 'what the hell is going on'. It helps to have sent material to a named editor. That way you avoid the risk of being sucked into the whirlpool of internal company communications.

There is no harm in canvassing several publishers at the same time. And there is no need to make a secret of so doing. A little friendly competition may help to stimulate interest.

And so to the next leap forward. Assume that a book proposal has sparked a response from a publisher – for the sake of argument, a middle of the range publisher with a respectable list of satisfied authors and a good name in the trade. (It is curious how few publishers are known to the general public, despite expensive efforts to achieve uniform designs and easily recognizable logos. Penguin is a rarity in that customers go for the imprint as much as for individual authors.)

It is at the point where a publisher shows interest that the unpractised author can fall into the error of assuming that he can now relax. It can never be.

The trouble is that every writer has an infinite capacity for self-delusion. The lonely occupant of a small back room, he likes to think that somewhere out there is a sympathetic counsellor and friend. In theory, the publisher is ideally suited to the role – he knows the problems, understands the pressures and, after all, he is the one who has to make the book work. But publishing is like any other business. The purpose is to make money. There are some well-publicized practitioners of the art who claim that their minds are on higher things, but I can't help noticing that those who shout loudest about the glories of literature and the evils of materialism end up with the biggest houses and the smartest cars. This is not to say they are dishonest. It is simply that in abiding by the first rule of elementary capitalism, they are out to maximize their profits.

Proceed, then, with caution.

For all but well-established authors the best that can be hoped for at this stage is an agreement in principle. The publisher may call for amendments to the proposal – more or fewer words or illustrations, a change of emphasis to help sharpen an argument or clarify an aspect of a plot. The timetable is bound to come up for discussion. Is it realistic? Can the author really turn out 80,000 words in two years? What other work does he have in hand?

If the outcome of the first meeting is encouraging, the next discussion should focus on the size of the advance. Any author who wants to make a living by writing must establish early on that his publisher is prepared to make a down payment on account of royalties. The bigger the advance the more likely the publisher will be to put his back into the marketing effort. Even if he winds up hating the book, he will want to earn his money back by pushing sales.

Overall, advances are well down on previous years. The recession made publishers cautious while the recovery is still too patchy for the accountants' liking. A first-time novelist is lucky to get more than £1000, while educational and academic writers may settle for a few hundred. A reasonable advance for all but the top names is a sum equivalent to 60 per cent of the estimated royalties payable on the first edition. The advance should be non-returnable, except when the author fails to deliver a manuscript. Usually, it is split three ways, part on signature of contract, part on delivery of the manuscript, and part on publication.

A popular misconception is that if an advance is not recovered by royalties on sales, in other words if there is an unearned advance, the publisher is bound to lose money. But the correlation between royalties and profit is not precise. A typical royalty is 10 per cent of the sale price of the book; a publisher's margin may be 15 or 20 per cent after overheads and trade discount are taken into account. It is possible, therefore, for an unearned advance to be absorbed into costs with the publisher still coming out at a profit. It all depends on the size of the advance, the level of sales and the publisher's margin over fixed costs. There are too many variables to produce a general rule. Just do not be too quick to assume that the publisher loses out.

Another unsafe assumption is that advances are bound to be higher if negotiated by an agent. This may be so for best-selling authors who put their work up for auction (though Jeffrey Archer is one of several who does his own bargaining) but down the scale there may not be too much room for manoeuvre. Where an agent really proves his worth is in knowing the pitfalls of a publishing contract and helping his client to avoid them.

The good agent understands the small print and, to greater advantage, spots the omissions – such as the failure to allow for higher royalties beyond a certain minimum sale. The agented author has a say on book-club deals, promotion budgets, cover design, the timing of publication, print number and on subsidiary rights – the latter capable of attracting earnings long after the book is out of print. The sheer range of potential subsidiary rights is mind-boggling – overseas publication (the publisher will try for world rights but when an agent is acting, US and translation rights are nearly always reserved to the ultimate benefit of the author), film and television adaptations, audio cassettes, video, information retrieval – to mention only the most obvious. Above all, the good agent keeps a watching brief long after the contract has been signed, always ready to challenge the publisher to do better on behalf of his author.

But where is the efficient and sympathetic agent to be found? There is more on this in Chapter 24 but for the moment, suffice to say, there is no sure way of matching a writer and agent merely by glancing through the list of names and addresses. The headline-makers exercise the heaviest clout but the most powerful agencies are not necessarily suitable for a beginner, who may feel the need for the close personal contact offered by a smaller agency. On the other hand, the smaller agency may already have taken on its full quota of newcomers. Those who are struggling for a toehold in publishing are by definition low earners who must, for a time, be subsidized by the more profitable sector of a client list. The agent who gets the balance wrong is heading for bankruptcy.

There are authors who, preferring to remain unagented, show a creditable talent for wheeler-dealing. Others – the misguided or the hopelessly optimistic – enter complex publishing agreements without so much as a glance at the small print. The chief victims seem to be in the areas of academic, professional and educational publishing, where contracts tend to be one-sided agreements.

Heed the words of Mark Le Fanu of the Society of Authors.

> Most of the contracts that we see from these publishers – at least the initial offers made to members – are shamefully bad. A significant number of contracts seek an assignment of copyright, the freedom to alter text, and the right to reject material without giving reasons. Most give no firm indication as to when the book will be published (having demanded delivery of the typescript by a certain date), offer minimal advances even for the biggest projects, and pay royalties based on the publisher's receipts.

How can an author be sure that a contract is fair and above board? Horrors can evade the closest examination by an unpractised eye.

The writer who handles his own affairs is not entirely alone. After years of vigorous campaigning, the writers' unions have negotiated a Minimum Terms Agreement (MTA) with several leading publishers including BBC Books, Bloomsbury, Century Hutchinson, André Deutsch, Faber, HarperCollins, Hodder Headline and Penguin.

A copy of the MTA, which can be obtained from either the Society of Authors or the Writers' Guild (free of charge to members who send a stamped, addressed envelope), is a useful standard against which to judge a publisher's offer. When it comes to signing on the dotted line, you may feel you have had to give way on a few points, but if the general principles of the MTA are followed, the chances of securing a reasonable deal are much enhanced.

Whatever else you concede, do not give way on the delivery date. Agree only to a duration of work that is within your scope. It is so easy to submit to a publisher's plea to shave off a few weeks here and there only to find that keeping to an over-tight schedule can bring on a nervous breakdown.

Also, contracts often require the author to submit two copies of the typescript. However, publishers will usually agree to one copy, a saving if the author does not have word-processing equipment. It should also be possible to negotiate a fee if the author supplies the material on disk, marked up for the typesetter.

Probably the most important break from tradition contained in the MTA is the clause allowing for the length of licence granted by the author to the publisher to be negotiable. The custom is for the licence to run for the duration of copyright (i.e. the author's lifetime plus fifty years). (See Chapter 25) The writers' unions have pressed for a twenty-year licence and some publishers have agreed to this but an acceptable compromise is a review procedure which permits the contract to be revised every ten years. This gives the author the opportunity to claim, for example, improved royalties if the book has been a success.

Other basic principles covered by the MTA include:

➡ *Accounting.* Once the advance has been earned, a publisher must immediately pay over to the author income from the sale of subsidiary rights.

➡ *Indexing.* The cost of indexing should not fall entirely on the author. At the very least, the cost should be shared equally with the publisher.

→ *Free Copies.* The author should receive twelve free copies of a hardback and twenty free copies of a paperback with the option of buying further copies at a 45 per cent or 50 per cent discount.

→ *Print run.* The author is entitled to know the size of print runs.

→ *Proofs.* The author is required to read, correct and return proofs within a specified time, usually fourteen days. Corrections have to be paid for and it is often the case that an author has to bear a share of the cost of late amendments. The best advice is: having made a decision, stick to it.

→ *Reversion of Rights.* As well as the author being able to recover rights after a book goes out of print (when fewer than fifty copies of the hardback or 150 copies of the paperback remain in stock), the author may also pull out of the contract if sales fall below certain figures. This gives the author the opportunity to leave a publisher if a book is not being properly marketed.

The MTA offers some valuable guarantees on author involvement in the publication of their books. For example:

The contract should specify the length of the typescript, the number and type of illustrations, and so on. Clarification at the outset can prevent misunderstanding and dispute at a later stage.

Before signing the contract there should be full discussion on the availability of illustrations, the costs involved, and who is to pay for them. Normally, the publishers will make a substantial contribution and if illustrations have to be specially prepared, as for art books and some children's books, the normal arrangement is for the publisher to foot the entire bill.

There must be full consultation on the placing of illustrations, the jacket design, blurb, catalogue copy, the distribution of review copies, and publication date.

ROYALTIES

An author's earnings from a book comes from royalties, his share of the sale price as determined by the publisher. The standard hardback royalty scale is 10 per cent on the first 2500 copies, 12½ per cent on the next 2500 copies and 15 per cent thereafter. On certain small reprints the royalty may revert to 10 per cent.

On home (mass-market) paperback sales, the minimum royalty should be 7½ per cent of the published price, rising to 10 per cent after 30,000 copies.

Greater flexibility in the paying of royalties is almost certain to follow the abandonment of the Net Book Agreement – retail price maintenance by another name. If an author's work is heavily discounted in the shop, is he entitled to a royalty on the original recommended price or on the marked down price determined by the retailer? There is no set answer. Much depends on the author's negotiating muscle.

Overseas Royalties

Here again, generalizations can be misleading – there are so many different ways in which publishers handle export sales. But as a rule of thumb, if the royalty is calculated on net receipts (when the publisher has sold in bulk at a special price), the percentages should not be less than the home royalty percentages. If the royalty is calculated on the British published price, it should be not less than half the home royalty. Whatever the basis, a rising scale is usually adopted.

Translation Rights

These rights should never be underplayed. They can sometimes produce a large proportion of the income from a book. If the author uses an agent, the agent will almost certainly exclude translation rights from the publishing contract and market them himself. If no agent is involved, the publisher is probably in a better position than the author to market the rights effectively. The publisher's percentage of the proceeds should not normally exceed 20 per cent, any sub-agents' commission being paid out of this share.

US Editions

More complications arise. All depends on how the publisher deals with this potentially most lucrative of markets. If the publisher has a subsidiary or parent company in the US, the royalty percentages should be much the same as those for home sales. But the calculation may be based on the US published price.

When an American publisher is licensed to produce a separate edition, normal US royalties should be paid. The MTA recommends that an author should receive 85 per cent of these.

A third and, for the author, the least attractive option, is for the UK publisher to sell unbound copies to an American distributor. Since the deal rarely covers more than the manufacturing cost, there is not much leeway for a payment to the author. The time to sort this out is when the contract is negotiated.

Subsidiary Rights

By way of an example, the author should get 90 per cent from the first serial rights, TV and radio dramatizations, and film and dramatic rights. Other percentages to the author include: anthology and quotation rights, not less than 50 per cent; TV and radio readings, 75 per cent; merchandising, 80 per cent; sound and video recording rights, not less than 75 per cent.

Bear in mind that the royalty percentages noted here do not necessarily apply to all books. For example, heavily illustrated books are excluded and there are occasions when publishers pay lower royalties on such as long works of fiction published in short print runs for libraries.

Book Clubs

If a publisher sells copies to a book club for an all-in price (a 'royalty inclusive' deal), the author should receive at least 10 per cent of the publisher's receipts. But on a royalty exclusive deal, when royalties are paid on sales, the author should receive at least 50 per cent of the royalties paid by the book club. The MTA suggested split is 60:40.

WARRANTY AND INDEMNIFICATION

The author is usually expected to indemnify the publisher against the risks of libel and infringement of copyright. It is important to watch the wording of the contract.

Example:
The Author hereby warrants to the Publishers that the said work is in no way whatever an infringement of any existing copyright and that it contains nothing libellous and the Author will indemnify the

Publishers against loss, injury or damage (including any legal costs or expenses properly incurred) occasioned to the Publishers in consequence of any breach by the Author (unknown to the Publishers) of this warranty.

The inclusion of the phrase 'unknown to the Publishers' could be important. The Society of Authors argues that if the publishers know that the book contains prima facie libellous passages, they cannot expect the author to indemnify them if successful libel proceedings are brought. (See Chapter 26) There is a growing tendency among publishers to demand that this clause should also cover obscenity, and to give themselves the right to alter the text to remove any material which they or their lawyers think might be actionable. A useful countermove is for the author to insist that, should the publishers so alter his work, the final text will be subject to his approval.

CHEAP EDITIONS AND REMAINDERS

There should be no cheap edition at less than two-thirds of the original price, remainder sales or destruction of stock within at least one year (and preferably two) of first publication without an author's written consent. The publisher should give the author first refusal on purchasing remainder stock and pay him 10 per cent of the net receipts. If surplus copies are to be pulped, the author should be offered the chance to obtain free copies within twenty-eight days of the notification.

ELECTRONIC EDITIONS AND AUDIO OR VIDEO CASSETTES

The right to publish in electronic form (as a database or CD) or as an audio or video cassette should be listed separately. Royalties and other terms must be agreed with the author.

ACCOUNTS

Whether the contract provides for royalty statements to be sent to the author twice yearly or only once – twice is usual (except with academic and educational publishers, shame on them) and should certainly apply for the first two years from publication – the monies due should be paid within three months of the date to which accounts are made up. Once the advance has been earned, money from 'sub-licences' over, say, £100, should be paid over to the author on receipt. In fact, publishers will normally do this on request, even if the contract does not specifically require it.

Example:

(a) The Publishers shall make up accounts at 30 June and 31 December and shall render such accounts and pay all monies due to the Author by the succeeding 1 October and 1 April, respectively.

(b) Any sum of £100 or more due to the Author in respect of sub-licensed rights shall be paid to the Author within one month of receipt if the advance has been earned.

(c) Each statement of account shall report the number of copies printed, the number of free copies distributed, the number of copies sold during the previous accounting period, the total sales to date, the list price, the royalty rate, the amount of royalties, the number of returned copies, the gross amount received pursuant to each licence granted by the Publishers, and itemized deductions. Each statement of account shall be accompanied by copies of statements received from sub-licensees.

(d) The Author or his authorized representative shall have the right upon written request to examine the Publishers' books of account in so far as they relate to the work, which examination shall be at the cost of the Author unless errors exceeding £50 shall be found to his disadvantage, in which case the costs shall be paid by the Publishers.

Authors who are registered for VAT should inform the publishers of their VAT registration number on signature of the contract.

If provision is made for the publishers to 'make a reserve against returns' (i.e. hold back a percentage of the royalties due to an author in anticipation of unsold copies of the work being returned by booksellers), the reserve should be limited to not more that 10–15 per cent of the royalties on the hardback edition, or 20–25 per cent of the paperback royalties. The publishers should only be entitled to withhold any reserve at the first accounting date following publication or reissue of the work and the balance should be repaid to the author not more than twelve months later.

COMPETING WORKS

It is only reasonable that an author should be deterred from publishing with another firm a book which is virtually an abridged or expanded version of the work covered by the contract. The difficulty is in choosing a form of words that leaves the author – particularly the specialist author – free to publish other books on his particular subject.

> *Example:*
> The Author shall not prepare any work which may be an expansion or an abridgement or of a nature similar to the said work published in such a style and at such a price as to be likely to affect prejudicially the sales of the said work.

It is often wise to exchange letters setting out the interpretation of any clause relating to competing works.

ASSIGNMENT OF CONTRACT

It is advisable to have in writing that the publishers shall not assign the rights granted to them in the contract or the benefit of the contract without the author's written consent.

AND FINALLY . . .

As a spot check on the acceptability of a contract, confirm five essential points before signature.

First, there should be an unconditional commitment to publish the book within a specified time – say, twelve months from delivery of the typescript or, if the typescript is already with the publisher, from signature of the agreement. It is also as well for the approximate published price to be noted.

The obligation to publish should not be subject to approval or acceptance of the manuscript. Otherwise what looks like a firm contract may be little more than an unenforceable declaration of intent to publish. It is equally important to watch that the words 'approval' or 'acceptance' do not appear in the clause relating to the advance payment. For example, if the advance, or part of it, is payable 'on delivery and approval' of the script, this might qualify the publisher's obligation to publish the work.

This point about the publisher's commitment to publishing a book is of vital importance, particularly since publishers' editors change jobs with increasing frequency. An author who has started a book with enthusiastic support from his editor may, when he delivers it, find he is in the hands of someone with quite different tastes and ideas. The publisher should have satisfied themselves at the outset that the author is capable of writing the required book – if necessary by seeing and approving a full synopsis and sample chapter. Provided the book, when delivered, follows the length and outline agreed, the publishers should be under a contractual obligation to publish it, subject, possibly, to reasonable and specified changes to the typescript.

Second, there should be a proper termination clause. This should operate if the publisher breaks the contract or if the book goes out of print.

When rights revert to the author it should be without prejudice to any claims for monies due. Occasionally, a termination clause is made dependent on the author refunding any unearned advance or on fulfilling some other obligation. Any such proviso should be struck out.

Third, the contract should not contain any unreasonable restrictions on future work. If an option clause is unavoidable it should be limited to one book on terms to be mutually agreed (not 'on the same terms') and enforceable only within a specified time limit – say, six weeks after delivery of a novel, or of submission of a synopsis and specimen chapter in the case of non-fiction.

Next, get it in writing. A recent article in the *Author* says it all:

> Your editor may be wonderful. Your faith in human nature may be undented. It may seem pedantic, pushy, bossy. But if you ever agree something important with a publisher which is not in your contract – be it regarding deadlines, amendments, publicity or, especially, money

– follow up the meeting or conversation with a friendly letter, confirming the salient points. If things go wrong and all you have is the memory of an airy promise on the telephone that the publisher has since 'forgotten', you will be in a much stronger position if you can produce a copy of a letter as evidence of that promise.

Finally, the author should not be expected to contribute towards the cost of publication. Every writers' organization warns against subsidized or vanity publishing. (Self-publishing is another matter; see Chapter 11) It is expensive (some vanity publishers charge up to £8000 for a modest print run), the quality of production is often inferior to that offered by conventional publishers, and the promises of vigorous marketing and impressive sales are rarely borne out by experience.

SETTLING DISPUTES

With the best will in the world – not to mention the best advice – disputes between author and publisher do occur. Generally problems arise from misunderstandings which can be settled amicably over a large drink with, maybe, the agent acting as go-between.

When the issue is serious – the flouting by one side or the other of a central clause in the contract, for example – it may be necessary to bring in the lawyers. But this can be a costly business in which success as much as failure can lead to a hefty bill.

For claims under £1000, there is the cheap and cheerful option of going to the Small Claims Court where it is not even necessary to hire a solicitor. Most cases heard in the Small Claims Court (really an offshoot of the County Court) are disputes between parties to a contract, claims for compensation for defective goods or for the return of property such as manuscripts or illustrations, the recovery of debts and claims for damages caused by negligence.

Say there is an outstanding debt, such as a stray royalty cheque. The routine is to write to the miscreant warning him that you will go to the court if the money is not paid in a specified time. The letter should set out your complaint in some detail, giving references to all relevant invoices and correspondence. Do not even hint that you are ready to settle for a sum less than you are claiming. If this is so, leave it until later.

If the deadline passes without a satisfactory result, the next step is submit to the court a 'request for summons'. This can be done on a standard form available from the court. A copy will be sent to the defendant telling him what he has to do. You also need to set out the 'particulars of claim' (another standard form), sending off two copies with a covering letter asking for proceedings to be served on the defendant and a self-addressed envelope which the court will use to notify you of the day of reckoning. A modest fee is payable at this stage.

Once the defendant receives the summons he has fourteen days to do one of four things. He can ignore the summons and have judgement entered against him. He can admit the claim and pay the money into court or offer a compromise such as payment by instalments. He can admit part liability, which puts the onus on you, the plaintiff, to accept or reject. Or he can contest the claim. If the latter, there follows a pre-trial review, a private discussion between the registrar and the warring parties as to how the action is to be dealt with. Often settlement is reached without further ado, the registrar acting as arbitrator, possibly hinting, ever so gently, that to go further is a waste of everyone's time. If the case does continue, the registrar will hear the arguments of both sides and come to his decision.

Witnesses can come to court and in specialist areas expert evidence may be called. The risk here is that fees and expenses may outweigh the value of the claim, although in the event of a successful conclusion, the defendant may have to meet your costs, including court fees.

An alternative for authors in dispute with their publishers is to refer to the arbitration process offered by the Publishers' Association (PA). The first essential is that both parties must agree to arbitration. They can then refer to the PA for an Informed Disputes Settlement, which binds them to the decision of an impartial referee selected by the Association. A statement of case must be drawn up by each party and all necessary documentation sent to the referee. As part of the judgement, the referee decides which party shall bear part or all costs: referee's fees and expenses and a modest fee to the PA.

Going for Bust

THE ART OF THE BESTSELLER

WRITERS ARE FOR EVER being told what to write, usually by people who find it hard to string together a dozen words to make a coherent sentence. Take Publisher A. Urged on by his accountants, he decides to cut the dead wood from his list. Out go all those dodgy titles, like first novels, that sell just a few hundred copies. From here on, Publisher A wants bestsellers, and nothing but.

His marketing team think they know what the public will buy, at least in broad terms. They have all browsed at the airport bookshops. These are far better indicators of literary stardom than the bestseller lists published in the Sunday papers. Two per cent of all books sold in Britain are sold at Heathrow and Gatwick. For general fiction, the proportion is higher, probably closer to 5 per cent. Ranging across the shelves in an airport shopping arena shows that what the typical punter really wants is a thick novel with a sufficient number of words to sustain a transatlantic flight (around 150,000 words should do it), larger than life characters in exotic locations engaging in plenty of action spiced with sex, intrigue, corruption, treachery, betrayal and sex. A mega-bestseller has, in addition, an eye-catching cover and a memorable title. And that is the recipe handed on to Publisher A. All he needs now is a writer.

It is at this point that the marketing plan begins to fall apart. Few writers can write to order and those who do invariably fail to live up to their publisher's expectations. There are writers who turn out the same type of book, with minor variations in plot and setting, time and time again, to profitable acclaim from all their fans – Jilly Cooper and Barbara Taylor Bradford spring to mind – but wherever these authors started you can be sure it was not with a publisher's blueprint in front of them. Like others in the trade they write what they want to write. It is too easy for a publisher to say, why don't we find another in the same mould, but no one can know who that will be until the novice appears in print and the public gives its verdict.

This is precisely the risk that Publisher A is seeking to avoid – he has too many on his list who turned out not to be another Jilly Cooper or Barbara Taylor Bradford to feel comfortable with the suck-it-and-see formula. Instead, he calls in the money men to back him in poaching best-selling authors from other publishers. Hence, the multi-million-pound, multi-book deals that are the gossip of literary gatherings.

The policy of buying in talent can pay dividends, though it is argued that frenzied competition has pushed up the price of some famous authors beyond their true market value. There is the related risk of paying too dearly for a talent that is past its best. It is here that a good editor proves his worth. Several well-known authors are known to trade heavily on the rewriting skills of their editors to make the proverbial silk purse. Another ruse for reducing the odds on manufacturing a bestseller is for the publisher to recruit a celebrity to act as the highly marketable image of an unknown, but competent ghost-writer (see Chapter 7). This is what happened with *Swan*, a novel 'by' Naomi Campbell, who made no secret of her minimal contribution, except when it came to promoting the book. If the celebrity happens to catch the urge to write, so much the better. Quality is irrelevant if the name on the cover is big enough. So it is that Eddy Shah, press entrepreneur, has entered into fiction, Kirk Douglas has turned from the spoken to the written cliché and Prince Charles and a gaggle of lesser royals have been persuaded to share their life-enhancing reflections.

But as Publisher A soon discovers, none of this is a sure-fire guarantee of success. Just look in the remainder shops to see the piles of 'bestsellers' that have somehow failed to connect with the popular imagination. The truth is hard to take. Beyond a few generalizations, nobody really knows what makes a bestseller. Not even the authors.

As Cyril Connolly observed in *Enemies of Promise*, there is an abundance of examples of writers who 'without knowing it, have hit upon the contemporary chemical combination of illusion and disillusion which makes books sell well'. Writing from a prewar perspective, Connolly identified *The Bridge of St Luis Rey*, *Decline and Fall*, *Brave New World*, *The Postman Always Knocks Twice* and *Goodbye Mr Chips* as books that were expected to sell respectably but were never treated as bestsellers, least of all by their creators, before the floodgates opened. Connolly went on to warn of unrealizable expectations of a succession of bestsellers from the same author. It can happen; but it may not. In our own time, it will be interesting to see if Stephen Hawking, whose *A Brief History of Time* has sold an incredible 620,000 hardbacks, will feel able or inclined to try to beat his own record.

But reverting to popular fiction, surely the characteristics identified earlier go to make a formula which can be replicated by any writer with a narrative gift. Maeve Haran (*Having It All*, *It Takes Two*) accepts this argument, up to a point.

> Most popular books reflect the author's voice (that odd blend of personality, observation and style that marks out a Cooper or a Binchy or a Cookson); they are strong on drama and storytelling; and they are often optimistic. I always know how I want my novels to end before I start. Endings are, to me at least, what a really good story is all about.

But then she goes on to say that the encouraging thing about bestsellers 'is precisely that they aren't predictable'. It took her a little time and experience to discover what really goes to make a best-selling author.

> Five years ago I gave up my job, nipped into WH Smith and scooped up an armful of gold-blocked one-word titles. I proceeded to analyse them in search of the key to the genre then known as 'sex 'n' shopping'. I followed this process with great diligence and precision working out exactly how many bonks, guilty secrets and lovers who turned out to be the heroine's father were needed per book. It never occurred to me that a mother of two small children who had forgotten what sex was and always shopped in Marks & Spencer might not be the ideal candidate to write a sex 'n' shopping masterpiece.
>
> After six months I sent off outline plus sample chapters (just as it tells you in the handbooks) to an agent and waited for the offers to flood in.

The eventual feedback made me wish I'd hung on to the day job. It was, said my agent, formulaic, dull and passionless. What was more, the genre I had naïvely adopted was already dead on its feet.

It was only when I chucked away the formula and wrote passionately about a subject that really interested me (the attempt to balance career and motherhood) that the bestseller lists beckoned. By following my own preoccupation I'd hit upon a theme that preoccupied thousands of others, and *Having It All*'s sales reflected that.

The triumph of the individual over the consensus is precisely what makes publishing a chancy business – and ensures that it will remain so despite the efforts of the marketing people to achieve safe predictability. Even if they manage, eventually, to produce a formula list that does tolerably well in the charts they will have cut themselves off from the mighty bonanza that every publisher craves – the sales triumph that defies all prophecy. A 400-page parable about rabbits rejected at first sight by forty-six other publishers, say, or a weird fantasy by a day scholar whose only previous work was an Anglo-Saxon Grammar – *Watership Down* and *The Hobbit*.

The only way for a publisher to achieve such triumphs is to trust to judgement and a wide range of titles, hoping that one or two will emerge from the crowd to justify the also-rans. Which is where we came in.

How should we judge bestsellers? Intellectuals may sneer at the passing fancies of a mass readership but sales figures are not without merit. And, my, how they sell. Barbara Taylor Bradford has disposed of 40 million copies of her romantic sagas to eighty-two countries in twenty-four languages. Robert Ludlum does even better: 195 million copies in thirty-two languages. The cumulative sales from Catherine Cookson are close to 100 million, while John Grisham, the biggest seller of them all, is said to earn more money than a minor Eastern European country.

Is there any more to it than that? Ken Follett is one who believes that best-selling authors – like himself – suffer unfairly the sneers and derision of the literary toffs who fail to recognize their own limitations.

Bestsellers are about murder, money, revenge, ambition and sex, sex, sex. So are literary novels. But bestselling authors give you more per page: there are five murders, three world financial crises, two bankruptcies and a civil war in *A Dangerous Fortune*. There is more drama in it than a literary writer will deal with in a lifetime of work.

Follett readily concedes that he is not into nuance or ambiguity: 'The worst crime I could commit is to make you read a sentence twice.' And he does admit to a certain predictability of style. As Deborah Moggach remarks, 'Bestsellers write in clichés so you know where you are.' But literary novels are by no means free of these vices or virtues. And if one sides with Cyril Connolly in believing that the up-to-dateness of a bestseller too easily passes for originality, it is still the case that many literary novels praised for true originality pass quickly into oblivion.

At a public debate at the Royal National Theatre on the Culture of the Bestseller, Ken Follett demonstrated the fallibility of literary criticism by displaying copies of *The Times* book pages of fifty years ago. Not one of the highly praised novels featured there has survived. On the other hand, the same can be said of one-time bestsellers. Whatever happened to Hugh Walpole, who half a century ago was a sure-fire winner on both sides of the Atlantic. Or Dornford Yates? Or John Buchan?

The only safe conclusion is that it is unwise to generalize. A bestseller may be a potboiler, an embarrassment to all except those who profit directly by its exploitation. Equally, the best-selling writer can enrich the culture – as Dickens, Trollope and Hardy did in their day. How would you judge John Le Carré, a bestseller who made spy fiction an art form with his departure from Bond-like preconceptions? Or Joanna Trollope, whose stories of middle-class domesticity have introduced another dimension to romantic fiction? Or Roddy Doyle, Booker Prize winner, who has nonetheless achieved best-selling status by becoming the first contemporary literary novelist to sell more than 100,000 hardbacks?

True quality and bestsellers can go together. So too can formula writing – or what is near as dammit formula writing – climb to the top of the charts. You can never quite tell.

Surprise. Surprise. That is what publishing – and writing – is all about. Surprise.

Love Story

THE UNKNOWN BESTSELLERS
OF ROMANCE

ROMANTIC FICTION is a large part of the British book market, accounting for sales of £70 million a year. Up to 10 per cent of adults buy at least one romance or love story a year. The readers are nearly all women and according to Book Marketing Ltd (Books and the Consumer) they come from all social groups though they are unlikely to be highly educated.

The market leader is, without question, Harlequin Mills & Boon (HMB), the Canadian-owned publisher, which has 4 million loyal readers in this country alone. Worldwide, HMB sells well over 200 million copies a year. Print runs start at 100,000 (the average paperback run is more like 10,000) and many titles break the half-million barrier.

Even those who dismiss the simplistic format – boy and girl meet, fall out, come together again, live happily ever after – cannot deny the success story that is HMB. It is a unique achievement.

Unique also is HMB's readiness to help aspiring writers. While other mainstream publishers despair at the size of their postbags and have been known to return unsolicited material with barely a glance at the title page, HMB editors go out of their way to offer constructive criticism. Their motto is, 'send it in and we'll look at it'. For true beginners, there is even a practical guide with booklet and audio tape (see end of chapter for details).

To start with the essentials, HMB novels are written almost exclusively by women. An occasional male author is allowed into the fold but the editorial consensus is that 'men find it almost impossible to identify with women's fantasies'. Thereafter:

We are looking for novels which focus principally on the developing romantic relationship between the hero and the heroine. The story should be written from the heroine's point of view but in the third person. An upbeat tone and a happy ending are essential but the story must be presented in a believable way.

There are four identifiable ingredients: characterization, dialogue, plot and background.

Are your characters the sort of people you would like to meet in real life? Is your hero the sort of man you dream about?

Be convinced, in other words. Take writing as a serious job. Rosalie Ash, a regular on the HMB list, offers Golden Rule No. 1:

Never assume that what is simple to read is simple to write. The reverse is almost always the case. With the rare, lucky exception, a rapid 55,000 words of tongue-in-cheek romantic fiction aimed at what's rumoured to be an 'easy' or lucrative market will almost certainly be rejected.

A sympathetic heroine is desirable. Readers are liable to grow impatient if they do not like the main character. She does not have to be beautiful but she should be young – the mid-twenties is the preferred age range – and with a mind of her own.

In recent years some changes have been detected in the kind of heroine our readers enjoy meeting. For example, although a heroine need not be a career girl, she is likely to have a job she enjoys, sometimes quite a high-powered, unfeminine-sounding one. The commercial airline pilot, the doctor in a busy hospital, the television producer, and the garage mechanic have all featured in Mills & Boon's books.

The hero is defined quite simply as a man women dream about.

That is why he never seems to have a shortage of girlfriends. Although he doesn't have to be classically handsome or a millionaire or a tempestuous Mediterranean type, it is important that he is over-whelmingly attractive. This probably means that if he is to appeal to most readers, he won't be very short or fat or bald. But as well as a good body, he should have a compelling personality and he should be an achiever, successful in his own field. In other words, he should be a strong character. No one dreams of marrying a wimp, but he doesn't have to be aggressive or domineering.

The HMB advice on writing dialogue could apply to any novel in any genre.

> Three lines of dialogue, if it is appropriate and to the point, is often worth a page of narrative . . . Let your characters speak for themselves instead of doing it for them in narrative paragraphs. The reader will often remember dialogue better than several paragraphs of narrative. Don't place yourself between the reader and the characters and prevent that sympathetic bond from taking place. Dialogue can make or break a character's credibility.

To say that dialogue should flow easily and not sound stiff and stilted is to state the obvious. Yet it is here that newcomers are likely to be weakest. They put words and phrases into the mouths of their characters that they themselves would never dream of using in real conversation. The best writers of dialogue are good listeners. What they hear in everyday life transfers easily to the printed page – with allowances for the tendency for people to say more than they need to get their meaning across. Too many words spoil the plot.

And speaking of plots: a romance must have a conflict and a happy ending.

> Most basic plot conflicts fall into two types, which can be called internal and external. For example, in an external plot, the heroine's father has financial problems with his business so the hero buys in to bail him out. The heroine resents this because, inevitably, it reduces her father's self-respect. It is an issue which is outside their usual lives but which impinges with some force, changing the course they would normally take. An internal plot involves character type – some emotional or moral issue which puts the hero and heroine at odds with each other and their sense of integrity. These issues are resolved, sometimes with great heart-searching, by an acceptance of each

other's differences, their basic needs and a willingness to compromise without destroying their beliefs.

Conflict must not overwhelm the love interest. Some writers become so involved in the machinations of peripheral characters they quite forget that the purpose of the exercise is to bring Jack and Jill together in a happy embrace.

Now comes the critical question. Should the embrace be vertical or horizontal? Popular romances have always contained love scenes but until recently sex has been treated rather as an optional extra – occasionally signalled in the story line but rarely described.

The skill was in stoking up the reader's imagination to a point where she no longer needed the author to fill in the details. Victorian writers were best at this. Their melodramatic style lent itself to vivid images which the moralists could not specify without themselves appearing to have dirty minds. Here is the prolific Victoria Cross (if anyone can identify the lady behind the pseudonym, I would dearly like to hear more about her) midway through her steamy saga *The Greater Law*.

Roland drew his chair very close to hers, and they sat in silence while the band played with all its own Italian passion and fervour the wonderful song 'Musica Proibita'. It was known to both of them, and the throbbing notes of the melody, as they came floating in, seemed to speak to them, also the familiar words. In silence they waited for the last grand final strain, the appealing cry, *Stringemi, stringemi al tuo cuor, fa mi provar l'ebrezza del'amor* (Press me, press me to your heart, make me feel the intoxication of love), and as it was flung on to the air by the violins Roland suddenly leant forward over her, and caught her to him in an embrace that seemed to the girl to have the agony of death in it.

'Darling, darling do you love me enough to stay with me? Tell me, shall I have your warm arms round me tonight, or shall I be out there alone in the darkness?'

'You know how I love you, enough to die for you.'

'Then live for me. Stay with me now. Let us have paradise for these weeks in the present, and then pay the price that the future may demand of us.'

He kissed her on her soft, parted lips, and the fire of supreme happiness, of that joy that only comes rarely in a lifetime, and never from any other source than love, of an ecstasy that seemed parting soul and body, took possession of her. It formed her resolution. What price that the future could ask from her would be too great for such a gift as this?

She put her arms round his neck. 'I will stay.'

'My sweet! My very, very own.'

There was silence for a moment in the shaded flower-scented room, as the two warm living hearts beat tumultuously against each other, and from without came the music, now changed into a wild gay dance; it seemed to translate into sound the joyous leap of their pulses.[1]

Victoria Cross romances sold in hundreds of thousands of copies up to the First World War and beyond. No lending library could afford to be without her.

The successors to Victoria Cross, of whom Barbara Cartland remains the undisputed doyen (cumulative sales run into hundreds of millions), promoted the submissive heroine searching for and finding the man who would soothe away all cares in a wonderland of cosy domesticity. But there was less passion than of old and more of a Barbie Doll primness that reflected the aspirations of suburban gentility. What changed were the circumstances in which love thrived. Injured heroes home from the war set the scene for medical romances, a market cornered by HMB in the 1950s. With the affluent society came exotic settings on cruise liners and Caribbean islands.

Curiously, however, popular romance was virtually untouched by the sexual revolution. While the rest of fiction leaped into physical gyrations of ever greater explicitness (and improbability), HMB contrived to thrive on a mix of idealism and innocence. Even with the arrival of the bonkbusters in the 1980s (Jilly Cooper, Jackie Collins, Celia Brayfield, *et al.*), Ruritanian fantasies held their appeal. References to sex remained heavily muted or euphemistic – the 'gossamer barrier' becoming a substitute for a condom, for example.

[1] Victoria Cross, *The Greater Law*, John Long Ltd, 1914

But now the pattern is changing. An early sign was the demise of three long-lived romance magazines – *True Romances*, *Love Story* and *True Story* – after their combined monthly circulation fell below 50,000. The absence of raunchy narrative was blamed for their fading attraction. More significant was the fact that these magazines were supposed to appeal to young readers. Their main competitors, *Loving* and *True*, both with an older readership profile, managed to keep going, albeit with dips in circulation.

The message was not lost on HMB, where the first corporate redesign in ten years was unveiled in 1993. An elegant rose of romance made its appearance, along with photographic illustrations aimed at the youth market. The latest imprint, Temptation Romance ('passionate, sensual novels where larger than life characters face temptation and make difficult choices') was given a high profile, while Medical Romances were renamed Love on Call. No one was greatly surprised when, a few months later, there was a shakeout of senior editors. A former colleague opined, 'With these people going it really is the end of the old world of Mills & Boon.'

Well, not quite. Competition is hotting up with Hodder Headline, HarperCollins and Bloomsbury, among others, getting their romantic act together. But much of their output is essentially conservative, even echoing the sighs and whispers of Victoria Cross.

He took a slice of toast, buttered it using a tiny silver knife with a rounded blade, spooned caviar lavishly onto one edge of the toast, squeezed lemon over it and leaned towards her. 'Bite it off,' he said, and popped it into her mouth. It was the first vaguely intimate moment they'd shared that day. He watched her. 'Well?'

'Mm.'

'You need more.' He spooned more onto her toast. 'Your tongue needs more.'

Laura let him feed her. 'You're right,' she said after a few seconds. 'It's very different.' She licked her lips. 'It's good.'

'Now a sip of champagne,' Roger said. 'They're beautifully matched.' He poured for them both from the Dom Pérignon bottle in the ice bucket beside him, and handed her a glass. 'To you.'

They were sitting on the semi-circle of white leather seating in the stern, the food on a low table before them. The sun was very warm, the air a little more sultry than it had been when they'd left the harbour.

'Laura,' Roger said suddenly. 'Come a little closer.'

'All right,' Laura said. She slid across the leather towards him. 'But it's okay, I can feed myself now.'

His eyes were very blue. 'Your taste buds,' he said again, 'need another new experience.'

'Do they?' she asked, softly.

He took the champagne glass out of her hand and put it on the table, and then he took her face between his hands again as he had the previous night, and kissed her. But this time, it was a different kind of kiss, searching, lips parted, stronger, more forceful. Laura did not pull away. It was what she wanted, her lips, her mouth, her tongue, all of her. Her arms went around him, his hands left her face and he pulled her closer, and the kiss grew more passionate, so that their teeth grazed, and their tongues mingled.[2]

But elsewhere on the romance shelves, steamier passions are released.

Pete's eyes swept from the damp tendrils of jet-black hair dangling on her forehead down to the V-necked opening of her robe. Her skin still glistened a pale, pearly pink from the steaming effects of the bath. Nice. His gaze took in the lush fullness of her breasts, the long curve of hips and legs sweeping down to her delicate bare feet with their pink-polished toenails. Stunning. Once again his gaze slid up and down the sensuous length of her lilac-perfumed body in one slow, appreciative glance.

'Don't mind if I do.'

Monique drew in her breath. Her heart had only barely recovered from the start he'd given her, and now it leapt again at the thinly disguised innuendo. Silhouetted against the darkness of the terrace, Pete Lambert looked even taller and more rugged than ever. And right at home.

In gray sweats, with his fair hair tumbling carelessly, he looked

[2] Hilary Norman, *Laura*, Coronet Books, 1995

ready to stretch out in front of the fireplace with the evening
newspaper, a glass of brandy, and a labrador retriever. Not *my*
fireplace, she thought, but she couldn't help admiring the ripple of
muscle beneath his easy-fitting casual clothes, the firm slant of his
jaw, and the undeniable power of those cobalt-blue eyes.

And she couldn't help but feel the spark flying between them, a
spark that made her acutely aware of his potent masculinity and of
her own vulnerability as she stood there barefoot, and naked beneath
the terry robe.[3]

Both these extracts are from Hodder Headline imprints. Now move
on to Black Lace (Virgin) and X Libris (Little Brown), both recent
entrants to the romantic fiction market whose offerings are so explicit
that to describe them as romance seems almost a contradiction.

Pulling her mouth away from his, she threw back her head and cried
out, sure she could not bear the intensity of it. Dominic held his hand
tightly against her pulsating core, prolonging the sensation until she
begged him to let her go.

She cried out again, this time in anguish as he took his hand away,
but he did not abandon her for long, entering her quickly, before her
orgasm had completely ebbed away.

Anna wrapped herself around him, tears of joy, love, gratitude; she
did not know what emotion, streaming down her face as she was
filled by him. She could feel him moving inside her and she met him,
thrust for thrust, grinding her hips against his as he raced towards his
own climax.

Her cries of ecstasy mingled with his as they rolled together, still
enmeshed, on the bed. And the one thought that played over and
over through Anna's mind was that this was it, the thing that she had
always suspected she had been missing. And she knew that never
again would she be content to settle for anything less.[4]

And if that is still a little on the tame side here we go with Mariah
Greene.

[3] Jillian Karr, *Something Borrowed, Something Blue*, Headline Book Publishing, 1994
[4] Nina Sheridan, *Arousing Anna*, X Libris, 1995

The first inch or two of a new cock was always Andrea's favourite
and she did not want to rush things. Keeping her legs as far apart as
she could so as to widen her pussy, she guided the tip into her. When
it was just in, she stopped and sighed, feeling the joy of what was in
her and anticipating what was to come. It was as though from the
position she was in, straddling Mike with his cock just inside her, she
could tell what kind of fuck it would be. The way the cock would
slowly fill her, pound at her and finally release itself inside her.

Inch by inch it entered her. She lowered herself delicately and
gently, her pussy lips against his shaft, the walls of her vagina
expanding blissfully. Eventually she felt his balls against her rear. She
reached round and felt them, small and stone-like. He groaned as she
tickled them. They held their position and he looked up at her,
reaching his hands out to her breasts. She touched his cheek and ran
her fingers along his jawbone.[5]

It takes another couple of pages for Andrea to climax and another 200
pages for her to complete her full cycle of sexual permutations. X Libris
and Black Lace turn out two new books a month, every one a hot seller
and an even hotter read.

Responding to a *Daily Mail* interviewer, Kerri Sharp, editor at Black
Lace, had this to say about titles like *The Captive Flesh* and *Moon of Desire*.

Until now, if women wanted a really raunchy read there was only
men's pornography – colossal penises and impossibly proportioned
nymphomaniacs – which doesn't really appeal to women's sensibilities. Women needed their own erotic fiction. And it wasn't difficult,
either, to find women to write it. We sent a circular to authors'
agents and they came flocking.

There are three categories of plot.

1. The Naive's Progress. An ever-so-slightly reluctant, passive young
woman, suddenly projected into a glamorous world, is initiated into
all sorts of carnal practices by terribly sophisticated and good-looking

[5] Mariah Green, *Back in Charge*, X Libris, 1995

libertines of both sexes. By the end, we are led to believe she has become a person of supreme sexual confidence.

2. The Powerplay. A 99.9 per cent independent woman falls for a terribly rich and handsome control freak who obliges her to Face Her Own Secret Desires – sex with strangers, sex with inanimate objects, sex in public, lesbian sex, group sex. In the end, either she and the main man prove to be equals and fall in love – or she gets the best of him and strides off into a 100 per cent emancipated future.

3. The Gothic Panto. This invariably features pirates/bandits/sheiks/barons, desert islands/harems/castles with torture chambers/chateaux with secret corridors and feisty heroines. Most are just bawdy romps. Others are excuses for Gothic S&M, some of it very grim – forced enemas, for example.

No one denies the trend or the pace at which the market for women's erotica is developing. But it is far too early to write off the time-honoured romantic novel. The continuing buoyancy of HMB sales proves the durability of the traditional market. Anyway, the shock of discovering that women may actually enjoy reading stories with a strong sexual content should not detract from the essence of all romantic fiction, erotic or anodyne – the ideal of true and, political correctness notwithstanding, submissive love.

Janet Allison, a young writer who has already had a crack at a Harlequin Mills & Boon novel, put it this way:

However intelligent a woman, there is always an inbuilt desire to be dominated by an authoritarian, good-looking, intelligent man. It's embarrassing to admit, and I should deny it wholeheartedly, but it's true.

Remember, please; she said it; not me.

The Harlequin Mills & Boon guide to writing a romantic novel includes a booklet, *Behind the Hearts and Flowers*, priced at £2.95 (including p&p) and an audio tape, *And Then He Kissed Her*, at £4.95

(including VAT and p&p). The double pack of booklet and tape is available at £7.50 (including VAT and p&p) from the Editorial Department, Harlequin Mills & Boon Ltd., Eton House, 18–24 Paradise Road, Richmond, Surrey TW9 1SR.

Catching Them Young
BOOKS FOR CHILDREN

EVERY FOOL THINKS that any fool can write for children. They don't try it for themselves – no time for such nonsense – but this does not detract from the conviction that the wealth coined by the books of Roald Dahl and other stars of the children's list is easy money. All you have to do, runs the argument, is to find a simple plot line, add a few pious sentiments, illustrate lavishly and Bingo or, as an adult in this type of children's story would say, Bob's your uncle.

Except that he isn't. It is never that simple.

Reality is a volatile market of ever shifting fashions. What children enjoy reading is an intriguing topic for publishers, who, being adults for the most part, have only the haziest notion of the cultural undercurrents driving the younger generation, even that part of it under their own roofs. They are further confused by propaganda from various pressure groups who think they know what children *ought* to read.

A prime example of adults getting it wrong, and how, goes back to the seventies when progressive education was all the rage. It was argued then that what children really wanted and needed (in this context, the two verbs were often treated synonymously with disastrous results) was 'relevance'. The black spot was put on stories that harped on middle-class values, of which most youngsters had no direct experience, and on adventure that promoted outmoded assumptions of national, racial or sexual superiority. Badges of approval were awarded to recognizable characters facing up to everyday challenges in realistic circumstances. The progressives were then left to wonder why it was that young readers did not respond, indeed showed every sign of being bored out of their minds.

The explanation is to be found in a standard thesis of child psychology. It is at least thirty years ago that a Harvard academic, Jerome S. Bruner, tested his theory of the teaching of civics with two contrasting syllabuses – one based on life as we know it to be, the other on an anthropological survey of a tribe of Eskimos. The Eskimos won hands down. Bruner concluded that children learn more when their imagination is stretched beyond their immediate experience. They enjoy more too when stories venture beyond the familiar. That is why Enid Blyton reigned for so long over generations of children whose families could never have aspired to the cosy gentility of the Famous Five.

The latest attack on freedom to read comes from the forces of the politically correct. Books thought to be sexist have to be given a shot of feminism. Even Thomas the Tank Engine is destined to meet his Thomasina in a controversial departure from the Rev. W.V. Awdry's concept of all boy engines together. In the United States, much-loved Roald Dahl characters are modified to satisfy the demands of the moralizing minority. So it is that the gluttonous Augustus Gloop, whose 'great flabby folds of fat bulged out from every part of his body' and whose face 'was a monstrous ball of dough with two small greedy currant eyes peering out upon the world', has had to lose much of the bulk to avoid offending the weight-disadvantaged. Much more of this and Roald Dahl stories will lose the very features that give them universal appeal.

The truth is that Dahl is the children's top favourite (with eight out of ten of the most popular library borrowings) precisely because his characters offend adult sensibilities. He is part of a noble tradition. Barrie, Carroll and Lear appealed to the subversive instincts of their young readers. Beatrix Potter and Kenneth Grahame mocked adult values (though many parents failed to notice because the provocative words were spoken by animals). The politically correct, with their scrupulous attempts not to say anything out of the way, can never reach out to reluctant readers who respond only when they are jolted by the unexpected. When Paul Jennings had to cope with a book-shy son, he fought back with a succession of macabre and risqué stories with titles like *Uncanny! Unbelievable! and Unreal!* Now Jennings is making impressive inroads into a whole generation of reluctant readers. They like his punchy, no-nonsense style.

There is always a market for irreverence and fun. An example at random is William Taylor's *The Worst Soccer Team Ever*, which, as a book-club offer, outsold the Dahl books. Sue Townsend has a teenage following for her Adrian Mole books every bit as loyal as her adult readership. For juniors, the comic naughty style of the Ahlbergs, Allan and Janet, has produced long-stayers like *Mrs Wobble the Waitress* and *Mr Biff the Boxer*.

As a small publisher, Piccadilly Press has scored heavily with a collection of weird and wonderful titles like *The Very Bloody History of Britain Without the Boring Bits, I Was a Teenage Worrier* and, for those with an interest in contemporary etiquette, Jane Goldman's *For Weddings, A Funeral* and *When you Can't Flush the Loo*.

One of the few constants in children's literature is the appeal of horror, starting with the brothers Grimm. It is not that children are cruel; on the contrary, the traditional horror story line offends nature, hence its fascination. It is the reverse of the old joke of the man who rejected violence on the screen because he got enough of that at home. Newspaper headlines notwithstanding, horror and violence are not part of ordinary domesticity, which is why they exercise such pulling power in print or on film. It is the unfamiliar that sells, as proved by Scholastic, which publishes a Point Horror title every month, and by Puffin, the traditional-ist's favourite publisher, which has attracted a new audience with its all-male Fighting Fantasy characters.

But the liveliest demand in the children's market is for non-fiction, in particular, lavishly illustrated co-editions created by a production team in which the writer shares equal status with a designer and illustrator. The trend towards collaborative effort continues with the recent tailing off in picture-book sales in the wake of multimedia and the ubiquitous CD-ROM (see Chapter 5).

A singularity of the children's book market is that it has long been free from the trade's self-imposed restrictions on where books should be sold and at what price. The alliance between booksellers and leading publishers to enforce the Net Book Agreement traditionally excepted many chil-dren's books, particularly those with an educational content. Come the entrepreneurial 1980s the go-ahead publishers saw their chance. The first break came when the late Sebastian Walker of Walker Books struck a deal with Sainsbury's. It had often been said that books could be sold like cornflakes. Well, here was the chance to prove the argument by actually placing books alongside the cereal packets. It worked. Thanks largely to Walker and the publishers who followed his lead, the children's book market grew by half again from the mid-1980s. By 1993, retail sales of children's books topped £260 million and accounted for some 10 per cent of total UK book sales.

The growth was not entirely in the supermarkets. Book clubs played a big part in the expansion. Though this was once the exclusive realm of Puffin, there are now ten or more clubs specializing in children's books, selling through schools or individual membership. Red House, a fifteen-year-old player in this highly competitive game, has over 400,000 family members and 8000 school members. About the same age and size is Books for Children (BFC). These were the two dominant players until Book Club Associates launched Children's Book of the Month Club. On the school side, the clubs run by Scholastic bestride the market.

The combined force of supermarket and book-club sales has made children's books more than usually price-sensitive. Hence the decline and, in the case of fiction, the fall of the hardback. What the customer wants is value for money, which means quality books at prices that attract the casual sale. To say as much is dangerously close to platitude for it leaves unanswered the most important question: who exactly is the customer?

For the book clubs, the purchasing power is concentrated on parents and teachers, while the supermarkets aim directly at children. To complicate matters, there is a rapid spread of overlap between educational and leisure reading.

Children represent formidable purchasing power with, according to a Henley Centre report, £1.6 billion a year to spend on their own account. Add to this the £8.4 billion put on the value of children's influence over parental purchase, and we have a £10 billion consumer market. Clearly there is scope for publishers to expand their market still further. How this might be done is suggested by research carried out by Book Marketing Ltd. These are the main points:

➙ four in ten of the adult population and just over half of all book buyers bought books for children in the last year;

➜ about one-third of all books bought are bought for children;

➜ buyers are more likely to be women – 63 per cent of those who bought were women, 37 per cent were men;

➜ those in the 25–34 age range are the heaviest buyers of children's books, accounting for nearly two in five purchases;

➜ a quarter of those who buy for children buy only for children;

➜ a quarter of those who bought books for children in the last year are over 55;

➜ preferred places of purchase were 47 per cent books/stationery stores, 38 per cent specialist bookshops, and 33 per cent other non-specialist outlets such as supermarkets;

➜ of those buying books for children in the course of a year, 62 per cent bought at Christmas, 45 per cent bought for birthdays, 41 per cent bought 'for no particular occasion', and 17 per cent bought for 'school-related purposes';

➜ buying for children shows little class variation – unlike other sectors of the market.

The conclusion must be that it is the children themselves who need to be persuaded to buy more books on their own behalf. It only reinforces the need to think young. Writers new to the scene are likely to do best if they aim directly at their readers rather than trying to satisfy adult conceptions of what a child's book should be.

The Daleks are Coming

MULTIMEDIA AND THE
YOUNGER GENERATION

MULTIMEDIA IS A REVOLUTION in the making and it is the young who are making it. Growing up with the technology they have an instinctive feel for its possibilities and are eager to try new products.

This is why Dorling Kindersley, already famous for highly illustrated information and how-to books, has teamed up with Microsoft for a joint venture into multimedia. It is, says Alan Buckingham, a natural extension of his company's existing output.

Now, instead of the still and silent world of books, we can offer an experience that appeals to more of our senses than the eye and the intellect. Publishers have been trying to create artificial worlds in words and pictures since printing began. The addition of sound, animation and video helps create information that more closely resembles the real world. Not only that, but it makes the transfer of information easier and more enjoyable.

The first challenge, however, is to get a handle on multimedia, to appreciate its potential and its limitations. Coming to multimedia from a book-editing background, Alan Buckingham likes to stress that he regards CD-ROMs as books.

There's nothing illogical in stretching the words we've got. CDs are still books that need good design, good writing and editing, good typography and good structure. There's something reassuring about regarding them as books and it is also important to stress that they're not games.

Quite so. But, to put it mildly, these are books with a difference. *The Way Things Work*, for example, has 70,000 words, 1000 illustrations, 1500 pop-up windows, 300 animations and video clips, and an hour of audio. Then again, the start-up costs of a CD-ROM enterprise are enormous – around £1000 a megabyte, if that means anything to you.

Estimates published in the *Electronic Author* put the average cost of developing a jazzy CD-ROM title at between £200,000 and £300,000.

> From signature of contract to finished disk takes 8 to 12 months, and the gross return per unit (to publishers) is 20 to 30 per cent (of which, at a guess, 5 per cent might go to the author). The percentage is worked out on an average selling price of £50. It means a publisher must sell between 30,000 and 50,000 units to break even.

Authors who want to break into this sector are urged to study the market. Recent titles include *The Kingfisher Children's Micropedia* (ESM/Sparrowhawk & Heald, £88.12), *Roots to Reading* (Philips Media, £24.99), *Solar System* (Philips Media, £29.99) and, every child's favourite, *Disasters* (Media Design, £39.99), a detailed examination of all the great man-made catastrophes. Take your choice from an ever increasing range which goes way beyond the adaptation of existing material in print form.

Writing opportunities abound for the technically skilled. Alan Buckingham advises the prospective multimedia author to talk to a programmer or software developer to see how an idea can use the power of the computer.

> It is as important to know what the limitations are as to know what marvels you can achieve. For example, we are at present restricted to the 386 processor as the bottom line. That is to say we have to guarantee to our customer base that the title will work on a 386 PC (or Mac equivalent), and that immediately means that all kinds of things you might want to do with 3D graphics or video are not yet possible.

That will change of course.

The state of the industry in Britain is small beer as compared to the US, where, last year, over 2000 CD-ROM titles were on sale for the

Christmas season. And this is only the start. Recent figures released by
the European Community suggest that up to 25 per cent of children's
literature will be in electronic form by the end of the decade. By then
prices of CD-ROMs will be down to casual sale level. In the States list
prices are falling at around 20 per cent every six months. In his latest
book, *Being Digital*, the director of MIT's famed Media Lab, Nicholas
Negroponte, sees a future in which more and more information will be
contained within a single disk.

> A CD used as read-only memory (ROM) has a storage capacity today
> of five billion bits. This capacity will be increased to 50 billion on
> one side within the next couple of years. Meanwhile, five billion
> alone is huge. It represents about 100 classics or five years of reading,
> even for those who read two novels a week.
>
> From another point of view, five billion is not so large; it is only
> one hour of compressed video. In this regard, the size is modest at
> best. One likely short-term result is that CD-ROM titles will use a
> lot of text – which is economical bitwise – many stills, some sound,
> and only snippets of full-motion video. Ironically, CD-ROMs may
> thus make us read more, not less.

Now take another fast-forward leap.

> The longer-term view of multimedia is not based on that fifty-cent
> piece of plastic, five billion or fifty billion bits, but will be built out
> of the growing base of on-line systems that are effectively limitless in
> their capacity.

At this point . . .

> A fundamental editorial change takes place, because depth and breadth
> are no longer either/or. When you buy a printed encyclopedia, world
> atlas, or book on the animal kingdom, you expect very general and
> broad coverage of many far-ranging topics. By contrast, when you
> buy a book on William Tell, the Aleutian Islands, or kangaroos, you
> expect an 'in depth' treatment of the person, place, or animal. In the
> world of atoms, physical limits preclude having both breadth and
> depth in the same volume – unless it's a book that's a mile thick.

In the digital world, the depth/breadth problem disappears and we can expect readers and authors to move more freely between generalities and specifics. In fact, the notion of 'tell me more' is very much part of multimedia and at the root of hypermedia . . .

Think of hypermedia as a collection of elastic messages that can stretch and shrink in accordance with the reader's actions. Ideas can be opened and analyzed at multiple levels of details. The best paper equivalent I can think of is an Advent calendar. But when you open the little electronic (versus paper) doors, you may see a different story line depending on the situation or, like barbershop mirrors, an image within an image within an image.

For the writer it means learning a whole new technique, not to mention a whole new language, for a whole new set of working relationships.

Having completed his second interactive screenplay for Disney, writer Michele Em set down his experiences for the benefit of his Writers' Guild colleagues.

An interactive script differs in a number of ways from a linear narrative script. The parameters are different from film or television. Depending on your target platform (CD-ROM, Sega Saturn, Genesis, floppy disk, on-line, to name a few), the limitations of playback are going to affect your dialogue. Sometimes your dialogue is going to be in text form for one platform and spoken for another.

It's tricky to write for text, but harder, as we all know, to write believable dialogue for actors to speak. The dialogue also needs to be brief. Very brief. In some cases, such as where the player addresses a character repeatedly, the same line may be heard over and over again. What starts out clever can become aggravating through no fault of yours. All too often, due in part to storage limitations, each and every line has to have a specific purpose, making it very difficult to casually build a character. Every line has to contain the information needed to move the story forward. After that it's in the hands of the actors.

If your dialogue is going to be shown on screen you must bear in mind such things as that there are only 80 characters to a line of 12-point type and that the text may be displayed even larger. Inform yourself about the issues pertinent to your work. The technical team, the producer and the designer won't necessarily have your time or craft in their minds. You need to look out for yourself. All they'll know is whether your dialogue worked for them or didn't. But they are not used to giving direction. So ask for it.

Even writers who stay aloof from multimedia, preferring to concentrate on print, will be unable to ignore the potential for selling on their creative output to feed the hungry technology. And we are not talking here simply of CD-ROM. If multimedia means what it says – more than one medium – then a host of other subsidiary rights come into play. Look what is happening over at the recently created BBC Children's International where the Disney example has inspired the acquisition of the rights to the Noddy series of books.

> The subsequent revival of the popular Enid Blyton creation has resulted in the sale by BBC Books of over one million Noddy books, the sale by BBC Video of over 300,000 Noddy cassettes, over 200 licensed Noddy toy products in the shops and sales of the Noddy television series to some 26 countries worldwide.

What next, a Noddy video game? It would fit the pattern. The European video games market – just ten years old – is today worth more than the entire feature film industry.

Surveying the world economy with an eye to the millennium, Peter Norman, Economics Editor of *The Financial Times* believes that 'Multimedia could prove to be as significant in the development of mankind as the harnessing of steam and the development of the railways in the 19th century or the exploitation and spread of electric power in the early years of this century'.

And for the first time in momentous economic change, writers will move from the periphery to the centre of the action.

With a Little Help From the Experts

LEARNING TO WRITE

TEACHING PEOPLE TO WRITE is a mammoth growth industry. It extends all the way from the postgraduate degree in creative writing pioneered by Malcolm Bradbury and Angus Wilson at the University of East Anglia to correspondence courses of dubious provenance pitched at would-be contributors to *Cat Lovers' Weekly*. In between are the writing holidays in rural retreats, adult education courses run by local education authorities, and seminars given by transatlantic gurus. Throw in the proliferation of writers' circles and you have an awful lot of people eager to improve on their literary skills.

The question is, what do they gain from their efforts? Heavyweight opinion says, not much. There is no objective formula for a prize-winning novel or for any other literary masterpiece. The art of stringing together the best possible words in the best possible order reduces to an individual gift for dovetailing with a particular market. What makes one writer in a thousand click with his readers is lost in the mysteries of cultural evolution.

In other words, those who can, do. There is a story of the American writer Sinclair Lewis appearing, after a few drinks, at a university seminar for incipient authors. 'Hands up, all those who want to be writers,' he shouted. A forest of hands waved back at him. 'Then why the hell aren't you at home writing,' he demanded, and staggered from the room.

He had a point. A sure sign of a writer who is bound to fail is one who grabs at any excuse to delay the moment when thoughts must be made real.

Yet there are basics of narrative and dialogue that must be learned, if

only at school. The feel for English that makes it an art form must follow
on an appreciation of the language and the richness of its potential. Artists,
composers and actors have their own colleges where they benefit from
the experience of their mentors and the inspiration of their peers. Why
not writers?

The year-long writing courses at East Anglia and other academic
institutions are founded on this premise. There is no attempt to establish
a particular style. Students are acknowledged to have their distinctive
qualities, otherwise they would not be accepted. As Malcolm Bradbury
puts it:

> I have no doubt that the essential qualities needed by the writer are
> independent of anything that can be taught. There has first, I believe,
> to be a passionate motivation. Writing is a solitary, obscure, frequently
> disappointing way of pursuing a life, and it must be driven by
> profound commitment. Then there must be distinctiveness of vision.
> And since writing, in the end, is a form of exploration and discovery,
> there must be an instinct to discover and explore the world and
> human nature.

Still, Bradbury believes that writers can draw on a stock of cumulative
wisdom.

> For the novel, the story or the screenplay are complex forms and the
> making of narrative a complex process. It benefits most from a deep
> knowledge of the resources and the many varied means of writing
> and from the analysis of the work of others, above all the great
> practitioners, and of the nature of the writing process itself . . . The
> complicated history of narrative and its various forms and possibilities
> has to become an instinctive part of the repertory of the serious
> writer. And this is an important part of the business of teaching.

Or as Andrew Motion, Bradbury's successor at East Anglia, comments
succinctly, 'If imagination cannot be taught, the craft of writing can'.

The biggest single complaint against university writing courses is their
tendency to take on the irritating features of academic life; irritating, that
is, to students who have no time to stand and stare. At a recent seminar

on creative writing held at the Royal Society of Literature, a lecturer from Sheffield gave the game away when she was talking about feedback as the most important aspect of her course. A middle-aged student wanted to write a novel about a man watching a blackbird polluted by industrial waste. 'Man meets poisoned animal.' His tutor thought it might, at best, make a short story but encouraged him to develop his theme. It took six months for him to find that he was wrong – the idea was a non-starter. This example was offered as a benefit of the course; it set the student off on the path of self-discovery. But six months! Come on. Surely life in the cloisters can move a little faster than that.

The criticism is taken up by Michèle Roche, who, last year, joined the MA course at Manchester.

> The day of registration finally came. It was badly organized. This was an ill omen but one I missed at the time. We were aged between 22 and 67, and were fourteen in number – which made for a big circle in the longer-than-it-is-wide Writing Centre, where all the classes and workshops were held. It was not a room particularly conducive to thought and imagination, being rather untidy much of the time, with chairs left scattered from one class to the next. We met over nine months for two sessions a week, each lasting a couple of hours: one a workshop, the other a lecture or seminar on the thirty or so novels we had to read. Two novels were discovered to be out of print.

The chance to meet established writers was welcomed by this student, as too was the experience of blunt criticism and realizing 'the simple premise that writing can be a perilous and pernicious profession'. But was it all worth the £2500 fee?

> All the sweating over applications, the trials and the treats? I can't say I got all I was hoping for and expecting. It was certainly preferable to struggling alone. This said, after 15 years away from academia, it wasn't long before I was thinking to myself: Christ, what's academia like? Can we get real here, please, someone? I feel like I'm floating around in space, with almost two-and-a-half grand floating round with me. Please Sirs! More direction. More order. More sense of

purpose. These elements are amiss. I mean . . . how long does it take to mark an essay? I'm the customer you know!

If achieving publication is the criterion for success, then the university courses score around 70 per cent *failure* rate. As P.D. James observes, 'In any other faculty, the teachers would be sacked.'

Short courses vary hugely in standards and objectives. Some of the best are reckoned to be offered by the Arvon Foundation, a residential arts centre which organizes five-day courses in Devon, Yorkshire and Inverness-shire. As a visiting tutor, the novelist Beryl Bainbridge has this to say

> You can't teach people to write novels: that's down to temperament and simply getting on with it. You can analyse where people are going, maybe even suggest a change of direction, and give construc- tive advice. Novice writers are often unsure of their strengths and may need help to believe in their writing.

This realistic approach is in contrast with the wild ambitions of many lesser-known but pricey writing schools. When Hilary Mantel, who inspired the Royal Society of Literature seminar on creative writing, appealed through *The Daily Telegraph* for readers' experiences of creative writing courses, she was appalled by the arrogance of some of the tutors who wrote in. They seemed to think of themselves as therapists guiding their patients to self realization; the writing course as a substitute for the psychiatrist's couch.

One third of the responses came from retired people, many of whom still felt the disappointment of a childhood education that stifled creativity under a dead weight of rote learning. For them, writing courses can act as a release for ideas that have been held back for years. The chances of satisfaction are reduced in almost direct relation to increased expectations of making money. One letter Hilary Mantel received was from a man who had been writing for thirty-five years and had earned only £15. 'If I had known then what I know now, I would not have wasted half a lifetime.' Another correspondent sadly conceded, 'Over the years, I might well have produced more if I had spent time actually writing instead of just talking about it.'

As a self-confessed 'sucker' for writing courses, Peter Guttridge is among those who accept the limitations of short courses while applauding their attention to practicalities.

I have learned some mantras: screenwriting is structure, a novel is change, don't forget the back-story, remember to plant your seeds early. And I've been offered sound practical advice. Of a dizzy Victorian adventure set in a Grand Guignol Venice that I wrote, the tutor remarked: 'If your hero has his hand cut off early in the book, you must remember later. When you have him attempt to escape under cover of darkness down the Grand Canal in a rowing boat won't the villains find him at dawn rowing in circles?'

Such modest achievements are well within the scope of a long weekend – if the teachers are up to standard. Having attended creative writing classes organized by her local authority, the journalist Mary Kenny wrote approvingly of her lecturers.

Both teachers were sensitive, conscientious literature graduates who took seriously the work offered by their pupils; and the work ranged from the scarcely intelligible to the notably gifted. I was touched indeed by the way the teachers showed patience and encouragement to individuals struggling to put words on paper, people who blushed with inarticulacy and bashfulness.

'Their writing classes,' said Mary Kenny, 'gave some students exactly the kick-start they needed: the discipline of the deadline, the focus of a standard and a measured response to their searching efforts.' But attempts at literary analysis left her unimpressed. Greater value, she felt, could be got from the rules she had been taught as a young reporter.

Be simple. Be sincere; if you don't believe in what you're saying, neither will the reader. Write about what you know. Never assume knowledge on the part of your reader ('Mr Harold Wilson, the Prime Minister . . .' I was taught to write, on the grounds that there is always someone who does not know who the PM is), but don't patronise. Don't preach. Never, under any circumstances, use irony. Jane Austen can, but you can't. Ninety readers out of a hundred take ironical allusions at face value. Don't try to run before you can walk; don't be too ambitious. Read good writing every day.

This last bit of advice would seem to be stating the obvious yet it is frequently ignored. Non-fiction writers are particularly at fault, as Steve Jones admitted when he launched last year's *Daily Telegraph* Young Science Writers' competition. He attributed a large measure of his own success as a writer to his pleasure in reading beyond his subject.

I almost never read science for relaxation. It seems a contradiction in terms, a busman's holiday. To unwind, I go for biography, travel or novels (as well as spending a quite unreasonable amount of time reading newspapers). To count the thousands of hours I have spent over the *Guardian* and *The Daily Telegraph* during the past 30 years fills me with horror. But – at least, so I flatter myself – some of the form, if not the content, of all those millions of forgotten words has rubbed off.

Most people who share the same unhealthy habit can, when pushed (or paid), turn a sentence or two. In that statement lies perhaps the most important qualification for becoming an author – without reading for pleasure, it is impossible to write for profit.

Professor Jones has his own rules for effective writing.

Never use a long word when a short one will do. Given the choice, choose one with an Anglo-Saxon rather than a Latin root. Use the active rather than the passive voice. Cut down on the adjectives and kill the superlatives. To quote Samuel Johnson's college tutor: 'Read over your compositions and wherever you meet with a passage which you think is particularly fine, strike it out.'

The sheer diversity of 'golden rules' suggests there is room for a few more. In the end, it is all a matter of value judgement. But knowing what other writers believe is important can be a powerful aid to self-criticism – a step on the way to finding our own 'golden rules'.

Sitting at the feet of Socrates is not essential to the learning process. If you enjoy going away on courses or attending evening classes, fine, but there is no scarcity of opportunities for home study. Ignore the correspondence courses for the moment. Concentrate instead on books about writing, starting with those written by undisputed masters of the craft. There are plenty to choose from, though some of the best are out of print and will need tracking down in libraries or second-hand bookshops. A case in point is the work of the American writer William Saroyan, whose short stories from the 1930s and 1940s are overdue for rediscovery. Saroyan was in his creative prime when his *Writer's Declaration* appeared as a preface to his collection of short stories *The Whole Voyald*. While he is dismissive of writing courses ('they are entirely useless') and refuses to give advice on particulars ('the writer who *is* a writer needs no advice and seeks none'), his philosophy of commitment to his craft comes close to conveying the essence of great writing.

> The writer is a spiritual anarchist, as in the depth of his soul every man is. He is discontented with everything and everybody. The writer is everybody's best friend and only true enemy – the good and great enemy. He neither walks with the multitude nor cheers with them. The writer who is a writer is a rebel who never stops. He does not conform for the simple reason that there is nothing yet worth conforming to. When there is something half worth conforming to he will not conform to that, either, or half conform to it. He won't even rest or sleep as other people rest and sleep. When he's dead he'll probably be dead as others are dead, but while he is alive he is alive as no one else is, not even another writer. The writer who is a writer is also a fool. He is the easiest man in the world to belittle, ridicule, dismiss, and scorn: and that also is precisely as it should be. He is also mad, measurably so, but saner than all others, with the best sanity, the only sanity worth bothering about – the living, creative, vulnerable, valorous, unintimidated, and arrogant sanity of a free man.

Saroyan's passion for freedom points up the difference between a writer who writes to make a living or to see his name in print and a writer who writes because he has 'an obsession to get to the probable truth about nature, and art, straight through everything to the very core of one's own being'.

Too high-flown? Possibly, but newcomers should go to Saroyan for inspiration. He won't say how to do it but he will say why. There is also

a lesson in Saroyan the failure – an indisputably fine writer who went out
of fashion in his own lifetime and is now almost totally ignored outside
San Francisco. The contradiction was discussed recently by Keith Waterhouse in a review of *Saroyan Memoirs,* a reissue of some of his best work,
edited by Brian Darwent. Waterhouse describes Saroyan as a 'hit or miss,
never revise a line operator' who had a marvellous facility for hiding the
join between fact (chiefly biographical) and fiction. And the fatal
weakness? In the end, Saroyan did not have much to say. 'He was more
interested in writing than in what he had to write about.' Still, in his time
Saroyan was wont to describe himself as 'the greatest writer in the world'.
And nobody laughed.

For the nuts and bolts of writing turn to John Braine, whose eminently
sensible *Writing a Novel* was published in 1974. To follow Braine is to
avoid the usual mistakes committed by novices. His advice, neatly
parcelled into memorable axioms, applies across the range of literary
endeavour, from fiction to faction, from documentary to drama. For
example,

> a good beginning means a good book. A good beginning is one
> which takes the reader straight into the action. It must also tell us
> who and what the novel will be about. It doesn't give away the story,
> but it doesn't leave us in any doubt. It shouldn't ever begin with a
> foreword, nor should it be leisurely and discursive. Summary – 'This
> is the story of what happened to an ordinary English family in the
> year of the Apollo Moonshot' – must never be used. It need not
> mention the main characters, but it's much preferable that they be
> brought in straight away.

Dialogue, says Braine, must always be speakable. If you can't speak it
aloud, it's no good. Interposing on Braine, writers spend too long on
dialogue. The attention to detail needed to develop a story with a
consistent theme can produce stilted dialogue which would never be
spoken in real life. On the other hand:

> those who can't write credible dialogue can't write good prose either.
> And there is an inextricable relationship between the fact that Scott
> Fitzgerald writes superb narrative and superb dialogue. It isn't that the

dialogue is merely an extension of his narrative. It could never be so, for its function is to give us words that we can accept as having been spoken in real life. But the same standards of craftsmanship apply to both. I suspect that the reason that the ability to write good prose and good dialogue go hand-in-hand is simply that a good writer knows how to listen.

There is much more on the same lines. Sound common sense on writing clear and understandable prose – from compiling synopses and creating characters (people who make a novel happen) to cutting down on the adjectives and rejecting clichés.

Braine and Saroyan come together on the need to write from experience. The brilliance of Saroyan's short stories springs from a diverse life, never far from the edge of insolvency. He was at various times a sales assistant, a vineyard worker and a post office counter clerk who became manager of a branch office.

I have always been a little proud of that, for I was the youngest manager of a Postal Telegraph branch office in America, nineteen years old and without a high school diploma. Yesterday I walked through the Crystal Palace Market and visited the stand at which I once hustled potatoes and tomatoes, the *Fiore d'Italia*. I went into the building at Market and Sixth where the offices of the Cypress Lawn Cemetery Company are located. I worked there, too.

The vice-president said: 'Do you intend to make Cypress Lawn your lifetime career?'

I said: 'Yes, sir.'

I got the job.

I quit a month later but working there was a valuable experience. I remember the arrival of Christmas week and the vice-president's bitter complaint that owing to the absence of an epidemic of influenza the company's volume of business for December over the previous year had fallen 22 per cent.

I remarked: 'But everybody will catch up eventually, won't they?'

The vice-president lifted his glasses from the bridge of his nose to his forehead in order to have another look at me.

'I'm a writer,' I said. 'Unpublished.'

He asked me to look at some slogans he had composed for the company: *Inter here. A lot for your money.*

I said he had a flair.

Saroyan is worth quoting at length to show how easily he slipped over from essay into storytelling. In writing about how his stories came to be written he writes a story, complete in itself.

But the real point to be made is that a writer's experience does not have to be exotic to be serviceable. Here is John Braine.

It doesn't matter how limited your experience has been. (It is hardly possible for it to have been more limited than mine.) If you've lived in the same house all your life, if you've had the same dull routine job ever since leaving school, if nothing remarkable has ever happened to you, if you have never even had such basic experiences as making love or seeing someone close to you die, you still have the material for a thousand novels.

The evidence for believing that a little experience goes a long way can be found throughout literature. What is needed, argues Allan Massie, is a combination of experience and imagination. An example is Hemingway's First World War masterpiece *A Farewell to Arms*.

Hemingway's experience of battle was brief and limited – he had served with an ambulance unit for a few weeks until he was wounded. Yet, drawing on this, he imagined battle so well and thoroughly that he convinced his readers, and in time also perhaps himself, that he was a veritable veteran and war hero: an interesting example of the imagination coming first, and the presumed experience only after the creation of the work of art.

The truth, sadly ignored by many biographers, is that the essential part of a writer's life is lived in the imagination. Of course all his experience, of a variety of sorts – everything that he does, everything that happens to him, everything that he sees, hears, touches, feels and importantly – reads – may serve as food for the imagination to brood on and transform.

Yet, just as innumerable people have remarkable experiences which they remain unable to transmute into imaginative literature, so also a very little experience, the merest whiff of a situation or story, may be sufficient stimulus for a writer's imagination. Stendhal found the germ of *Scarlet and Black* in a newspaper report a couple of paragraphs long. Tolstoy also found his inspiration for *Anna Karenina* in a similarly brief report.

The only condition that John Braine puts on the exercise of imagination is that the writer does not go out of his way to be wildly experimental. In words that should be up in lights over every publishing house, Braine proclaims the simple truth:

> There is nothing which you cannot say within the framework of the straightforward realistic novel. It is the people in your story who should astound us. The great failing of the novel in England is a self-imposed restriction of subject and its stereotyped attitudes towards every aspect of life, particularly class. To be shockingly original with your first novel you don't have to discover a new technique: simply write about people as they are and not as the predominantly liberal and humanist literary Establishment believes that they ought to be.

Of his own choice of books that seem to improve our understanding of the creative process, Braine puts Dorothea Brande's *Becoming a Writer* at the top of his list. First published in 1934, it is still in print. You can see why. Her advice is specific; she avoids abstractions. And she faces up to problems every writer has encountered. Here she is on the Four Difficulties in getting going as a writer:

> First there is the difficulty of writing *at all*. The full abundant flow that must be established if the writer is to be heard from simply will not begin. The stupid conclusion that if he cannot write easily he has mistaken his career is sheer nonsense. There are a dozen reasons for the difficulty which should be canvassed before the teacher is entitled to say that he can see no signs of hope for his pupil . . .
>
> Second, there is the writer who has had an early success but is unable to repeat it. Here again there is a cant explanation which is offered whenever this difficulty is met: this type of writer, we are assured, is a 'one-book author'; he has written a fragment of autobiography, has unburdened himself of his animus against his

parents and his background, and, being relieved, cannot repeat his tour de force ... His first impatience at being unable to repeat his success can pass into discouragement and go on to actual despair; and an excellent author may be lost in consequence ...

The third difficulty is a sort of combination of the first two: there are writers who can, at wearisomely long intervals, write with great effectiveness ... Those who suffer from these silences in which not one idea seems to arise, not one sentence to come irresistibly to the mind's surface, may write like artists and craftsmen when they have once broken the spell ...

The fourth difficulty has a technical aspect: it is the inability to carry a story, vividly but imperfectly apprehended, to a successful conclusion. Writers who complain of this are often able to start a story well, but find it out of control after a few pages. Or they will write a good story so drily and sparely that all its virtues are lost. Occasionally they cannot motivate their central action adequately, and the story carries no conviction.

Dorothea Brande set herself the task of remedying these four disabilities. But she adds the rider 'If you fail repeatedly [at the exercises she commends] give up writing. Your resistance is actually greater than your desire to write, and you may as well find some other outlet for your energy early as late.'

There are dozens of how-to books on the market, two of which, *Character & Viewpoint* by Orson Scott Card and *Plot* by Ansen Dibell, have been given a lift by Michael Ridpath who credited them with helping him to land a £750,000 deal on his first novel, *Free to Trade*. But with honourable exceptions the content of many of these instructional guides is painfully banal.

From books to correspondence classes is another leap towards the lower depths. The skill of these so-called 'educational' institutions is to present modest achievements ('I was paid £19.99 for my article on hill climbing in the Cairngorms') as major triumphs. Satisfied customers are those who are pleased to see their names in print. They would even pay for the privilege; indeed they probably do pay to the extent of failing to earn enough to cover the course fees.

For more accurate pointers to a future in writing, return to the base rules set forth by those who are undisputed masters of the craft. Evelyn Waugh identified three essential qualities:

Lucidity – which can be acquired.
Elegance – which you can strive all your life to achieve.
Distinctive voice – for which you can only pray.

To which George Orwell adds six practicalities:

Never use a metaphor, simile, or other figure of speech which you are used to seeing in print.
Never use a long word when a short one will do.
If it is possible to cut a word out, always cut it out.
Never use the passive where you can use the active.
Never use a foreign phrase, a scientific word, or a jargon word if you can think of an everyday English equivalent.
Break any of these rules sooner than say anything outright barbarous.

Orwell's last rule does seem to endorse the view of those who hold that there are no rules. The wisdom of modesty comes over with terrifying clarity in Hugh Leonard's autobiography *Out After Dark*.

Writing is neither profession nor vocation, but an incurable illness. Those who give up are not writers and never were. Those who persevere do so not from pluck or determination but because they cannot help it. They are sick and advice is an impudence.

Making Ends Meet

A WRITER'S GUIDE TO
SUPPLEMENTARY INCOME

IT IS A WELL-KNOWN axiom of the writing trade that few live by words alone. For every full-time author or dramatist, there are hundreds, maybe thousands of scribblers who also do proper jobs. The reasons are not entirely financial. Writers who depend on experience for their raw material need to get away from the laptop to remind themselves how the rest of the world lives. The risk for the desk-chained professional is that having nothing else to contemplate except his own outpourings he ends up writing about the traumas of writing, the victim of literary ennui.

But there are writers who are driven from their garrets by economic necessity. They would dearly like to be more creative, if only they could think of ways of making money at the same time. It can be done but the trick is strictly conditional on junking fancy ideas about pure art.

FREELANCING

Susan Elkin, an experienced freelancer, compares her trade to prostitution. 'The more clients the better and you can't afford to be too particular about who they are.' Here is someone who makes a full-time living from placing articles across and beyond the national press.

> The variety is exhilarating. I visit schools and education centres all over the country. I've written articles about the English wine industry, keeping pets in 19th-century Paris, travel pieces about Germany, Northumberland, South Shields, Kent and Sussex, and children's fairy tales. I've also done book reviews, fiction and biography.

I have interviewed two famous peers in their country homes, observed musicians at work, watched the making of an animated opera in a Soho studio, been shown round several nature reserves and met dozens of fascinating people.

There is another type of freelancer, one who offers specialist knowledge – 'A Doctor Writes', for example, or 'Cookery by Numbers' – and yet another who has an opinion on everything and is only too ready to share it with you. The latter are generally well-paid columnists with star names.

The link between all these writers is their experience of the market and the multiplicity of their contacts. As travel writer Adam Hopkins reflects:

It is extremely difficult, perhaps impossible, to start up as a media freelancer unless you are on good terms professionally with a number of people who actually commission the kind of work you do. This is normally achieved by working full-time in a media organisation. A few years with a publisher, newspaper or similar is almost always a necessity for successful freelancing. As a journalist I say this feelingly, having watched a number of perfectly intelligent and literate people, with no journalistic background, trying to contribute to newspapers which had no previous knowledge of them. The results are far too often negative, leading first to frustration and then to loss of confidence.

His view is endorsed by Kent Barker.

In a busy newspaper office, with editorial conferences and coffee machine chats, story and feature ideas proliferate. The freelancer working alone at home has to better them to be in with a chance. Then there is knowing whom to approach. National papers have a plethora of page editors, section editors and specialist correspondents. All can commission a piece but few have the ultimate say on whether it will be published. One colleague phoned the *Independent*'s Saturday magazine with a proposal for a regular column slot. 'Great,' said the column's editor, 'I'd like that.' Three hours later she phoned back to say the magazine's overall editor did not feel it was suitable, so the commission was off.

And editors change. No sooner have you built up a good working relationship with one person than he or she is posted to Washington and the successor will not even answer the phone to you. 'Put the idea down on paper,' says a secretary or assistant, 'and he'll look at it.' Well, he might or might not, but he will probably only bother to tell you if he is definitely interested.

Seen from the point of view of an editor, the reluctance to take on unknown freelancers on trust is understandable. Adam Hopkins again:

Plenty of people can write so why take chances on an unknown in whom you have established no confidence? What if the article is a tissue of lies? What about dear old Bloggins whose piece will have to stay out of the paper if this one runs tonight? It takes the outsider a while to learn the disconcerting truth – all freelance work is sold in a buyer's market and no concessions are made to inexperience. It is true that every now and then a features editor may spot an unusual quality in the offerings received from a particular supplicant and may then decide to give that supplicant a try. One or two well-established writers have started in this way. But those whom I know personally have all been academics or specialists of some kind, with particular things to say, a reason for trying more than once to say them, and a regular salary to pay the phone bill in the meanwhile.

The upside, and this is in no way a contradiction of the preceding arguments, is that freelancers are more in demand today than ever before. Visit any newspaper office and you will see why. There are editors everywhere – news editors, features editors, section editors, supplement editors, picture editors, managing editors – even the occasional editor's editor, the top man, when he can spare a few moments from lecturing the nation on *Today* or being assertive on *Question Time*. But ordinary staff journalists are thin on the ground. There are two reasons for this.

First, there is not much call for news journalists nowadays. Much of what passes for hard news in the national press is adapted from the Press Association with a little help from CNN. Second, and as a consequence of television and radio taking over as the main providers of news, the space between the advertisements is occupied predominantly by features and columns. Feature writers and columnists do not have to work from a central office. In fact, it is far better for the overhead and profit margin that they work well away from the office – on the kitchen table at home, for example, where they have to pay for their heating and make their own coffee. Hence the increase in the number of freelancers. Some may be tied to particular newspapers by monthly pay cheques but, like the freelancers who spread their talents across several publications, they know the terror of job insecurity and compensating pleasure of managing their own lives.

And the market is growing. There are more papers with more pages and there are far fewer obstacles to getting into print. Time was when you had to have a union card to qualify as a regular contributor to any national publication. Today, no one bothers to ask if you are a fully paid-up member of the labour movement. The closed shop has been consigned to history.

This brings us back to the 64 thousand-dollar question. What is the best way for a writer to extend his money-making into freelancing, short of starting over as a tea boy for the editor? Susan Elkin advises buying *The Writer's Handbook* for 'outlets and other valuable information', which is nice of her, and goes on to urge a study of the market by assiduous reading of newspapers and magazines. Telephone skills are vital.

> When you ring an editor, try saying 'Is this a convenient moment or would you prefer me to ring back later?' If the response is 'yes' then you are bound to be granted long enough to explain yourself. If the answer is 'later please' then the same will apply when you call back. Work out when people's busiest times in the day or week are and avoid phoning on non-urgent matters at those times.

She adds cannily:

> It's an editor's world. However cross an editor makes you, you cannot afford to quarrel. Swear after you've put the phone down and not before.

Possessing a reasonable claim to an area of expertise is a great advantage. University teachers lucky enough to have impressed bright students who subsequently achieve editorial power invariably find themselves called upon to parade their knowledge for a wider public. And we all know of authors who become critics, retired generals who hold forth on military strategy and doctors who advise on healthy living.

But experts should beware experts. To turn out a marvellous piece on, say, the winemakers of England or feminism in the theatre is to risk coming up against a newspaper's regular wine correspondent or theatre critic. A journalist – freelancer or staffer – who occupies a comfortable niche is unlikely to make room for a possible rival. The best policy is to identify a specialization which has popular appeal but which, for one reason or another, a particular newspaper covers inadequately or not at all. To take an obvious general example, all newspapers are in hot pursuit of younger readers to boost their flagging circulations. Yet, so far, the race is still wide open. Anyone with a bright idea to win over the youth market without deterring older readers has to be on to a winner.

A more radical suggestion for freelance advancement appears in a NUJ advice sheet which urges readers to 'plan an entire new life'.

> One of the fastest ways of making a name (and finding things to write about) is to set off for a year or two to somewhere exciting where there aren't too many journalists working for British publications (the Far East looks promising at the moment) and vow to cover everything you can find in the area.

Other NUJ-inspired pointers to successful entry into print include writing about yourself ('Whether presented humorously, treated as confessionals – or as awful examples – the activities of you, your family and friends might be turned into subjects for articles.'); using aspects of your life to trigger off research into general topics (adopting a child, for example, might lead to an article on adoption agencies); and trawling through other people's articles.

> You see an odd little item in a local newspaper. Could the people involved be interviewed at greater length and an article for a national

publication be conjured up? You read an article in an American magazine – is there a British equivalent that you could do?

The principle of following on has strong application even with stories that first appear in a national paper. Editors are easily incensed by a scoop in a rival publication and are eager to beat the competition by producing an even better story on the same theme. This is why a report on town hall corruption, say, is soon followed by a succession of revelations of the nefarious ways of local politicians. But you have to move smartly to take advantage of a follow-on. Today's hot story can be tomorrow's reject.

Looking ahead, an anniversary is generally good for an article. There is a magic in a fifty-, twenty-five- or even ten-year retrospective. The recent blockbuster example was the fuss surrounding the fiftieth anniversary of the ending of the Second World War. But lesser events qualify for extensive coverage – the anniversary of an artist's death, say, or the construction of a famous landmark. The next biggie is in four years' time. Maybe we should all be writing now for the millennium.

EXTRACTS FROM THE NATIONAL UNION OF JOURNALISTS' GUIDE TO FREELANCING

When commissioned, a freelancer should record the name and position of the commissioner and check the authority to commission – useful information if, say, a newsdesk later denies knowledge of ordering an item.

Freelancer and commissioner will need to agree a number of matters which may include:

→ the work to be carried out

→ the fee to be paid or the rate at which payment will be calculated

→ the length for written or recorded material or time to be spent on an assignment

→ expenses to be paid

→ insurance against libel risks

→ deadlines to be met

- form of delivery – whether by typescript or photographic print, for instance, or some form of electronic filing
- rights to be licensed to the client
- arrangements for insurance and return of illustrations, transparencies and the like
- when payment will be made

A commission is a contract in law. A word-of-mouth contract – when a commission is given face to face or over the phone – is legally binding but, to avoid later problems, should be confirmed in writing.

At the very least, the freelancer should send a letter or a fax to the commissioner (while keeping a copy) outlining the agreement reached and stating that the letter records the contract unless queried or disputed within seven days.

When delivering material, freelancers may ask for written acknowledgement or use the Post Office recorded delivery service. When posting valuable materials, such as negatives or colour transparencies or cartoons or illustrations, freelancers should use registered post and check the level of insurance.

Speculative material

Freelancers often work up material on their own account and do so on the basis that rates and conditions negotiated in the past will continue. Even so, the freelancer should send a covering note making this clear.

When approaching a possible client for the first time, or when circumstances change – perhaps when submitted work has greater news value than usual – this covering note should state that offering the material does not in itself constitute a licence to publish: terms must be agreed between editor and client. These terms will cover matters such as the fee to be paid, rights required and any allowance towards expenses, just as with a commission. And, just as with a commission, this agreement, including the fact of acceptance, should be confirmed in writing.

An editor may reasonably be expected to inform a freelancer whether speculatively offered material is accepted or rejected within two weeks of receipt. Where a faster response might be required – with news-based material, event previews or whatever – the covering note should make this clear.

Rejected material should be returned immediately. If unable to decide, an editor should negotiate a holding fee with the freelancer.

Freelancers are advised not to send valuable or irreplaceable materials, such as colour transparencies, original tapes or cuttings, until an editor or client has confirmed an interest.

Regular Contributors

Where a freelancer makes regular contributions, whether as a columnist or as undertaking to produce a certain amount of work, the arrangement should be formalized with a written contract providing for, amongst other things, agreements on fees, annual revision of fees, notice of termination, redundancy and a retainer where applicable. Such a contract will normally be a contract for services, to protect the freelancer's self-employed status and ownership of copyright.

Seeking work

Freelancers have to judge what form of approach will seem reasonable to clients. With news-based material, a fax or phone call may be essential. With slower-moving material, commissioning editors may prefer a letter outlining the project.

Brain picking

Editors wishing to buy information or solicit ideas from a freelancer should expect to pay, just as they would for material. If asked to supply background information, contact numbers and so on, a freelancer should negotiate an agreement in the same way as for a commission.

Although there is no copyright in ideas, there is copyright in memos, letters, synopses and so on that give expression to these ideas. Ideas can be further protected by marking submissions confidential.

Copyright

Freelancers, whether writers, photographers, broadcasters, cartoonists, illustrators or whatever, automatically own the copyright in material they create. They should retain that ownership in any agreement for use of the material, whether commissioned or speculatively submitted. Ideally, freelancers should grant a licence covering the specific conditions of publication, say for one-time use in the United Kingdom.

If offering first rights or first British serial rights the freelancer guarantees that the material will be appearing in that market for the first time. As a working practice, the freelancer would expect to agree a specified period during which the client would make use of the material and after which, even if the client has not published it, the freelancer would be free to offer it elsewhere.

Where further rights are required, these should be specifically requested and paid for at an agreed fee. Such rights might include:

→ repeat fees or repro fees, where the client pays for each use of the material

→ syndication rights, where the client sells on the material to other users – a freelancer granting syndication rights would expect to receive at least 50 per cent of gross sales

→ geographical rights – typically a freelancer might negotiate extra fees if a publication is distributed in the United States, the English-language market worldwide or in foreign-language markets

Freelancers should try to avoid granting blanket licences covering, say, the various forms of electronic distribution where the full value of material is yet to be discovered.

Some clients demand all rights – insisting on a contract where the freelancer assigns the entire copyright to the client, giving up control and hope of future earnings. Whether done as a matter of choice or because the client organization presents a take-it-or-leave-it ultimatum, a freelancer selling all rights should look to charge at least double the one-time use fee.

A licence to publish can be granted by word of mouth, although, as with any agreement, this should be confirmed in writing. If the licence confers some exclusive rights it needs to be in writing to be fully effective. A licence should be specific, setting out limits on time, territory or language, number of copies or editions, and the purpose, such as inclusion in a magazine or a television programme. As part of any agreement, a freelancer may require his or her own copyright notice (a line stating copyright belongs to the freelancer) to appear with the published work in order to prevent it being picked up by any automatic lifting, reprinting or syndication network operated by the publication.

Freelancers should check carefully the wording of any document they are asked to sign. Some media organizations include clauses assigning all rights within payment releases or acknowledgements, or even in endorsements on the back of cheques.

By-lines and credits

Published material should carry a by-line or credit unless the freelancer agrees otherwise.

Payment

Ideally, payment should be tied to the delivery of a specified commission or acceptance of speculatively offered material: freelancers deliver, fulfilling their side of the contract; clients pay, fulfilling theirs. Payment should be made within thirty days of delivery or acceptance. Should an editor choose to delay publication, or should the material not be used at all, payment will still be due, as agreed, within that thirty-day period.

Freelancers should be wary of agreeing to be paid on publication as this may lead to a long wait, particularly if the material is not used as expected. If a freelancer does agree to be paid on publication, a date should still be set when payment will be triggered if publication is delayed or cancelled.

When a commission covers a long period, freelancers should negotiate an advance towards the total fee or staged payments for editorial work.

Expenses

Expenses should be paid to freelancers on at least the same basis as to staff and should cover matters such as phone calls and other communication costs, full subsistence, travel costs including car mileage (using the AA assessment of 36p per mile upwards depending on the size of the car), necessary entertainment and so on. Where freelances pay out expenses and claim them back later, a handling charge of 10 per cent may be added where agreed.

When reclaiming expenses, freelancers may need to obtain VAT receipts in situations where they would not otherwise bother – for taxi rides and train journeys, for instance. Also, freelancers may need to keep photocopies of receipts to satisfy both clients and tax authorities.

Payment of expenses should be made part of any contract. Where they are a significant amount, perhaps on an assignment involving extensive travel, some agreement as to their likely level should be reached beforehand and a reasonable proportion paid to the freelancer in advance.

Insurance and libel

Client organizations should insure commissioned freelancers, at the same level as staff journalists, against personal injury, sickness or any loss or damage to equipment incurred on assignment. Freelancers should check insurance cover, particularly when going abroad, perhaps charging it on the same basis as other expenses. In deciding whether to take on speculative work, remember the useful adage: if you can't afford the insurance, you can't afford what will happen if you're hit.

Clients should indemnify freelancers against damages for libel, and freelancers should check that they are covered by the client's insurance. Freelancers should keep interview notes and copies of all material supplied to protect themselves against situations where client organizations introduce libellous material during editing.

Cancellation or kill fee

If a commission is cancelled before the work has been completed, a cancellation fee of at least 50 per cent should be paid. Where work has been delivered to a specified commission, or accepted when being offered speculatively, it must be paid for in full even if circumstances change and the client does not use it. Only where delivered material demonstrably fails to meet the agreed brief would a kill fee of less than 100 per cent be acceptable.

Freelance check list

→ Make sure you clearly understand what each commission or contract involves

→ Record the names and positions of people you deal with – particularly those responsible for payment

→ Confirm fees and conditions, including copyright arrangements, in writing

→ Follow up where necessary to confirm that material has arrived and is acceptable

→ Send in an invoice as soon as possible – or confirm that an effective self-billing arrangement operates

→ Check that payment arrives as promised. If it doesn't, start telephoning to find out why – and think hard before working for these people again

→ Keep records so you can see who owes you money and satisfy the Inland Revenue and VAT collectors

TRANSLATIONS

A writer with a second language can make a supplementary income, or, indeed, his chief income, as a translator. Formal qualifications are not essential. Some translators start with the advantage of being raised in a bilingual family, others acquire linguistic skills by working overseas. A university education in modern languages can be helpful but is not in itself a badge of competence.

The ideal translator is also a gifted writer. He needs to have a feeling and fascination for language and the talent to convey the essence of the original work, echoing its style and tone. A word-for-word literal interpretation is bound to fail.

Because the translator is a creative artist in his own right, copyright law recognizes the 'original' nature of his work with copyright protection that is distinct from the copyright of the author. This opens up the possibility of a recurring income over many years, even when the duration of the author's copyright is exhausted. For example, a writer knowledge-able in Russian might produce a marvellous new Chekhov translation thus bringing a play back into copyright for the benefit of the translator.

The downside to any such enterprise is that there can be no exclusive right to the translation of a particular work. Where one translator has trod profitably, another may soon follow in his footsteps. Working from the same source text, the result is likely to be two different but equally valid renditions. Nonetheless, for a popular book or play, the possibilities for argument between translators as to who owns what are legion. In the theatre, such disputes are further complicated by the tendency of some translators to rely rather too heavily on existing English-language versions of a play to achieve their own interpretation. It has been known for a 'translator' to possess only the haziest notion of the language he was supposed to be working from. His defence was that he had a good dictionary.

Ideas for translating books or plays invariably start with a publisher or producer. It follows that the best chance of a commission comes from sending out sample material. But it is open to anyone to offer proposals. A writer who is bilingual in, say, French or German should watch the reviews and publishing lists for likely projects. The trick here is to secure an understanding with a prospective partner before trying to negotiate a commission. This is at least some protection against a publisher who might thank you profusely for the idea before sending it off to one of his regular panel of translators.

Like every other form of writing, translating is subject to fashion. A few years ago French drama was in; now it is quite definitely out. It is said that there are few modern French plays worth translating.

Knowledge of a rare language can help, though it is no longer enough to be conversant with one of the minority European languages like Dutch or Danish. The use of English in these countries is now so extensive that writers are inclined to do their own translations or compose in English as the first language.

Payment for translation can be by royalty or by fee. If it is in the form of a lump sum, it should not be for the translation but for a specified use of the translator's work; for example, for the right to print 5000 copies for sale in the UK. Such an arrangement makes fair allowance for additional fees to be paid if further copies are sold or if the licence is extended to include America. For the translation of a book, the Model Contract drawn up by the Translators' Association recommends that there should be an advance payment on account of royalties and a share of the proceeds from the sale of subsidiary rights such as serialization. In the case of a play, the translator should receive a percentage of the gross box-office receipts. The translator should be able to obtain additional payment if asked to edit a literary work as well as translate it; and there should be an additional fee for the preparation of an index for the translated edition. When translations are borrowed from public libraries, the translator receives a 30 per cent share of the full Public Lending Right payment (see p. 86).

Usually the rights owner, either author or publisher, accepts lower royalties on the translated edition, say a 7 per cent royalty on sales of a translated book compared with 10 per cent on sales in its original language. On a theatre production the original author might receive 6 per cent instead of 10 per cent. The author may also forgo a share of secondary rights; for example, of the proceeds from the sale of American rights. This means that some or all of the payment received by the translator is money that would otherwise have been paid to the original author. To that extent, the *author* is the person who is paying the translator.

Sometimes the foreign author of a work is so keen to see it translated that he will offer to pay the translation costs directly. In this case, a written contract between author and translator should specify the respective rights and set out how any proceeds from publication or production are to be divided.

Bursaries and Prizes

A number of residential bursaries are offered by the British Centre for Literary Translation at the Department of Modern Languages and European History, The University of East Anglia, Norwich NR4 1TJ. For up-to-date information about bursaries abroad, contact the Cultural Attaché of the relevant embassy or bodies such as the French Institute, the Goethe Institut and the Italian Institute. The Arts Council offers bursaries to theatre translators under its Theatre Translation Schemes. The Translators' Association administers several prizes for already published translations and the Arts Council sometimes contributes towards the cost of producing translations.

The Translators' Association

The Translators' Association is a subsidiary group within the Society of Authors. Published translators can apply for full membership. Translators in the making may apply for Associate Membership either when they have received an offer for a full-length translation or if they have had occasional translations of shorter material, such as articles, short stories and poems, published or performed commercially.

The Association's Model Contract, with explanatory notes, is available free to members; and the Association also issues guidelines for translators of dramatic works. The Association's journal, *In Other Words*, contains a wide variety of articles, reviews and information.

COMPANY HISTORIES AND SPEECH WRITING

Industry and the public services are much in need of capable writers – though they can barely bring themselves to admit it. There are jazzy-looking publications carrying the imprint of leading companies, from shareholder reports to product brochures, that defy rational analysis by anyone who is unfamiliar with the corporate patois. Yet they are distributed without a trace of embarrassment or shame.

Foolishly optimistic customers are led to believe the promise of 'simple instructions' to assemble a piece of furniture, say, or to operate a new appliance when the reality is hours of patient effort to key into the manufacturer's tangled logic. But the problem goes largely unrecognized.

All credit then to those organizations which do treat communication skills seriously. It is no coincidence that most of them are not too proud to engage professional writers. More might be encouraged to do so if writers pushed their services. An apparent reluctance to double up as salesman may derive from a wariness of the unfamiliar (the hard commercial world can strike fear into the uninitiated) but may equally originate in the snobbery of creative artists who cannot bring themselves to think in terms other than of the great novel.

This last category must settle for the garret and prolonged periods of self-reflection. There is no helping them. The rest, the shrinking violets, should get their act together. Seek out the prospects. A telephone call or letter to a local company or, more particularly, to the head of public relations or corporate affairs of that company – by name! – could well lead to an invitation to talk over ideas. There are many writers with enviable track records who make a respectable supplementary income working in the front line of marketing. It does not have to be advertising copy or the editing of internal memos. Other, more substantial projects are available.

Writing in the *Author*, Patrick Beaver proclaims the virtue of the company history. This type of book is often judged to be a product of the 1980s – when business was keen to assert its claims to approbation. But the tradition goes far back. The first company history was *A Short Account of the Bank of England*, published in 1695. It did not start a trend, it has to be said, and it was not until the late nineteenth century that the book of the firm became popular. Patrick Beaver reckons that over 2000 have been published in the last 25 years.

> Broadly speaking, company histories fall into two classes. There are the 'exhaustive' works, full of figures, tables, graphs, analyses and vital statistics. Sometimes running into two volumes, these can be powerful sedatives for all but company directors and professors of economics. The other kind (which are the subject of this article) are the 'popular', not-too-technical, usually illustrated books, written with an eye to a wide readership, and suitable for distribution not only to a firm's investors and business associates, but employees, friends – and the general public.

The advice to a would-be author of a company history is to check first the client's motive for producing a book.

> Some firms will see it as a stimulus to consumer loyalty and staff motivations; others as a monument to past and present achievements; some managements want a record of the past as their firms move away from family ownership. But without exception, all will want the book to express everything that management knows and feels about the company: its organisation and experience; its struggles and accomplishments; its policies and aims.

Payment is nearly always by direct fee. Even if the book is sold through the shops, the large number of copies given away to the firm's customers makes it hard to calculate royalties. Moreover, the author is usually asked to surrender copyright. This is fair given that the author is working directly for a specific client. Any consequent loss of earnings should be taken into account when negotiating a fee. A day-rate for research and writing, plus expenses, is the sensible way to proceed.

What to put in and what to leave out is a question that may trouble the author no less than the client. Patrick Beaver's experience suggests that the distant past has the edge on the present, 'for no one has an axe to grind'. For the rest, it all depends on the collective conscience.

> It is highly unlikely that the company will make available to the author details of an episode which it prefers to forget. The author, if he is worth his salt, will shoulder *his* responsibility and do his best to tell of things as they happened. On the other hand, he must recognise that no company can be expected to spend money in inviting ridicule or condemnation because of some indiscretion – especially if it is recent.

If the need to compromise disturbs the silent hours of the night consider the axiom that truth is to be found between two areas of value judgement. The alternative is to act as a court advocate putting over a client's case to the best of your ability because his version deserves to be heard. The problem is no more serious than that faced by a biographer of a living person.

Speeches have to be written, a time-consuming activity that top people hand over to the professionals. Some of these are stars in their own right. Sir Ronald Millar was best known as a playwright before he turned to speech-writing for Margaret Thatcher. He it was who gave her the words by which she is best remembered: 'The lady's not for turning.' A speechwriter for an American president can earn more than a member of the cabinet, and be treated with far greater respect.

The skill of the speechwriter is in being able to think in the same way as the speechmaker, but more lucidly and more memorably. Writing for someone with whom you are not in sympathy can be a painful, frustrating and, in the end, a fruitless exercise.

A good speech is like a good story. It must have a structure with a beginning, a middle and an end; a logical sequence of thoughts which leads to a satisfying conclusion. Clearly, a professional writer, particularly one with an ear for dialogue, has much to offer a speechmaker who is not himself a skilled communicator. Given the best material, even a modest speaker can make a strong impact.

The target clients are senior managers who are often called upon to grace a conference platform but have no idea where to start – or when to stop. Training sessions in public speaking are now part of every executive's further education. But the art of adding substance to the theory by finding the right words for a particular occasion can seldom be taught. It is the writer who gives coherence to diverse thoughts.

TALKING BOOKS

Writing and acting make a good combination. The advantages are usually seen from the actor's point of view. All that hanging about waiting to be called for rehearsal or to appear on a film set drives the actor to think of something more productive to do than the *Times* crossword. But it works both ways. The writer has much to gain from acting experience and the ability to hold an audience other than by putting words on paper.

Talking books are a case in point. After years of muddling along on story tapes for children and vintage radio comedy, this market is at last taking off. Its total value is anyone' guess – figures from £25 million to £50 million are bandied about. The best evidence of increasing buoyancy is the range of titles on offer – romance, thrillers, travel, biographies, even political memoirs, they are all there on cassette, read occasionally by their authors but more often by well-known actors who have cornered this profitable sector of the business. Naturally, there are star turns such as Martin Jarvis and Miriam Margoyles whose talent for creating images by voice alone is unlikely ever to be matched by the authors they serve. But judging by the results there are many in this game who treat it as an optional extra to their main living. Their performances are competent but hardly inspiring. The authors might do a lot better and could certainly not do worse. They should nurture whatever dramatic skills they may possess. Even a short course of voice training can do wonders.

The alternative is to risk being marginalized. It is already happening. While a talking books publisher will offer a modest advance to an author – £2000 on a cassette forecast to sell 5000 copies a year is considered generous – he will not blink at paying a reader £1000 for a day or two's work, not to mention a similar sum to an editor for cutting a text to the required length. The author does get a royalty, anything from 4 per cent of receipts to 15 per cent of the published price, but Equity, the actors' union, has caught on to what it sees as a discrepancy that must be corrected. In other words, the author will get less, and the actor more. The publishers say they have no room to manoeuvre. The production costs, including recording, duplicating and packaging, are higher than for the average printed book, while profit margins are correspondingly thinner, which begs the question as to why so many are keen to get into the business but, hey ho, that's free enterprise.

The best literary agents, primed on the knowledge that in the States the talking books market is roaring ahead and audio rights secure million-dollar deals, are beginning to fight back on behalf of their clients. Speaking to a conference organized by the Society of Authors, Anthea Morton-Saner of Curtis Brown urged resistance to any publisher who presses for world rights (the US should not be so lightly discarded) and recommended a five-year limit on the granting of options. Moreover, the right of consultation on production values and distribution deals should be enshrined in the contract.

As to delivering the full package, voice and all, judge the competition and set a standard by listening to Dirk Bogarde reading his latest volume of autobiography, *A Short Walk from Harrods* (Penguin) or to Alan Clark's *Diaries* (Polygram). In their different ways, the two old charmers are totally compelling. But, then, they have had to work hard to make it look easy.

SINGING FOR SUPPER

For those with something to say and an entertaining way of saying it, the performance circuit can be a merry money-spinner. There are some twenty agencies specializing in lectures, after-dinner speeches and confer-ence turns, of which Associated Speakers, Prime Performers, J.F. Sports, Taylor Made Productions and Marks Productions are the leaders. But speakers very often fix their own engagements.

It is the celebs who command the skyrocket fees. Bob Monkhouse, Sir David Frost, Alan Whicker, Ken Dodd, Sir John Harvey-Jones, Clive James and Barry Humphries are among those who can demand up to

£5000 an appearance. They are joined by those possessed of transient notoriety, such as a round-the-world balloonist lately dredged from the North Sea. Writers can find themselves in this category but they are usually one-book authors who have published an account of their adventures.

More typical is the writer/speaker who builds up a reputation for holding an audience on a subject dear to his heart. It might be a gardener with an unparalleled knowledge of roses, a weather forecaster with a sideline in water divining or a sports reporter with a fund of 'believe-it-or-not' stories. The possibilities are endless. Some years ago there was a demolition man called Buster Bates whose somewhat overripe anecdotes were so popular with after-dinner audiences that he advanced to making a long-playing record.

Skilled practitioners can link up this side of their activities to the point where they join the ranks of professional performers touring one-man shows. Robert Gittings, the multi-volumed biographer of Thomas Hardy, used to range the country with thematic readings from the master's collected works, often with an actor in attendance to give dramatic effect to his narration. It is unlikely that he made a fortune this way but he sold a lot of books.

There is a risk here, of course. Selling books is quite properly a collaborative effort between publisher and author. But in throwing oneself into the promotional maelstrom, the writer can become a hard-working but unpaid member of the sales team. Festival organizers, chairmen of literary groups and secretaries of this or that professional body are past masters at persuading publishers to sacrifice an author to a day of travel and talking. If the author resists, the offer of lunch is thought sufficient to clinch the deal.

Maybe the benefits show up on the sales returns but don't be too sure. A safer bet is to insist on a minimum fee – say, £100 plus expenses. It may not pay the mortgage but it is at least a sign that they really want you.

THE GHOST IN THE MACHINE

Literary ghosting is franchising by another name. A famous company sells to an outsider the right to trade under its logo; that's franchising. A famous personality parades himself as the originator of a book written by another; that's ghosting. In both cases, the advantage is in marketing – familiarity breeds sales.

The purists will have none of it. Naturally. They take the view that a real book should be written by the person whose name appears on the cover. It should not be 'told' to someone else. Why not? In other intellectual pursuits, the name on the invoice rarely acts alone. Artists have their apprentices, surgeons their nurses, scientists their research assistants, lawyers their clerks. What is so particular about a book that its value should be enhanced by the knowledge that its author works in isolation?

Then there is this curious assumption that ghosting is new, the invention of a profit-obsessed generation of publishers who think with their pocket calculators. True, our entrepreneurs have exploited ghosting but they did not invent it. Ghosting goes back at least as far as the Bible (how many unnamed scribes were engaged on that masterpiece?). Dr Johnson had 'six amanuenses' to help him write his dictionary, the forerunner of thousands of ghost-created reference works. It was in the late nineteenth century that ghosting really took off with the boom in self-justifying political and military memoirs. Closer to our own time, Winston Churchill employed a veritable army of back-up writers for his books and articles. And he won the Nobel Prize for Literature.

The latest development is the ghosting of novels. The example of *Swan* by Naomi Campbell is often quoted because the 'author' made no attempt to disguise the fact that the book was written by her 'editor'. After Simon & Schuster paid lavishly for two novels by Ivana Trump, she told the *Ladies Home Journal* that to have her ghostwriter follow her around on the international scene was 'so much easier than describing everything'. The first of the Trump novels sold 100,000 copies in hardback, which suggests that honesty is no deterrent to sales.

For really bad ghosted books one turns immediately to the life stories of those titans of the sports field who have little to say but take the long route in saying it. But for more serious subjects, it is at least arguable that the ghosted biography of a living character can get as close to the truth as autobiography or straight biography. The autobiographer has to live with his prejudices and illusions, which means that they are recycled as convincing rationalities. Given adequate sources, the biographer can see through these stratagems but he is invariably too far removed from his subject to be objective. The ghost, on the other hand, can play the interviewer, persuading the subject to say what he might otherwise have left unsaid. Enough. Even if the opponents of ghosting are not won over they should at least accept that a ghosted book is not necessarily inferior to other forms of literary enterprise and may be a sight better.

Ghostwriting can be far more lucrative than writing books under one's own name. Given that the personality blazoned across the dust jacket has the inbuilt interest to command large sales, the ghost can materialize after six months' work £20,000–£30,000 in pocket. The sum translates into 30–40 per cent of the advance on royalties (in America it is usually 50 per cent) and a similar share of serialization and other subsidiary rights.

The problem is in securing sufficient acknowledgement. It is an infallible rule of ghosting that the subjects always end up believing that they wrote the book themselves. This makes them touchy on the question of billing. Often the only hint of a ghost is a name on the copyright line or a passing reference to a 'loyal helper'.

But anonymity is not a precondition of ghostwriting. While it is fair enough for the name of the storyteller to be up front, the story writer deserves his credit, if not on the book cover, at least on the title page. Quite apart from the benefits of self-promotion (one ghosting job leads to another), a clear credit removes any misunderstanding over the share-out of Public Lending Right.

Over in the States they are less inhibited. Ronald Reagan's *An American Life* contained a fulsome tribute to Robert Lindsey, 'a talented writer who was with me every step of the way'. It was noted by Anthony Howard that the contribution of his co-writer was about the only thing the former President made a clean breast of in the entire book.

Particular care has to be taken with the contract. A sloppily worded clause can bring endless trouble and financial pain. Even when all known loopholes have been closed, others can be opened up by a sharp operator. Some time ago, I ghosted the biography of a well-known actor. Sadly, he died before the manuscript could be completed, which left me to sort matters out with his widow. By no means an automatic bestseller, the book promised its best return on serialization. I therefore settled for a low percentage on royalties against a decent share of the proceeds on two centre-page spreads in a Sunday newspaper.

So far, so profitable. But then, immediately after the first extract appeared, I was informed by the widow's agent that I would not gain from further serialization. This was because the newspaper had chosen, or been persuaded, to present the article as an interview. That the interview was, word for word, taken from the book and amended only by the addition of inverted commas, was said to be irrelevant. Letters were exchanged, anger vented before a none too amicable settlement was reached. Not for the first time I was grateful for a long association with a first-class agent.

PUBLIC LENDING RIGHT (PLR)

It is one of the amazing facts of literary life that there are authors – established ones at that – who have still not signed on for Public Lending Right. Maybe they feel they do not need the money, which is fine by the rest of us, or perhaps they think that the sums involved are too small to matter. On the second point, they could be right. A quarter of those registered do not qualify for any payment at all and the majority come in at less than £100. On the other hand, at the last count 116 authors received cheques of £6000, the highest maximum level, and 1700 authors made in excess of £500.

The curiosity is that you can never be sure which category you fall into until you test your popularity on the library shelves. For example, there are children's writers who earn modest royalties but clean up on PLR because they write books which are borrowed frequently and read quickly. A personal experience – I do best from a travel book which has been out of print for twenty years. Until it popped up on a PLR return I had almost forgotten I had written the book.

For the uninitiated, Public Lending Right allows for a modest payment to authors (writers, translators and illustrators) whose books are lent out from public libraries. The amount they receive is proportional to the number of borrowings credited to their titles over a year. The first payments under PLR were made in 1984, when £1.5 million was divided between 6000 authors. The latest funding (for 1994–5) was just short of £5 million and now 23,000 authors are registered.

These are the ground rules for PLR:

To qualify, an author must be resident in the United Kingdom or Germany (the latter as part of a reciprocal deal). For a book to be eligible it must be printed, bound and put on sale. It must not be mistaken for a newspaper or periodical, or be a musical score. Crown copyright is excluded, also books where authorship is attributed to a company or association. But – and this is where mistakes often occur – the author does not have to own copyright to be eligible for PLR. Anyone who has disclaimed copyright as part of a flat-fee commission, for instance, will still have a claim if his name is on the title page.

Under PLR, the sole writer of a book may not be its sole author. Others named on the title page, such as illustrators, translators, compilers, editors and revisers, may have a claim to authorship. Where there are joint authors – two writers, say, or a writer and illustrator – they can strike their own bargain on how their entitlement is to be split. But translators may apply, without reference to other authors, for a 30 per cent fixed share (to be divided equally between joint translators). Similarly, an editor or compiler may register a 20 per cent share provided he has written 10 per cent of the book or at least ten pages of text. Joint editors or compilers must divide the 20 per cent share equally.

Authors and books can be registered for PLR only when application is made during the author's lifetime. However, once an author is registered, the PLR on his books continues for the period of copyright. If he wishes, an author can assign PLR to other people and bequeath it by will. If a co-author is dead or untraceable, the remaining co-author can still register for a share of PLR so long as he provides supporting evidence as to why he alone is making application.

Three years ago the criteria for eligibility were amended slightly to allow for cases where an author's name is not given on the title page, or where a book lacks a conventional title page. In these instances, it will now be possible for a writer to register if he is named elsewhere in the book and can show that his contribution would normally merit a title page credit. Alternatively, proof of a royalty payment is acceptable. Where there are several writers, one of whom cannot prove eligibility, the co-authors can provide a signed statement testifying to their colleague's right to a share of the PLR payment.

The other significant change in eligibility concerns the former rule that books were disqualified if more than three authors were named on the title page. This has been abolished and there is now no maximum limit on the number of authors who can apply for part-shares.

One limiting factor has been introduced. Authors can no longer register books that do not have an International Standard Book Number (ISBN). Tracing them was simply too expensive.

A note on German PLR. Some authors wonder why their payments are so small. The answer is that under the German system, after the 10 per cent deduction for administrative costs, a further 10 per cent is paid into a 'social fund', which is set aside for making *ex gratia* payments to authors who are in need, and yet another 45 per cent is paid into a 'social security' fund. Foreign authors, however, are not entitled to benefit from either fund. After the 65 per cent deductions, the remaining amount is divided between the authors (who take 70 per cent) and the publishers (who take 30 per cent). Furthermore, under German law, the translator is entitled to 50 per cent of the author's share, and if there are editors involved, they are also entitled to a percentage of the fee.

There are various ideas for extending PLR. Much thought, for example, has gone into the question of rewarding authors of reference books which are consulted on library premises but rarely taken out on loan. Complex sampling procedures have been rejected as too expensive and time consuming. Instead, payment is likely to be based on the average number of loans of a book in the lending stock. Also, there is a good argument for extending PLR to all authors living in the European Union. This might persuade other European countries to follow Germany's example with reciprocity payments to UK authors.

Next in line for a claim on PLR are the authors and presenters of talking books. The only reason why the spoken word is currently excluded from PLR is that the producers of talking books are also the exclusive copyright holders. But a directive from the European Community suggests that copyright in audio and visual productions can be reclaimed by those responsible for creative input. Expect a settlement for the spoken word before long. Doubtless, this will start a debate on PLR for computer books. The queue of potential supplicants is never-ending.

Trouble is, unless funding is increased, which seems unlikely in the short run, more claimants means less money per author. One possible corrective is to raise the minimum payment level from £1 to £10, or possibly £20. But redistribution which favours the better off is not likely to go down well with the writers' associations. For now, they will not go above £5 as a minimum payment. Another possible saving is to cut the retention time for unclaimed PLR payments from six to two years. But we are talking peanuts here.

Maybe the solution rests with the libraries themselves. Once they have got their own economic house in order by winning concessions from publishers, say, or saving on administration, there might be a little left over from their £740 million budget to support hard-pressed writers.

PLR application forms and details can be obtained from: The Registrar, PLR Office, Bayheath House, Prince Regent Street, Stockton on Tees, Cleveland TS18 1DF (Tel: 01642 604699)

P.S. If all else fails on making ends meet, a writer might consider following the example of a well-known advertiser in the *Literary Review*:

> *Fiona Pitt-Kethley* seeks adjudication work, readings, light jobs on quangos, plus an influential sponsor to nominate her for literary awards in Britain and America.

Now there *is* a determined lady.

Making Sounds

THE WRITER ON RADIO

THERE HAS TO BE a computer printout somewhere which shows how many words are spoken on radio every day. Billions rather than millions, one would think. Allowing for all the spontaneous generation of sound – instant punditry, DJ chatter, 'And now back to the studio' – at least half the words transmitted must first be set down on paper. What a market for writers! Newspapers, even books, are shaded by comparison.

And yet. Those who do best by radio are themselves broadcasters who spend most of their working hours in front of a microphone or bent over a tape recorder.

Long-established and wide-ranging programmes like *Woman's Hour* or *You and Yours* have a pecking order of contributors. The editors do not actively discourage material from unknown outsiders. But much depends on sheer good fortune – catching the right producer with the right idea at the right time. It also helps to boast expert knowledge, which explains why certain voluble academics are for ever taking to the air.

The challenge for the newcomer is to acquire a degree of professionalism through self-education. Those who run the airwaves give little in the way of practical help to budding broadcasters. To start with news and current affairs, a radio journalist in the making should first become familiar with the mysteries of the tape recorder. Investment in a Sony Professional or a recorder capable of broadcast standards is a good start; so too is a short course in editing. Cutting and splicing fill a large part of the radio journalist's life. Listen to the experts, the big names on radio, and try to understand how they do it (they themselves often find it hard to explain how they achieve their results; success can come by simple trial and error). Listen, too, to the sound of your own voice. The initial experience can come as a shock. Most of us have no idea how we sound to other people. Regional accents stand out more prominently than we ever expected while verbal mannerisms and the repetition of stock phrases – 'I mean to say', 'You know', 'At the end of the day' – can grate on the listener every bit as irritatingly as a one-tone voice that makes a dramatic story sound like a reading of the livestock prices.

The obvious place to start for real is local radio. There are now around 200 BBC and Independent local radio stations in Britain, all eager to fill the waking hours with compelling sounds. Phil Sidey, one-time maverick boss of Leeds Radio and the originator of much that is best on the local network, points to the opportunities.

> Many of the BBC stations are genuinely trying to find places for local writers, but they, or their subjects, really must be local. Some stations have 'back doors' labelled religious, drama, countryside and similar programmes; most of them, admittedly, not in prime time. If young, try the youth programmes that, in some areas, give very inexperienced youngsters freedom of the microphones.
>
> Local issues come top in acceptability but local history, straight, or based on some anniversary, is not that far behind. There is always some anniversary around, and the station might well be too busy to root it out and spend time building a programme about it. But it will all take a lot of your time to make it attractive to the station . . .
>
> Perhaps the easiest way to aim your telephone voice at the listeners' hearts is via a sports report. Most stations need a huge number of these, and if you specialize in a slightly unusual sport to start with, the broad way may be opened up to the ultimate discussion of England's soccer hopes in due course.

The key to success, says Phil Sidey, is clarity of voice.

> Accents are fine as long as the meaning can be grasped by all listeners including those who may hear the output passed on via other stations, network radio and television and may not be over-familiar with the local patois.

As to making a pitch, the informal approach seems to be the most effective.

> You may gain from visiting the station to talk to the staff. You will find most of them very friendly and informal, and you might pick up a tip or two about any gaps in their staffing. But do not waste too much of their time. Most local radio staff are very overworked; they are burdened by having to be jacks (or, hopefully, masters) of all trades. They also tend to be so much in touch with so many listeners that they find themselves being unpaid social workers.

Black marks are awarded to those who think it is so easy.

> Many writers suffer the delusion that if they come up with a story, they are creating a cheap few minutes for the station. They forget that a producer might have to put a lot of work into making it sound comparable to a network radio story – and the author may not be the best person to read it.

News reports on local radio are generally the province of journalists experienced in the ways of the regional press. It is not simply the reporter's skill that is at issue here; credit has to be given for knowledge of the finer points of the laws of defamation and contempt of Court. If an item goes out live from a rookie with a microphone and a determination to make a splash, there is no chance for the studio to correct potentially expensive mistakes.

Nobody earns much from local radio but the experience of working with the medium stands the freelancer in good stead when national radio beckons.

A useful entrée to the bigger time is provided by Educational Broadcasting. Hot in demand are subject specialists with teaching experience who can bring the touch of magic that makes learning a joy. Constraints are imposed by school and college syllabuses but within these limits there are great possibilities for innovative broadcasting. Programmes are often recorded by listeners – and may be used time and again – and can be designed for individual study, possibly in conjunction with another medium.

RADIO DRAMA

Writers who are content that others should speak their words are inevitably attracted to radio drama. In theory, every local radio is a potential market for plays and stories. But, in most cases, the operating margins are too narrow to allow for halfway respectable productions. The occasional playwriting or short story competition crops up, usually in association with a sponsor looking to a one-off public relations campaign, such as a supermarket chain with a few tricky planning applications in the pipeline.

The good news is Independent Radio Drama Productions, a non-profit-making organization which has inspired a playwright festival, runs workshops for aspiring writers and, more to the point, produces up to forty-five plays a year by new writers which are transmitted on Independent and BBC local radio. (Independent Radio Drama Productions Ltd can be contacted at Manningtree, Essex CO11 1XD).

Meanwhile, over at the BBC national network, billed as the drama centre to beat all, the accountant-led efficiency drive has thrown writers and producers into a tizzy of confusion. It is still a matter of fact that the BBC produces nearly 2000 radio plays a year, with one new play somewhere on radio every day, but nobody is quite sure how these plays come to be chosen.

Time was when unsolicited material was channelled through to a Script Unit where a body of professional readers was on hand to deliver considered verdicts. A writer might have quarrelled with a reader's judgement – nobody welcomes a thumbs down – but it was something to know that hard graft yielded more than a nod of acknowledgement.

The drawback to the Script Unit from the BBC's point of view was that its very existence attracted submissions from every punter in the business – 15,000 unsolicited scripts a year – the vast majority of which were barely up to the standard of amateur night in the Scout hut. Alan Drury, one-time literature manager of BBC Radio Drama, admits to a touch of paranoia on turning up day after day to face a deskload of unusable scripts.

> When you sit in a room with a pile of plays and you read ten or more a day and most of them are absolutely dreadful, you begin to think 'They're doing this deliberately.'

The dedicated labours of the Script Unit led to fewer than twenty productions a year. Clearly, a reorganization was called for.

Out went the Script Unit and in came the Literary Unit, which switched the emphasis from reactive to proactive commissioning. Instead of waiting for ideas or scripts to come to them, producers were encouraged to shape up their own proposals while matching appropriate writers to particular jobs. To concentrate minds there was to be a Commissioning Cycle, with most of the buying taking place in May and September.

'The department's needs will be discussed with producers and writers in the Spring and late Summer,' said Caroline Raphael, Head of Drama. 'Ideas obviously continue to be discussed throughout the year; if material is to be turned down, that will be done as quickly as possible.'

The response from writers and independent producers was, to put it mildly, overwhelming. Propelled by a flood tide of ideas, the commissioning cycle span out of control. Within months, all available drama slots were filled up to three years ahead. In an effort to restore a semblance of organization, tight controls were imposed on producers, who, having been assured that their freedom to commission was sacrosanct, now found themselves subject to the restraining power of editors and controllers. And that is how it has remained.

If, after all this, you feel inclined to try your luck with the BBC, the lines of communication are open to the Chief Producer of Plays, the Chief Producer of Series and Serials and the Producer of Readings. Outside London, the critical names for plays are Nigel Bryant (Midlands and West Country), Pam Brighton (Northern Ireland), Jane Dauncey (Wales), Patrick Rayner and Hamish Wilson (Scotland). Established writers in search of a sympathetic producer should make their pitch to one of the drama editors who are ready to act as marriage brokers.

It is easy to understand why radio drama attracts so many talented writers. Even with the restraints on subject matter, there is the chance on radio to let the imagination fly in a way that would be impossible in live theatre or on screen. Then there is the comforting knowledge that the words will be spoken by masters of their craft. Many a modest radio play has been lifted above its station by the quality of the actors. The best of them work on radio and, like writers, tolerate the miserable fees because they enjoy the freedom to play against physical type and age. It also helps that they do not have to put on costumes or learn lines.

For every newcomer the critical pointer is an understanding of the potential and the limitations of sound. Even established writers fall into the error of including too many characters (confusing the listener, particularly if they talk over each other), or failing to ring the changes in pace and location. The longer the sequence the more difficult it is to sustain interest.

Probably the best advice is encompassed in the list of questions producers must consider before recommending a play:

→ Is it basically a good story?

→ If it is, are the characters and dialogue equally good?

→ If they are, will it make good *radio*?

→ If it will, to which spot is it best suited?

→ If the script is viable on all the counts listed above, is it the right length? If not, can it be cut or expanded without artistic loss? If so, where?

→ Even if the script is still viable, how might it be improved? Is the cast too big? Does it maintain dramatic tension? Is everything that should be conveyed sufficiently well planted in the *dialogue*?

→ If it's a good story, well told in radio terms, are there any special problems (e.g. controversial themes liable to misunderstanding by the audience; foreign settings calling for difficult or expensive casting; technical backgrounds likely to attract expert criticism; etc.)?

→ If the play passes on all these counts, it's obviously a strong possibility for broadcast. How could the author make it better?

The New Playwrights' Trust suggests five technical features which make a good radio play stand out.

1   QUALITY OF CHARACTERIZATION. Can the listener imagine the experience of the character through the script? Is the character

immediate to the listener and can they empathize with her or him? Do the characters undergo some significant change through the course of the drama and does that change encompass conflict?

2   QUALITY AND ORIGINALITY OF SOUND DESIGN. Is your script uniquely suited to the radio medium? Have you created a sound atmosphere and 'sound set' that enhances and complements the mood of the writing, the characters and the plot? Is sound used symbolically, ironically, surrealistically, or satirically and does it form part of the texture and artistic fabric of the play?

3   QUALITY AND ORIGINALITY OF DIALOGUE. Are the characters created by the idiom and speech rhythms of their lines? Are characters developed by effective and revelatory dialogue? Is there a sense of reality in the speeches? If you are writing about real people do they sound like them?

4   QUALITY AND ORIGINALITY OF THE PLOT. Are you able to keep the listener on tenterhooks? Do you leave the listener determined to hear the play to the very end? How logical and believable is the story? Is the listener sure of what is happening in each of the developing scenes?

5   EFFECTIVENESS OF THE BEGINNING of the play in making the listener want to continue listening. Remember some drama producers insist that the writer has only a minute to engage the listener before they are liable to turn off!

More help on 'putting it together' appears in a BBC information leaflet.

1   *Act 1, Scene 1.*   **NO!**

Radio has no 'scenes' in the way a stage play has. A sequence in a radio play might be one line long, or last for 20 pages. But no single sequence should go beyond its natural length. Beware of boring the listener. Radio is fatally easy to turn OFF.

2   *Geoff, Carol, Alice, Roger and Richard are in*   **NO!**
    a crowded pub with some other friends.

The only means of establishing a character's presence is to have them speak or be referred to by name. If there are too many characters in a scene the listener will lose track.

3 *Geoff (looking angrily at Irene, his pale face*   **NO!**
   flushed) 'I will not.'

'Stage directions' for the producer's or actor's benefit are to be avoided. If it is important it should be there in the dialogue.

4 *A car draws up. Engine off. Door opens and*   **NO!**
   shuts. Feet walk to the front door. Key in the
   lock. Door opens. Feet walk down the hall to
   the kitchen. 'I'm home darling.'

Sound effects should be used sparingly. They should work with the dialogue. Out of context they will mean little. Effects must be useful in setting a scene, but the signposts must be subtle.

5 *Geoff's breathing in the phone box becomes*   **YES, think in**
   more laboured; painful. Behind him a   **sound!**
   symphony orchestra, at first quietly, plays
   Mahler's fifth. Bring up interior Albert Hall.

A *variety* of sound is essential for holding the listener's attention and engaging their imagination. This variety can be achieved by altering the lengths of sequences, number of people speaking, space of dialogue, volume of sound, background acoustics and location of action. On radio, one room sounds very like another, if they're about the same size, but the difference between an interior and an exterior acoustic is considerable. The contrast between a noisy sequence with a number of voices and effects and a quiet passage of interior monologue, is dramatic and effective.

Then there is the question of presentation. Adrian Mourby (formerly a drama producer with BBC Wales and now a freelance producer) has developed a set of guidelines for spotting the duds.

Beware the script that has been professionally printed or bound in Leathertex, is preceded by a telegram and delivered by Securicor.

Beware the play that uses every available word processor typeface or
has the stage directions typed in.

He goes on to warn colleagues about name-droppers – 'John Birt
suggested I pass you this play' or 'Steven Spielberg has expressed an
interest'. The tactic, says Mourby, is a sure sign of an irredeemably bad
play.

For making a good first impression, it helps to follow a few basic rules.

→ Type on one side of the paper only (preferably A4 size)

→ Make sure all the pages are firmly fastened and numbered
consecutively

→ Use plenty of spacing

→ Put your name and address on the title page

→ Give names of characters in full throughout the script and clearly
separate them from speech

→ Clearly distinguish technical information such as location changes
and sound effects from speech

→ Attach a synopsis of the play to the completed script together with
a full cast list and notes on the main characters

There is no need to embellish the text with detailed studio instructions
– they are bound to be changed anyway – as long as it is clear who is
speaking to whom and in what circumstances.

These are the chief slots for BBC Drama:

Radio 3

DRAMA NOW – *Up to 75 minutes* – Dedicated to new and challenging
work.

STUDIO THREE – *Up to 45 minutes* – Exploratory and experimental use
of sound. Aims at innovative new writing.

THE SUNDAY PLAY – Stage classics and major dramatizations.

Radio 4

Up to 20 per cent of work broadcast on Radio 4 is by first-time writers.

SATURDAY PLAYHOUSE – *75 and 90 minutes* – Drama Department Editor: Marilyn Imrie. A traditional slot for 'family entertainment'. Strong narrative is essential for this strand, which can include original plays, adaptations of stage plays and dramatizations. Aims to provide a mix which has a strong emphasis on original comedy, stories retold from real-life adventure and history, and significant events in the lives of ordinary, extraordinary and infamous people, living or dead. It includes a selection of dramatized material from the best writers of crime, detection and romance, and from the worlds of science fiction, mystery, travel and exploration, and espionage. Writing for women is particularly welcomed as well as proposals from writers new to radio.

THE MONDAY PLAY – *60, 75, 90 and 120 minutes* – Drama Department Editor: Jeremy Mortimer. Aims to provide a place for original writing on complex themes. It is also one of the showcases for classic stage plays and occasional dramatizations of novels. Offers should be for fresh and challenging original radio plays by writers with a track record within or outside radio. This is radio's main new-writing slot. More comic writing is needed, along with writing by women and writers from the black and Asian communities.

THIRTY MINUTE THEATRE – *Tuesday (twenty-six weeks of the year)* – Drama Department Editor: Jeremy Mortimer. This slot aims to be accessible and life-enhancing. Themes can be challenging, but plays should be relatively straightforward. Writers new to radio can try for this slot. Particularly wanted are more comedy and first-class one-character plays. There should not be too many scenes or characters (in general, casts should not exceed six people).

THURSDAY AFTERNOON PLAY – *60 minutes* – Drama Department Editor: Jeremy Mortimer. Offers should be for fresh and challenging original radio plays by writers with a track record, new writers and writers new to radio. This slot aims for a miscellany approach. Some plays will be challenging (although the afternoon placing will never have the freedom for use of language possible on occasion in the Monday Play), others will fall within the well-established genres. Again, there is a particular need for comedy and women's writing and writing from the black and Asian communities. Dramatizations will not be considered. This slot should have a more contemporary or authentic sound, perhaps making use of authentic accents and different recording and acting techniques.

CLASSIC SERIAL – *60 minutes/Sunday, repeated Fridays* – Drama Department Editor: Marilyn Imrie. This slot aims to broadcast a wide selection of dramatized material with a strong narrative which has achieved classic status as either a published novel, an epic poem, a ballad, a short story, a film or an event from history and legend enshrined in memory as being of lasting significance. The works can range from the well loved, through the neglected or undiscovered, to the perhaps once popular but now fallen from favour. The strand reflects the literature of all cultures and there is a need for new translations and translators – suggestions of writers new to this skill would be considered.

THIRTY MINUTE SERIES AND SERIALS – Drama Department Editor: Marilyn Imrie; Drama Department Chief Producer: David Hunter. *Thursday 10 a.m.* – this slot seeks to present sharp, stylish and arresting drama. It is mainly original writing with a good dash of comedy, with some dramatizations of currently popular fiction which reflects bestseller lists. It needs vivid work that bridges the gap bewtween *The Moral Maze* and *Woman's Hour* and holds listeners. *Wednesday 12.25 p.m.* – somewhat gentler and more accessible, this slot offers strongly narrative drama and comedy that may focus on historical and literary concerns. It can carry solid popular dramatizations for the more traditional Radio 4 audience on themes such as travel and romance. *Thursday 11 p.m.* – this slot features ground-breaking work that reflects the breadth and energy of the best new writers and performers. It can include dramatizations of cult books and the racier end of the popular-fiction market. There should be an element of surprise, with quality drama reaching and engaging a new, younger audience, and prepared to take risks.

FORTY-FIVE MINUTE SERIES AND SERIALS – *Wednesdays 2 p.m.* – Drama Department Editor: Marilyn Imrie. This slot features dramatizations of well-loved or rediscovered popular fiction, for example from the detective, mystery, romance and comedy genres. Original work will also be considered but a strong narrative is essential. There will be room for one community drama project – perhaps a project that features the retelling of the history of a community. As with all the series and serials slots, more women's and black writing and more writers new to the skills of dramatization are needed here.

CHILDREN'S BBC RADIO FOUR – *30 minutes/Sunday 7 p.m.* – Drama Department Editor: Caroline Raphael. For a short time Radio 5 was an exciting market for young writers. But drama is no more on this channel. Instead, Radio 4 is making a pitch for the 10–13-year-olds with a combination of original series, serials and single plays and dramatizations of classic and new work. Many of the very best-known children's books have already been dramatized or are in the process of being dramatized. The subject matter should not cover the problems of adolescence. The focus is very much on adventure, strong narrative, with children leading and driving the action. Children of this age group expect major protagonists of the same age as themselves and older, but not younger. The production style is strong and direct. The narrative linear, passages of time and change of scene clearly signposted through sound and dialogue. Children do not understand the grammar of radio drama that we often take for granted. Serials or series should not be longer than four episodes.

There are then the established series like *The Archers* with a rota of contributors. Those hoping to break into this market should beware the pitfalls of a quarter-hour episode – never try for more than five scenes and seven characters, for example. The discipline of tight plotting can come in handy. Tom Stoppard, whose *Artist Descending a Staircase* remains a classic of radio drama, started his career writing for *The Archers*.

Short Story, formerly *Morning Story*, is one of those institutions with survival on its masthead. It has lasted for forty years and looks good for another forty. Each week *Short Story*'s producer, Pam Fraser Solomon, sifts well over a hundred unsolicited submissions. Many fail at the first hurdle, revealing a fatal weakness of plot.

> The sort of domestic trivia in which so and so's in the backyard and Gloria comes down the stairs and the sun is shining through the lattice window casting strange shapes on the dining room table. That's what happens on page one and that's what's still happening on page five.

Length is critical. With a quarter-hour slot, anything more than 2500 words is overwritten. *Short Story* has got braver of late. Last year, in the Romance Season, there was even a story of gay love (*The Sticky Carpet* by Frank Ronan), though it was not billed as such in the *Radio Times*. The fee is anything between £100 and £200; not generous, but the exposure is more important than the money. *Short Story* has a fair line-up of success stories of contributors who have had their first break with the programme and then gone on to greater things.

With at least a thousand submissions under consideration at any one time, nobody should expect a quick response from the BBC. A two- or three-month wait is common even for a straight rejection. A further wait suggests that the writer has become part of the BBC's internal politics. Somebody for some reason is nervous of saying 'yes' but reluctant to say 'no'. A telephone call might help to clear the blockage.

World Service

Much of the drama material comes from elsewhere in the BBC. Last year the World Service commissioned only six plays.

RADIO COMEDY

The one area in broadcasting where they go out of their way to encourage newcomers is radio comedy. All ideas are welcome – the zanier the better. There is even an open meeting held once a week at Broadcasting House when novices can join with the old hands in creating laughter for programmes such as *The News Quiz, I'm Sorry I Haven't A Clue, Week Ending* and *The News Huddlines*. Jonathan James-Moore, who heads up the department, sees himself as running the Cape Canaveral of comedy, a launch pad for talent, and Dirk Maggs, producer of *Comic Strip* and former producer of *Huddlines,* is on record as saying: 'We solicit unsolicited material.' It's no way to get rich (standard pay is £20 a minute with a 65 per cent repeat fee) but it is a way to get on, as Griff Rhys Jones, David Hatch, John Langdon and Ian Hislop, all graduates of *Week Ending*, can testify.

For a pointer in the right direction, study the comedy classics, the cassettes and the published scripts.

INDEPENDENT PRODUCERS

They come and go so quickly it is hard to keep track of them. At the last count there were some 300 companies with a link to radio production – however tenuous. Many of these operate on the margin with one-off commissions and need to be distinguished from operations like Hat Trick, Ladbroke and Unique, which are substantial businesses. Radio 4 Drama, for example, has regular contact with just nineteen independent companies and the list is not expected to grow substantially in the months ahead.

Many of the independents have had a hard time of late, suffering from BBC prevarication in clarifying its commissioning policy. There are complaints, too, of the BBC favouring corporation old boys for the best commissions, with inadequate budgets for the rest. But it is unrealistic to expect the BBC to adjust overnight. As one producer put it, 'You don't change the religion that is the BBC by sending out a memo – it takes time.'

Current BBC policy is for radio to take up to 10 per cent of its output from the independents by the end of next year. The contact names for commissions and all other matters relating to independent production are:

Radio 1 – Andy Parfitt, Editor, Commissioning & Planning, Radio 1, Room 230, Egton House, London WIA IAA. Tel: 0171–765 5406.

Radio 2 – David Vercoe, Managing Editor, Radio 2, Room 113, Western House, London WIA IAA. Tel: 0171–765 2123.

Radio 3 – Martyn Westerman, Commissioning Editor, Radio 3, Room 407, 16 Langham Street, London WIA IAA. Tel: 0171–765 2791.

Radio 4 – Mary Sharp, Special Assistant, Radio 4, Room 4119, Broadcasting House, London WIA IAA. Tel: 0171–765 3732.

Advice to independent producers on submitting proposals is sent out on a mailing list or by request. This, by way of summary, is what Mary Sharp of Radio 4 has to say:

Before you submit formal offers for the dramatising of existing published material please check that the rights are in p inciple available and that your proposal demonstrates an informed, critical view of the book under offer.

If the offer is for an original storyline, or comes with the name of a dramatist attached to existing material, you should include a treatment and synopsis.

Suggestions for casting are critical and ideally you should have gained the agreement in principle of your leads. Also include details of the production team you are offering for each production . . . and . . . indicate a budget for each proposal though detailed breakdowns are not needed at this stage. Upon commission there will be an opportunity to adjust the figure if necessary but please be realistic in your estimates.

There is a note at the end warning that the new arrangement should not be taken to mean a change in the Radio 4 power structure. The final decision on all commissions rests with the Controller, Michael Green.

This Gun That I Have in My Right Hand is Loaded

BY TIMOTHY WEST

When Timothy West tried his hand at creating the worst possible radio play, he was so successful that his catalogue of errors was adopted by the BBC for induction courses. As a teaching aid it is unrivalled. With the generous permission of the author, This Gun That I Have in My Right Hand is Loaded, *is reproduced here as a classic of misconception.*

ANNOUNCER: Midweek Theatre.

(*Music and keep under*)

We present John Pullen and Elizabeth Proud as Clive and Laura Barrington, Malcolm Hayes as Heinrich Oppenheimer, Diana Olsson as Gerda, and Dorit Welles as The Barmaid, with John Hollis, Anthony Hall and Fraser Kerr, in 'This Gun That I Have in My Right Hand is Loaded' by Timothy West, adapted for radio by H. and Cynthia Old Hardwick-Box. 'This Gun That I Have in My Right Hand is Loaded.'

(*Bring up music then crossfade to traffic noises. Wind backed by ship's sirens, dog barking, hansom cab, echoing footsteps, key chain, door opening, shutting*)

LAURA: (*off*) Who's that?

CLIVE: Who do you think, Laura, my dear? Your husband.

LAURA: (*approaching*) Why, Clive!

RICHARD: Hello, Daddy.

CLIVE: Hello, Richard. My, what a big boy you're getting. Let's see, how old are you now?

RICHARD: I'm six, Daddy.

LAURA: Now Daddy's tired, Richard, run along upstairs and I'll
              call you when it's supper time.

RICHARD: All right, Mummy.

(*Richard runs heavily up wooden stairs*)

LAURA: What's that you've got under your arm, Clive?

CLIVE: It's an evening paper, Laura.

(*Paper noise*)

              I've just been reading about the Oppenheimer
              smuggling case. (*effort noise*) Good gracious, it's nice
              to sit down after that long train journey from the
              insurance office in the City.

LAURA: Let me get you a drink, Clive darling.

(*Lengthy pouring, clink*)

CLIVE: Thank you, Laura, my dear.

(*Clink, sip, gulp*)

              Aah! Amontillado, eh? Good stuff. What are you
              having?

LAURA: I think I'll have a whisky, if it's all the same to you.

(*Clink, pouring, syphon*)

CLIVE: Whisky, eh? That's a strange drink for an attractive
              auburn-haired girl of twenty-nine. Is there . . . anything
              wrong?

LAURA: No, it's nothing, Clive, I—

CLIVE: Yes?

LAURA: No, really, I—

CLIVE:	You're my wife, Laura. Whatever it is you can tell me. I'm your husband. Why, we've been married – let me see – eight years, isn't it?
LAURA:	Yes, I'm sorry Clive, I . . . I'm being stupid. It's . . . just . . . this.

(*Paper noise*)

CLIVE:	This? Why, what is it, Laura?
LAURA:	It's . . . it's a letter. I found it this morning in the letter box. The Amsterdam postmark and the strange crest on the back . . . it . . . frightened me. It's addressed to you. Perhaps you'd better open it.
CLIVE:	Ah ha.

(*Envelope tearing and paper noise*)

Oh, dash it, I've left my reading glasses at the office. Read it to me, will you, my dear.

LAURA:	Very well.

(*Paper noise*)

Let's see. 'Dear Mr Barrington. If you would care to meet me in the Lounge Bar of Berridge's Hotel at seven-thirty on Tuesday evening the twenty-first of May, you will hear something to your advantage.

(*Crossfade to Oppenheimer's voice and back again immediately*)

Please wear a dark red carnation in your buttonhole for identification purposes. Yours faithfully, H.T. Oppenheimer.' Clive! Oppenheimer! Surely that's—

CLIVE:	By George, you're right . . . Where's my evening paper.

(*Paper noise as before*)

Yes! Oppenheimer! He's the man wanted by the police in connection with this smuggling case.

LAURA: Darling, what does it all mean?

CLIVE: Dashed if I know. But I intend to find out. Pass me that Southern Region Suburban Timetable on the sideboard there. Now, where are we—

(Brief paper noise)

Six-fifty-one! Yes I'll just make it. Lucky we bought those dark red carnations.

(Flower noise)

There we are. Well – *(stretching for fade)* – Lounge Bar of Berridge's Hotel, here . . . . . . I . . . . . . come

. . . .

(Fade)

(Fade in pub noises, glasses, chatter, till, darts, shove-halfpenny, honkytonk piano, Knees up Mother Brown etc.)

HAWKINS: *(middle-aged, cheerful, Londoner)* Evening, Mabel. Busy tonight, isn't it.

BARMAID: It certainly is, Mr Hawkins. I've been on my feet all evening. *(going off)* Now then, you lot, this is a respectable house, this is.

(Singing and piano fades abruptly to silence)

FARRELL: *(approaching, middle-aged, cheerful, Londoner)* Evening, George, what are you having?

HAWKINS: No, no, let me.

FARRELL: Come on!

HAWKINS: Well, then, a pint of the usual.

(Till)

FARRELL: Two pints of the usual, please, Mabel.

(*Money*)

BARMAID: (*off*) Coming up, Mr Farrell.

HAWKINS: Evening, Norman.

JACKSON: (*middle-aged, cheerful, Londoner*) Hello there George.
                  What are you having, Bert?

FARRELL: I'm just getting them, Norman.

JACKSON: Well, leave me out then, I'm getting one for Charlie
                  Illingworth. Two halves of the usual, Mabel.

BAINES: (*coming up, middle-aged, cheerful, Londoner*) Evening all.

JACKSON: Hello, Arnold, haven't seen you in ages.

(*Till*)

BARMAID: Your change, Mr Farrell.

(*Money*)

FARRELL: Thanks Mabel. Where's Charlie got to? Ah, there you
                  are. Charlie, you know Arnold Baines, don't you?

ILLING.:   (*cheerful, Londoner, middle-aged*) Known the old so-and-
                  so for ages. What'll you have?

JACKSON: No, I'm getting them, what is it?

BAINES: Oh, I'll just have my usual, thanks.

JACKSON: Who's looking after you, George, old man?

(*Money*)

BARMAID: There's yours, Mr Hawkins.

HAWKINS: Bung ho.

(*Till*)

FARRELL: Cheers George.

BAINES: Cheers Norman.

JACKSON: Cheers Bert.

ILLING.:   Cheers Arnold.

(*Till*)

BAINES: Well well, look who's coming over.

ILLING.:   Isn't that young Clive Barrington from the Providential
                Insurance?

BAINES: As happily married a man as ever I saw.

CLIVE: (*approach*) Evening Arnold. Evening Bert, Charlie,
                George. Evening Norman.

BARMAID: Evening Mr Barrington.

FARRELL: Evening Clive.

BAINES: (*simul*) Long time no see.

JACKSON: Hallo Barrington old lad.

ILLING.:   How goes it.

HAWKINS: What ho then, mate.

HAWKINS: What are you having?

CLIVE: A whisky, please.

HAWKINS: Any particular brand?

CLIVE: I'll have the one nearest the clock.

HAWKINS: Half a minute. There's a bloke over there can't take his
                eyes off you, Clive. Over in the corner, see him?
                Wearing a dark blue single-breasted dinner jacket and
                tinted spectacles. A foreigner, or my name's not George
                Hawkins.

CLIVE: Yes, by George, you're right, George. Excuse me.

(*Peak chatter*)

OPPENHEIMER: (*middle-European accent*) So, Herr Barrington, you are
                here at last. I was becoming impatient.

CLIVE: Well, now I am here, perhaps you would be so good
                as to explain what the blazes all this is about?

OPPEN.:   Certainly, but not here. We will go to my place in
                Wiltshire where we can talk. My car is outside. Come.

(*Fade on pub background*)

(*Fade up car noise slowing, stopping, engine ticking over*)
                Excuse me, Officer.

POLICEMAN: Yes, sir?

OPPEN.:   Am I on the right road for Wiltshire?

POLICEMAN: That's right, sir. Straight on, then turn left.

(*Car revs up, moves off. Crossfade to car slowing down on gravel path and
stopping. Car door bangs eight times. Footsteps on gravel. Front door creaks open.
Distant piano, Moonlight Sonata*)

OPPEN.:   Ah, that is my sister playing.

(*Piano nearer. The Sonata comes to its close. Suspicion of needle noise at end*)

GERDA: Ha! Managed that difficult A flat major chord at last.

OPPEN.:   Gerda, my dear, we have a visitor. Herr Clive
                Barrington from the Providential Insurance
                Gesellschaft. Herr Barrington, this is my sister Gerda.

GERDA: I am pleased to meet you, Herr Barrington. Has
                Heinrich told you what we have in mind?

OPPEN.:   Nein, not yet, Liebchen. Herr Barrington, first a drink.
                Champagne, I think, to celebrate.

(*Champagne cork, pour, fizz, clink*)

CLIVE:	Thank you. Now, Mr Oppenheimer, or whatever your name is, don't you think it's time you did some explaining?
OPPEN.:	Ja, of course. The stolen diamonds about which your Major Kenwood-Smith has seen fit to call in Scotland Yard—
CLIVE:	Major Kenwood-Smith? You mean the Major Kenwood-Smith who's head of my department at the Insurance Office?
OPPEN.:	Right first time, Herr Barrington. As I was saying, the diamonds are safely in my hands.
CLIVE:	What! You mean to tell me—
OPPEN.:	One moment, please, let me continue. I intend to return them, but on one condition. Now listen carefully; this . . . is . . . what . . . I . . . want . . . you . . . to . . . do . . .

(*Bring up threatening music to divide scenes*)

(*Fade music behind Oppenheimer*)

. . . and I think that is all I need to tell you, my dear Herr. Now I must leave you: I have one or two . . . little matters to attend to. (*on mike*) Auf Wiedersehen.

(*Door slams immediately some way off*)

GERDA:	Won't you sit down, Herr Barrington.
CLIVE:	Thank you, Countess.

(*Sitting noise*)

Look, I don't know how far you're involved in this hellish business, but I would just like to say how exquisitely I thought you played that sonata just now. It happens to be a favourite of mine.

GERDA: Ja? You liked my playing, yes?

CLIVE: Beautiful, and yet . . . no, it would be impertinent of me . . .

GERDA: Please.

CLIVE: Well then, if you insist. I thought that in the Andante – the slow movement – your tempo was a little . . . what shall I say?

GERDA: Strict?

CLIVE: Exactly.

GERDA: (*coming in close*) I had no idea you knew so much about music.

CLIVE: Please, Countess, I beg of you. I don't know what kind of a hold that filthy swine your brother has over you, and I don't want to know, but you don't belong here. For Pete's sake, why not leave with me now, before it's too late.

GERDA: Nein, nein, I cannot . . . (*in tears*)

CLIVE: Why, Countess, why?

GERDA: I will tell you. It is better that you should know. It all started a long time ago, when I was a little Fräulein in the tiny village of Bad Obersturmmbannführershof, in the Bavarian Alps . . .

(*Fade. Bring up London traffic. Big Ben chimes the hour and then strikes twelve. As it strikes we move out of the traffic, a car stops, squeal of breaks, car doors, footsteps, newsboys, tugs, barrel organ, creaking door, more footsteps down a very very long corridor passing offices with typewriters until a small door opens at the end of the passage and we move into a small room on the last stroke of twelve*)

POWELL: Ha! Twelve o'clock already. Morning, Sergeant McEwan. Or perhaps I should say 'Good Afternoon'.

McEWAN: (*Scots*) Whichever you like, sir!

(*Good humoured laughter*)

POWELL: As a matter of fact, I've been out on a job already this
                 morning. I bet you just thought I'd overslept, didn't
                 you, Sergeant?

McEWAN: What, you sir? Hoots, no. Not Detective Inspector
                 'Bonzo' Powell, V.C., who went over the top at
                 Tobruk; one-time Channel swimmer, and one of the
                 toughest and at the same time one of the most popular
                 officers at Scotland Yard here? I should say not. Och.

POWELL: No, I got a line on our old friend Heinrich
                 Oppenheimer, at long last. Our chap at Swanage says
                 Oppenheimer has a private submarine moored nearby
                 – it's my guess he'll try and get the diamonds out of the
                 country tonight.

McEWAN: Havers! Where will he make for, d'ye ken?

POWELL: I don't know, but it's my guess he'll make straight for
                 Amsterdam. Come on, Sergeant, we're going down to
                 Swanage. And . . . the . . . sooner . . . the . . . better. . .

(*Urgent music. Then fade behind gulls, rowlocks, wash. Studio clock should be
particularly noticeable in this scene*)

(*Note: all the Germans in this scene are indistinguishable one from the other, and
indeed may all be played by the same actor as Oppenheimer*)

LUDWIG: We are nearly at the submarine now, mein
                 Kommandant.

OPPEN.:   Ach. Sehr gut. Tell me once more what you have done
                 with the prisoners; my sister Gerda and that meddling
                 fool Barrington.

LUDWIG: Karl found them attempting to telephone Scotland
                 Yard from the porter's lodge. They have been tied up
                 and taken on board the submarine half an hour ago.

OPPEN.:   That is gut. I will teach the fool Englishman to double
             cross me. Achtung! Here we are at the submarine. Karl!
             Heinz! Kurt! Lower a rope ladder.

KARL: Ja, mein Kommandant.

(*Feet on tin tray*)

OPPEN.:   It is four o'clock. We will sail immediately.

(*Change to submarine interior acoustic*)

HEINZ: The diamonds are safely locked in your cabin, mein
             Kommandant.

OPPEN.:   Jawohl. Kurt! Heinz! Karl! Prepare to dive!

(*Diving noises. Klaxon*)

             Set a course for Amsterdam.

KURT: Steer East North East eight degrees by north.

(*Cries of jawohl, Achtung, midships etc*)

OPPEN.:   Ludwig!

LUDWIG: Ja, mein Kommandant.

OPPEN.:   Take me to the prisoners.

LUDWIG: Ja, mein Kommandant.

(*More feet on tin tray*)

             They are in the forward hydroplane compartment.

(*Door opens. Forward hydroplane compartment noises*)

OPPEN.:   So, Herr Barrington, we meet again.

CLIVE: You filthy swine, Oppenheimer, you won't get away
             with this.

| OPPEN.: | (*becoming slightly manic*) On the contrary, my friend, there is no power on earth that can stop me now. You, I'm afraid, will never reach Amsterdam. There will be an unfortunate . . . accident in the escape hatch. |

GERDA: (*a gasp*) Heinrich! You don't mean . . .

OPPEN.:   As for you, my dear sister Gerda . . .

CLIVE: Leave the girl out of it, Oppenheimer. She's done nothing to you.

OPPEN.:   Charming chivalry, my English friend. But it is to no avail. Come.

CLIVE: All right, you swine, you've asked for it!

(*Blow*)

OPPEN.:   Aargh. Himmel! Karl, Kurt!

(*Running footsteps*)

CLIVE: Ah, would you? Then try *this* for size.

(*Blow. Groan*)

          If *that's* the way you want it.

(*Blow. Groan*)

KURT: Get him, Hans.

CLIVE: Ah, no you don't. Take *that*.

(*Blow. Groan. A chair falls over*)

GERDA: Look out, Clive. The one with glasses behind you. He's got a gun.

(*Shot*)

CLIVE: (*winces*)

(*Another chair falls over*)

	Phew! Close thing, that.
GERDA:	Clive! What happened?
CLIVE:	Just my luck; he got me in the arm. Luckily, he caught his foot on that bulkhead coaming; he must have struck his head on that valve group between the depth gauge and the watertight torpedo door.
GERDA:	Is he—?
CLIVE:	I'm afraid so. Right, now to get this thing surfaced.
GERDA:	Do you know how?
CLIVE:	It shouldn't be too difficult. Luckily I had a week on Subs in R.N.V.R. years ago. (*with pain*) This right arm being Kaput doesn't help, though. Right, now, just blow . . . the . . . ballast from the main . . . and . . . number four . . . tanks . . . adjust the Hammerschmidt-Brücke stabilizers . . . and up – we – go.

(*Surfacing noises. Sea. The cry of gulls. A few bars of 'Desert Island Discs' music. Cross – fade to chatter, clink of glasses*)

LAURA:	Have another drink, Sergeant.
MCEWAN:	Thank you, Mrs Barrington. I'll have a wee drappie.
CLIVE:	How about you, Inspector?
POWELL:	Don't mind if I do, sir. Charming place you have here, if I may say so; and a charming wife to go with it.
LAURA:	(*blushing*) Thank you, Inspector.
CLIVE:	Well, I don't mind saying, Inspector, there were one or two moments today when I wondered if I'd ever see either of them again.
LAURA:	Tell us, Inspector, exactly when it was you came to realise that Major Kenwood-Smith was behind it all?

POWELL: Well, for a long time it had puzzled us that the safe was
                 blown by a left-handed man – Oppenheimer and his
                 henchmen are all right-handed. Luckily one of our
                 chaps noticed Kenwood- Smith signing a cheque with
                 his *left* hand.

CLIVE: Aha.

POWELL: We asked him a few questions, and he broke down and
                 confessed. Sergeant, you can go on from there.

McEWAN: Ay, well, the diamonds aboard the submarine turned
                 out to be imitation. Oppenheimer must have been
                 double-crossed at the last minute, and someone in
                 Berridge's Hotel must have performed the switch.

CLIVE: Great Scott, the barmaid!

POWELL: Right, first time, Mr Barrington. We checked in our
                 archives, and she turned out to have a record as long
                 as your arm. She made a dash for it, but in the end she
                 broke down and confessed.

CLIVE: So everything turned out for the best in the end, eh?

POWELL: That's right, sir. And just think, Mrs Barrington, if it
                 hadn't been for young Richard here losing his puppy
                 on Wimbledon Common, none of this might ever have
                 happened.

(*Yapping on disc*)

RICHARD: Down, Lucky, down!

POWELL: Now then, young pup, none of that gnawing at my
                 trouser leg, or I'll have to take you into custody as well!

(*General laughter. Light hearted rounding-off music and up to finish*)

ANNOUNCER: (*spinning it out – the play has under-run*) You have been
                 listening to 'This Gun That I Have in My Right Hand
                 is Loaded'.

Radio Drama Agreement

IN COMMISSIONING original drama, the BBC is governed by the 1988 agreement negotiated with the Society of Authors and the Writers' Guild. The initial fee structure is based on a beginner's rate of £37.82 a minute and a minimum rate of £57.58 a minute for established writers. Residual payments are calculated as a percentage of the initial fee, for example, repeats attract 29½ per cent.

The purpose of these guidelines is to establish parameters for negotiation of individual fees.

Credits

A writer shall be entitled to spoken credits either at the beginning or end of the programme and where practicable a credit in the billings columns of the *Radio Times*.

Single Script Commissions

If a writer is commissioned to write a single script the BBC must pay half the initial fee within fourteen days of signature of a contract. Problems must be aired within thirty days from delivery. If the script requires alterations then the second half of the initial fee may be held back until amendments are agreed. A decision not to proceed because of a change of programme format or other reasons beyond the control of the writer is not in itself grounds for withholding the second half of the initial fee.

Other Single Script Contracts

If an uncommissioned script requires alterations to make it suitable for production the BBC will within fourteen days of signature of a contract pay half of the initial fee agreed upon.

Upon delivery of a revised version the BBC shall notify a writer within thirty days whether there are problems of policy which require further consideration by the BBC (such consideration not to be unreasonably prolonged), or whether the revised version is acceptable as it stands, or whether it requires alterations to make it acceptable for production, or whether it is to be abandoned altogether.

If a revised version of an uncommissioned script is acceptable as it stands the BBC shall pay to its writer the balance of the initial fee. If it requires further alterations then the second half of the initial fee shall not become payable until such alterations have been carried out.

If the BBC requires further alterations after fifty-six days from delivery of the revised version then its writer shall be entitled to receive payment of a further quarter of the initial fee.

Payment of the second half of the initial fee is contingent upon a revised version of an uncommissioned script being acceptable for broadcasting.

Plural Script Commissions

If a writer is commissioned to write more than one script then within fourteen days of signature of a contract the BBC will pay the initial fee agreed upon for script No. 1.

Within fourteen days of the acceptance of the first commissioned script the first half of the initial fees for the remaining scripts (up to a maximum of a further twelve) shall be paid.

If the BBC wishes to offer a plural-script contract to a writer who has submitted an acceptable uncommissioned script then within fourteen days of the signature of a contract the BBC will pay the initial fee for the uncommissioned script and the first half of the initial fee or fees for the other commissioned script or scripts.

'An Established Writer' means a writer who has satisfactorily completed within a period of three years three separate plays or dramatizations of at least thirty minutes each in duration, or two separate plays or dramatizations of an aggregate of 110 minutes, or two original or adapted serials, or material commissioned as dramatized features by Copyright and Artists' Rights Department of an aggregate length of not less than ninety minutes, or relevant dramatic material for Radio Schools programmes of an aggregate length of not less than seventy-five minutes, *or* is regarded as established for the purposes of the BBC's Agreements with the Writers' Guild for Television Drama.

Rights Licensed to the BBC

The right to give within two years from acceptance a First Dramatic radio broadcast and a second performance simultaneously or within any particular network non-simultaneously. The right to give at any time after the first two radio broadcasts, further repeat broadcasts subject to payment of an amount equal to $44\frac{1}{2}$ per cent of the initial fee.

BBC Exclusivity

The writer of a script covered by this agreement undertakes not to authorize any other radio or television broadcast or any public performance of such script in the United Kingdom before the First Broadcast.

During a period of one year from the date of the First Broadcast of such script or the Last Script not to dispose of book publication rights and/or rights in sound recordings in any format in such script without prior reference to the BBC (so that the BBC can make an offer for such rights if it so wishes).

Matching Rights

The writer of a script covered by this agreement agrees to grant to the BBC the right to match any offer made to the writer to broadcast such script on television, such matching rights to be exercisable from the date of signature of the commissioning agreement until the end of three months following the date of First Broadcast.

Warranty for Defamation

The writer of a script covered by this agreement shall warrant that such script contains no defamatory matter (provided, however, that the writer shall not be liable for any defamatory matter which in the opinion of the BBC was included without negligence or malice).

Provision of Scripts

The producer of a script commissioned under this agreement shall be entitled to request the writer of it to deliver the final script as a $3\frac{1}{2}''$ floppy disk in a format specified by the BBC in studio-ready form. If the writer agrees to such a request and a fee is agreed by the BBC and the writer for delivery in studio-ready form, the BBC shall pay the agreed fee upon delivery.

Attendance Payment

An Established Writer shall be entitled to a single attendance payment per script.

Attendance on Producer's Request

An additional attendance fee should be paid in respect of each daily attendance of an Established Writer.

Consultation on Director and Casting

The choice of director and cast should be discussed between the Drama Department and a writer so far as may be practicable given the constraints of time, a writer's availability and experience. Nevertheless the final choice of director, cast and other participants in the production of a work shall be in the BBC's discretion.

On-Air Credits

The writer should be named in any trails.

Guidelines for Dramatizations

For dramatizations which draw on the original not only for the basic construction but also for the majority of the dialogue, 65 per cent of the full rate is appropriate. For dramatizations which draw on the original for the basic construction but where more than half of the dialogue has to be invented by the dramatizer, 75 per cent of the full rate is appropriate. For dramatizations which require the dramatizer to undertake major structural changes and to invent more than half the dialogue, 85 per cent of the full rate is appropriate.

All is Vanity

WHAT WRITERS DO TO BE PUBLISHED

WHY WRITE? Some do it to make a living and get rich. Some do it to make a living and stay poor. Others write for pleasure and fulfilment. A Mori poll released last year to coincide with the launch of *Bookworm* on BBC2 found that three in ten people believe they have a book in them, while one in fifty has actually written a book. Rejecting Dr Johnson's testy opinion that no one but a fool writes for aught but money, most of these authors would be content to see their words in print between covers, selling in numbers sufficient to cover the basic costs. Can it be done?

The short answer is, yes. With the digitalization of printing technology, the business of producing a book is hardly a big deal. And there is no shortage of publishers eager to provide this service – at a price. This is where the problems start. A response to a small ad in the book pages appealing to unpublished authors with vague promises of literary fame invariably leads to disappointed expectations and a large bill. Horror stories mount up of substandard products, failure to promote, unexpected extra costs and piles of unsold copies. Kate Pool, deputy general secretary of the Society of Authors, has a thick file of complaints against vanity publishers.

'It frustrates me,' she says, 'to get letters from people saying: "Is this normal?" when it isn't normal. What's normal is that a publisher pays you. I tend to be very wary of anybody who advertises for writers. The best publishers don't do that.'

Where vanity gets its bad name and, arguably, oversteps the boundary of acceptable commercial practice is when beguiling compliments are handed out to likely prospects. The tendency of vanity publishers to be less than frank in assessing the commercial appeal of the literary offerings that come their way has been proved many times over. The latest exposé comes from Johnathon Clifford of the National Poetry Foundation, who sent three poems to fourteen vanity publishers. He went out of his way to make his poems as dreadful as possible, testing them against the judgement of established poetry editors, not one of whom 'would give any one of the poems house room or who did anything other than smile at examples of the weakest of poor ill-constructed verse'. Yet one after another the vanity publishers responded with glowing reports on such as:

> I held you in my arms at Christmas.
> You must have thought me very brash!
> The holly and the tinsel spoke to us,
> of love and all the presents too.
> I gave you socks of blue;
> you gave me undies of a different hue.
> And when we sang the carols me
> and you (such pretty songs)
> I blushed to think of
> later ons.

One who *was* cautious was Carol Bliss of the Book Guild. She pointed out that her company 'is a publishing service and that the critical difference between mainstream and us is that we are not choosing manuscripts on judgement of commercial success'. She went on to say: 'as an author's money is involved, it would be wrong . . . to give you glowing readers' reports on which you base your decision to publish.'

Interestingly, Miss Bliss is a recent contributor to the *Author*, where she offers this advice to any writer contemplating subsidy publishing:

→ Be sure you can afford it. If you recoup your financial investment, consider it a bonus

→ Visit the publisher's office if at all possible

→ See samples of the publisher's latest books

→ Ascertain that it has an in-house publicity staff

→   Ask to see review coverage on current books

→   Ascertain that it has proper distribution facilities

→   Don't simply take the cheapest offer

→   Forget about fame and fortune

→   Enjoy the experience

The first point is vital. Accepting that there is nothing inherently wrong in paying for one's book to be published, it must also be said that the expense can be horrendous. A vanity publisher can charge anything from £5,000–£10,000 for what in the end is a simple print operation.

One way forward is to clamp down on vanity advertising. Two years ago *The Sunday Times* ran a mordacious investigation into the less-than-honest ways of some vanity publishers. Following publication and the letters that flowed in, the paper decided to drop all advertisements appealing for manuscripts.

Maybe it is unnecessary to go quite so far, particularly now that the Advertising Standards Authority has distributed an advisory note on the permissible limits to vanity advertising.

Claims, whether explicit or implicit, that the publishers offer a 'joint venture', a 'co-operative', a 'co-partnership' or 'subsidy scheme' should be avoided unless there is evidence to demonstrate that all expenses are shared by the publisher and the author.

Advertisers should avoid such claims as 'Does your book deserve to be published?' unless (a) they can show that submissions will be considered on merit and that offers to publish are made only when the work is of a sufficiently high and therefore saleable standard and (b) they make clear in the advertisement that authors have to pay to have their work produced.

Advertisers should only make claims, whether explicit or implicit, about whether and the extent to which books will be marketed and promoted where they hold sufficient evidence to demonstrate their accuracy.

Claims which imply that authors are likely to gain from the venture should only be made where documentary evidence is held.

Claims such as 'Your investment should be recouped from the revenue of sales' should only be made when they can be supported. Claims such as 'Profits cannot be guaranteed' can also leave the impression that many authors do make a profit from the venture; they should therefore be made only where it can be shown that there is a reasonable likelihood of this.

Where does this leave the unpublished author? Assuming there is money to spend, but not on a vanity publisher, an alternative is to go in for self-publishing.

Jill Paton Walsh did it and was shortlisted for the 1994 Booker Prize for her trouble. An established children's author, her *Knowledge of Angels* is, as she admits, a 'strange book'. An unashamedly philosophical novel centred on a conflict between belief and tolerance, it was certainly strange enough to be turned down by fourteen publishers, including the author's regular publisher, Weidenfeld. Eventually, the book came out under the banner of Jill Paton Walsh's own imprint, Green Bay.

She was following an honourable tradition. Beatrix Potter, Virginia Woolf, James Joyce, Walt Whitman and J.L. Carr all engaged in self-publishing for some of their books. William Blake was entirely self-published.

The latest big name to enter the self-publishing lists is Timothy Mo with his novel *Bronmout in Breadfruit Boulevard*. He made his decision after publishers failed to come up with what he regarded as an adequate advance. But he insists he is not in it for the money.

> I could have got £175,000 at auction but turned my back on that figure because although I'm unlikely to make that much myself, I've got the control if I publish it myself. The book belongs to me. It's mine, and I'm getting three times my share of the profit.

And he likens self-publishing to jumping into a cold pool: 'quite nasty gearing up for it, but surprisingly easy actually'.

To succeed in self-publishing you need to have a knowledge of practicabilities like making sure that the title appears in the Publications of the Week column in the *Bookseller* and that it has an ISBN to distinguish it from all the other titles appearing in the same week. Numerous guides to self-publishing are now available. Centaur Press, for example, has *Publishing Your Own Book* by Jon Wynne-Tyson, who also happens to be the company's managing director. Stanley Trevor, coordinator of the Association of Little Presses can offer *Publishing Yourself, Not So Difficult After All* and Peter Finch is the author of *How to Publish Yourself*.

Last year, Richard Heller published his novel *A Tale of Ten Wickets*, about the secret lives of an amateur cricket team, under his appropriately named Oval imprint. The experience led him to frame a number of vital questions to anyone thinking of following his example.

Why Am I Really Doing This? There is a good chance that you have decided to self-publish because conventional publishers have turned down your book. Forget any idea of revenge. Do not imagine that your self-published book is going to become a bestseller and make all those publishers look foolish. This is very unlikely to happen . . . Self-publish because you are proud of your book and want to give other people the chance to read it.

Can I Sell This Book to a Total Stranger? Any bookseller has to ask this question before accepting your book. Ask it yourself and be honest in your reply . . . You need produce only a few hundred copies (to start with) and you can expect to sell or give them away without great effort. If you really believe that complete strangers might walk into a bookshop and pay for your book, self-publishing becomes a far greater enterprise. It will cost you a lot more money and may even take over your life.

Can You Handle Terminal Jealousy? Once you have self-published a book it becomes torture to visit a bookshop or read a newspaper or magazine. You will constantly see inferior authors displayed, reviewed or interviewed and you will develop paranoid fantasies about booksellers and the media. It is vital to develop a sense of perspective in these matters. My book is a lot better than Jeffrey Archer's latest and yours probably is too. This is irrelevant to a bookseller or a newspaper. Milord Archer is a phenomenon and a news story: you and I are not.

Adrian Hill, diplomat turned author, who self-published his thriller *The Tiger Pit* warns against underestimating the work involved, particularly when it comes to marketing.

A self-publisher has no sales team on the road. That makes life tough. Books will stand on the wrong shelf or sit in boxes half the summer because somebody was too idle to pick up a telephone and ask why they were sent! Remember, small independent shops that buy on firm orders show more concern for individual titles.

The Tiger Pit has sold 4000 copies so far. It is nowhere near enough to make a profit. Nonetheless, I have managed to sell more copies of a first novel than most writers with big publishers could hope to achieve.

One option is to take on a professional distributor (a list appears in a National Small Press Centre handbook, available from the National Small Press Centre, Middlesex University, White Hart Lane, London N17 8HR) but this can gobble up scarce resources.

It is rare to make money on self-publishing but it does happen. Not long ago an American advertising executive wrote a 90-page children's story about a busy father who learns to find a new love for his family. On first seeing the manuscript, publishers said that they found it naïve. So Evans brought it out himself and sold, entirely through word of mouth recommendations, 400,000 copies. Once the book had reached number two on the *New York Times* bestseller list, the leading houses stepped in, fighting a bidding war from which Simon & Schuster US emerged victorious with an offer of over $4 million.

A more familiar story comes from Hugh Popham who self-published his biography of an adventurous ancestor, admiral Sir Home Popham, the inspiration for C.S. Forester's Horatio Hornblower.

> We [Old Ferry Press] published 1000 copies in September 1991, rather less than a year after we had started work, and it had cost us £10,000 – which we hoped to get back. We had sent out our leaflets and review copies beforehand – and now we waited for the orders and the reviews. And waited . . .
>
> To date, 18 months after publication, we still haven't covered our costs, and have sold fewer than half of the 1000 copies, yet we remain surprisingly cheerful. Reviews and orders continue to trickle in, and there is no immediate danger of it being remaindered! Faith and patience are the chief requirements needed for those who essay to

publish their own books: given those, there are compensations. It is deeply rewarding, and great fun.

John de Falbe, bookseller turned author, is touted in the press as one of the successes of self-publishing. Certainly the reviews were good and 2000 copies were sold. But his profit on *The Glass Night*, a novel about a Jewish refugee from Nazi Germany published by his Cuckoo Press ('A lot of people thought I was cuckoo'), is modest and shows up at all only because he does not include himself, as author and editor, in the costs.

If self-publishing seems to be as expensive as vanity publishing and just as risky (you could be right) yet another possibility is to seek out a sponsor. This can work well for a specialist book which links in to the public relations concerns of a major enterprise. The Shell Guides are an obvious example. Less ambitiously, but on the same tack, I have on my desk a *Pallas Guide to East Anglia* by Peter Sager, which is sponsored by Norwich Union and Greene King. The big companies are quite used to supporting the theatre, ballet, opera and orchestral concerts. Why not books? You can but ask.

Front of House

WRITING FOR THE THEATRE

THEATRE HAS A WONDERFUL capacity for self-publicity. Write a novel and the chances of it being reviewed are remote. Write a play for a hundred-seater fringe venue in the outer suburbs and a dozen famed critics will turn up for the first night, eager to deliver their verdicts, often at inordinate length, for a national readership. Even if the audience stays away, media attention can do wonders for a playwright's self-esteem. Someone has noticed; someone cares.

The hard part is in persuading a production company to put on a new play. This is where the novelist wins out. The profusion of small, regionally based publishers has multiplied opportunities for getting into print. Theatres, on the other hand, are slicing back on new writing. The regions are particularly hard hit, with reps trying to reconcile the push for survival with the cutback in arts funding by filling their seasons with old faithfuls like *Noises Off*, *The Corn is Green* and *Murder at the Vicarage*. No need to sneer at popular entertainment – all of us would jump at the chance of creating a long-running money-spinner – but nervous concentration on the line-up at the box office does tend to put unknowns, albeit with mighty talent, at a disadvantage.

What can be done? Eighty-seven playwrights who signed a round robin to the directors of Britain's subsidized theatres know the answer. They want every venue to stage at least three new plays each year as 'the first step back from the brink of the absurd situation that we are very close to: theatres with no plays'. The bank manager style in which the demand is couched holds out no great hope of literary excellence undiscovered, but this is not really the point.

The point is, are we nurturing playwrights with the same assiduity as we give to other artists who set out to command our hearts and minds. Michael Billington, the *Guardian* critic who, post-Milton Shulman, must qualify for his profession's longest-service medal, leads those who think not.

Praising the 'striking exceptions (The West Yorkshire Playhouse, the Stephen Joseph Theatre in Scarborough, the Nuffield Southampton, Live Theatre in Newcastle and Hull Truck) that do a healthy quota of new work', he concedes the blunt fact that 'most regional theatres are either unable or unwilling to risk new work on main stages' and blames cuts in arts funding. Whether or not the cause of new writing would be served by enforced presentation of new plays is an issue Billington sidesteps. Others are less inhibited. Over on the *Telegraph*, Charles Spencer is certain that a quota system for new plays would fail disastrously.

> I suppose it must be the ideal of every playwright to have one new work staged each year. But of the 87 writers on the list, ranging from celebrated names like Harold Pinter, David Hare and Peter Shaffer to many more obscure dramatists, how many are likely to produce a *good* new play every year? Fifteen per cent would strike me as an optimistic success rate. The result would be that many theatres would be obliged to stage *bad* new plays, which would ultimately put them out of business.

But Spencer is not pessimistic.

> When a really good new play comes along, it tends to thrive.

This view is endorsed by, among others, William Rees-Mogg, who turns the tables by arguing that 'The 87 playwrights are themselves a sign of the relative health of the British theatre. I doubt if there has ever before been a period when one could have assembled a group of 87 serious British playwrights.'

He is led to conclude 'that British drama is now in better shape than the British novel, that the best six new plays of each year are better than the novels on the Booker Prize shortlist'.

This is most certainly true. Equally, periodic forecasts of doom over the past decade have proved to be way off the mark. In the mid-1980s, the Theatre Writers' Union was describing playwrights as 'an endangered species' and confidently predicting that before long new writers would be 'confined to the ghetto of small scale theatre, their work often misrepresented and rarely adequately remunerated'. The reality is nowhere near as bad.

Nineteen ninety-five was a year rich in new theatre work. Patrick Marber's *Dealer's Choice*, one of the best original plays to be seen in this decade, transferred from the Cottesloe to the Vaudeville. Terry Johnson's *Dead Funny* came in from the Hampstead Theatre, Jonathan Harvey's *Beautiful Thing* from the Bush, Kevin Elyot's *My Night with Reg* from the Royal Court, Kay Mellor's *A Passionate Woman* from the West Yorkshire Playhouse and Tim Firth's *Neville's Island* from Alan Ayckbourn's Scarborough theatre. In Newcastle the Live Theatre Company has made its mark with new plays that would put the frighteners on many a commercial producer. In Scotland, the Traverse Theatre and Communicado Theatre Company are busy nurturing exciting young writers like Iain Heggie and Liz Lochhead.

The Royals – the National and Shakespeare – come in for hard knocks from playwrights who fear the domination of directors' theatre. Says David Edgar:

> For the first time since 1956, there is a whole generation of talented young British directors who affect little or no attachment to the production of new work. Emerging RSC stars such as Phyllida Lloyd declare themselves only interested in the classics ... The National's Deborah Warner is well-known for her dismissal of contemporary plays and her hostility to the idea of a living writer in the rehearsal room.

And Arnold Wesker adds:

> The phenomenon may be new for Britain but it is old hat in mainland Europe and Scandinavia. This new generation of directors have, like Jonathan Miller, joined the ranks of a fiercesome [sic] breed of European directors who could be called The Necrophiliacs – those who prefer to practise strange acts on the dead without fear of protests. Living writers, vibrant with intellectual energies of their

own, answer back with matching, often more vivid theatrical imaginations. Most troublesome!

But there is a danger here of confusing the troubles experienced by new young writers in finding a showcase for their work with the frustration of older, established writers, like Wesker, who go out of fashion. The special pleading of dramatists who see themselves as having a claim to precedence is disputed vigorously by Max Stafford-Clark, former artistic director of the Royal Court.

I don't think there's an obligation on the part of any public theatre to stage the work of established writers. The Royal Court's primary task is to put on the work of new writers. Writers are like athletes. They have a shorter rather than a long career. They hit a particular moment, write about it, and things move on. Shakespeare, Shaw and David Hare are the exceptions in having long careers. Many of the great playwrights, Congreve for example, only wrote a couple of plays.

The pledge to encourage new writing is voiced frequently by the power brokers, including Richard Eyre who stands by his 'undiminished commitment' to regenerate the theatre, not least the National theatre, with new blood. And now we have an Arts Council ruling that a proportion of a theatre's subsidy must be set aside for new work.

So what is wrong? Why all the complaints? Maybe what we are talking about is a question of quality rather than quantity. Plenty of new work is being presented but it rarely matches the traditional criteria for excellence. There is a general moaning at the loss of drama that tackles the big issues and generates ideas that can shift popular opinion. The shortcoming is conceded by Max Stafford-Clark, who blames the way we live now.

A confident age supplies ringing answers that fill big stages. But the century has after all just turned the corner of a particularly nasty decade. It was a tough time. Those who failed were vilified, while those whose work succeeded were trivialised. The theatre had to have its wits about it to survive.

A rather more subtle explanation is offered by David Edgar:

Part of the crisis that new writing in the theatre now faces is that that conversation has hitherto been (largely) internal, which is why it has so often seemed invisible. Max Stafford-Clark enjoys remarking that the ideal Royal Court play would be titled something like *When I Was A Girl I Was Not Quite A Bent Catholic*. This is by no means just a quip. There is an aching need among theatre makers who align themselves with the women's movement, with gay sexuality, with the black and Asian community, to widen the conversation, to talk to each other, and indeed to society at large. As the binary polarities of class broke down in the eighties, and people appeared to define themselves through more specific (and various) forms of collective identity, so theatre artists aligned with those identities found themselves addressing particular constituencies rather than geographical communities. As those constituencies themselves attempt to break out of their ghettos, so the theatre should offer a space to question how their experience might inform and enrich the culture as a whole.

It would be simpler – and more truthful – to say that for the past fifteen years, all the intellectual ferment has been on the political right while theatre has remained resolutely bedded in the traditions of the old left. Yes, there are big issues – 3 million unemployed and 2 million homeless must be big enough for anyone – but if all that dramatists can come up with are variations on the platitude of 'them versus us', they can hardly be surprised when audiences prefer to stay home and watch the telly.

As one who knows a thing or two about bringing in the punters, Alan Ayckbourn urges writers to liven up the stage, to be less solemn and censorious, to concentrate first on entertaining audiences while allowing the more intellectual elements to creep up on them.

'All this modern stuff – the curtain goes up, three people dressed entirely in black point at the audience accusingly for ten minutes – only baffles the customers,' he says. 'Empty auditoriums are of no use or interest to anybody and will only hasten the demise of British theatre.'

Writers new to the theatre tend to go through a lengthy and sometimes destitute apprenticeship. The days are long gone when an overnight success could lead to West End stardom in one move (R.C. Sheriff's *Journey's End*,

Terence Rattigan's *French Without Tears*). The giants of modern theatre come up the hard way. Aspiring playwrights should read John Osborne's autobiography for pleasure and profit while contemplating the early experiences of Harold Pinter. It has been said that his first important play, *The Birthday Party*, was taken off after one week with receipts totalling £206 11s. 8d. A production of *The Caretaker* in Düsseldorf was booed off on its opening night, the cast doggedly taking curtain calls until there were only two people left in the audience, both still booing.

Most producing theatres have well-established routines for considering new work (see p. 144). But readers are not infallible and rejection is not death. Every playwright has his collection of producers' put-downs. When Peter Terson (*Zigger Zagger*, *Strippers* and *Good Lads at Heart*) made his first approach to the National, he wrote to the then literary editor, Kenneth Tynan, declaring, with the arrogance of youth, 'This is probably my finest work. I should like to give you the opportunity of being the first to produce it.' Tynan replied, 'I'm glad you admire your own talent. I wish I could share your enthusiasm.'

Two decades later, Terson made another assault on the National. This time the literary editor was more positive. He told the writer that while his play was not quite right for them, he should persevere. Terson might reasonably have thought that twenty years was long enough for anyone to stick at it but he took the advice and soon afterwards made his breakthrough. He still has not worked for the National but he did get a commission from the RSC.

At the New Playwrights' Trust they tell the story of Paul Godfrey sending his first play, *Inventing a New Colour*, unsolicited to his local theatre.

> It was sent back with a report which told him that he clearly had no idea of how to write for the stage and should stop doing so now. A little wrongfooted by this advice, he decided he would send it to one other theatre and if their opinion was the same he would indeed do something else with his life. The second theatre – the Royal Court – eventually produced the play and Paul went on to direct it himself at the theatre which had initially rejected it. He now lives happily in London with two commissions.

But, however dispiriting, a reader's report is worth careful study. Writers who are prepared to accept constructive criticism and are willing to look for ways to improve their skills are often those who eventually secure commissions to submit new work.

It is also worth mentioning that the New Playwrights' Trust has its own script-reading service which can turn round work in four weeks and give advice to a writer on where to send scripts. (Details from the New Playwrights' Trust, Interchange Studios, Dalby Street, London NW5 3NQ.)

Can playwriting be taught? As John Mortimer reminds newcomers:

> Writing plays, like any other literary pursuit, begins with sitting alone in a room. Unless the gift of creation is in you, no amount of talking to directors, sitting in rehearsals and studying stage techniques will come to your rescue.

But there are essentials of the craft to be absorbed. This is invariably done by trial-and-error experience and by picking up tips from the masters. A possible short cut to competence can come from the playwriting courses, the best known of which is David Edgar's postgraduate course at the University of Birmingham. David Edgar's own conversion from the cult of the amateur came 'when I was asked to teach an undergraduate playwriting option at Birmingham in the 1970s, whose students included Louise Page and Terry Johnson. It was at the very least clear from this experience that there were ways of thinking about dramatic problems (on the level of where scenes start and end, who's on the stage and how to get them on and off) which can be collectively explored and individually applied'.

Then there are the self-help groups such as the North West Playwrights' Workshop, founded in Manchester by the Theatre Writers' Union, and advice in plenty from those who have spent a lifetime honing their dramatic skills.

Here is James Roose-Evans, founder and one-time artistic director of the Hampstead Theatre and the begetter of many West End successes, including *84 Charing Cross Road* and *The Best of Friends*.

> Not surprisingly, dialogue is the key to the theatre. It must not be overly literary, unless, of course, the author is creating a particular

world based on language, as with the plays of Wilde or Shaw. A novel
can afford to be leisurely, even tangential, for the reader can easily
refer backwards or forwards or, if he chooses, step off the book and
go and do something else. If too much is explained by the playwright
in long rambling speeches then nothing is left for the actor to discover
or the spectator to imagine. What counts first and foremost in theatre
(and even more so on the screen) is the sub-text, that which lies
beneath the surface of what may even appear as banalities: the
unspoken thoughts, the unexpressed feelings, of a character which are
expressed primarily through the actor's use of nuances of tone,
silences, gestures and movements. Eva La Gallienne has described
how Eleanor Duse could hold a pause for two minutes and during
this time she would keep the audience entranced by her reactions and
interior thought processes.

It is important for the playwright to remember that acting is as
much about *re-acting* as it is about acting, *being* rather than doing.
Even the most ordinary of statements can be illuminated by a gifted
actor.

And he adds:

I have read thousands of plays and still, whenever a new script is sent
to me I approach it as though this were to be a new romance, hoping
to find the script that excites and fires me. All too many plays are
clearly not written for actors, with a knowledge of what actors can
achieve, or what makes for theatre rather than literature. This is why
it is important to read a script aloud. When I am sent a new script, if
it engages my interest, I will read it two or three times silently,
making notes, and then I will read it aloud, acting it out. This process
can also be invaluable for an author, unless she or he is wholly vain
and in love with their work. When I am working with an author on
a new play, perhaps in the early drafts, I will often act out a scene or
even the whole play, improvising with whatever furniture or proper-
ties are at hand. Having been an actor this is easy for me to do, and
very quickly an author, if receptive, will see where a scene is not
working, where perhaps it has got bogged down in words. Indeed
very often the author will discover that certain speeches are not

required because the action or a gesture, a silence, or even one word or phrase, will say it all.

Ten tips towards successful playwrighting are offered by Peter Cox, a judge of five years' standing for the Lloyds Bank Theatre Challenge.

1   When you are writing the play, watch it as well – in your mind. Do you find it hard to remember who is on stage, who has gone off or who has been sitting doing nothing for 20 minutes.

2   If you have become locked into the 'talking heads' syndrome start searching for ways to present the content of the play visually. As an exercise, rework the scenes you have already written using only visual images and action.

3   Beware the seductive 'easy option' of writing your play through the mouth of a narrator. But if you can't survive without your helpful storytelling friend, try at least to give them a strongly identifiable character and function in the play. Storytelling is for rocking chairs by the fireside. Think drama.

4   When pen hits paper or fingers hit the keyboard remember you are not in a one-to-one session with your psychoanalyst. Writing as therapy for the writer can make dire, excruciatingly squirm-provoking theatre.

5   Try not to show how clever you are. Too many ideas can kill a play as surely as too few. Invest in a pair of scissors and a red pen.

6   Remember you are writing for the stage, not television. Think music. Think of the difference between a live concert and a car radio. Think of a live human being beating a drum and making the air move.

7   Decide if you are a playwright or a playwriter. Are you trying to present a unique, individual vision in the play or are you devising the play with other people? Be clear what you are doing. If you are the playwriter for a group, beware of the 'too many cooks' syndrome.

8 Having managed to lose all your friends by slashing, hacking and brutalising their work (aka 'editing'), beware of the 'too much democracy' trap. You might find that, because *everyone* has been involved in making the play, *everyone* should have a little bit to say. This in turn can leave an audience experiencing a little bit of everything but an awful lot of nothing.

9 Do not listen to people who say, 'You should only write about what you know.' This is an ignorant, trite cliché. What you should be doing is finding ways within yourself, your experiences and your research to dramatise and express what your characters know about. If you only ever write about what you know, there will only ever be one character in your play – you.

10 Finally, be clear in your mind that making a play involves more craft than inspiration but that the best and most inspired plays you will ever see, or hopefully write, will show no signs of the craftwork involved.

After all that, remember that presenting a play is a collaborative effort. Director and actors are entitled to have their say. Good dramatists thrive on teamwork but recognize the extra labour, not to mention the diplomatic skills this entails. For a writer used to the self-containment of books, the rewriting on top of the writing can come as a shock. It certainly did to Sue Townsend, who adapted her novel *The Queen and I* for the stage.

I gave Max [Stafford-Clark] the first draft in a pub in Stratford. It was inside a sealed brown envelope. Max weighed the script in his hand and declared that it felt 'very light', and so it turned out to be. Literally and figuratively. I embarked on draft two, initially writing in all-night sessions at the kitchen table, eventually booking into a hotel, two miles from my own home, to finish it off.

I lost track of time; sleep was something I did when I could no longer hold my pen. I covered my king-sized bed in pages of A4 paper until the padded pink bedcover was obliterated. To sleep I removed Scenes I, II and III, and placed them carefully at the side of the bed. I did not get into the bed but lay rigidly on top, so as not to disturb Scenes IV, V and VI, etc. I think I became a madwoman. Occasionally I looked moodily out of my window and saw people below carrying their Christmas parcels. I longed to be one of them. To be a person who wasn't adapting a play from a book.

Incidentally, the play was a great success.

Minimum terms for dramatists, including fee and royalty structures, have been negotiated by the Writers' Guild and Theatre Writers' Union for every sector of British theatre. The agreements cover such matters as the right to attend rehearsals, the obligation on the producer and director not to change the text without the writer's permission, the right to be involved in casting and to be credited in all promotion.

In the old days, all playwrights, whatever their standing, were paid either by a straight box-office royalty or, more rarely, by a commission set against royalty earnings. This simple formula was undermined by the emergence of the subsidized theatre and its law of diminishing returns. The smaller the theatre, the higher the proportion of subsidy per seat and the more unrealistic the box-office takings on which the playwright's earnings were calculated. The writer's sense of injustice was accentuated by the knowledge that the salaries of directors, actors and managers were not subject to the same degree of risk.

As a result, the Arts Council devised a strategy whereby theatres were supposed to offer an outright commission fee backed by guaranteed minimum royalties. In reality commissions were few and far between and royalty supplements were last in line for payment.

A new technique was tried. The Arts Council specified a proportion of each of its theatre grants to be set aside for new writing. But when the playwrights' unions began negotiations on a minimum terms agreement it soon became clear that theatre managers were bending the rules to divert writers' money into their general budgets. The Arts Council duly tightened its rules by threatening to claw back funds that were misdirected away from theatre writing. The response was immediate. Most theatres affected by the change responded by spending more on writing than was actually expected of them.

Meanwhile, the Theatre Management Association accepted the need for setting out minimum terms for writers. The current agreement allows for four grades of commission related to the size of venue. The fees are £2776, £2271, £1766 and £1514. Royalties are open to negotiation but should not be less than 8 per cent.

Long term, the financial rewards of playwriting can satisfy the sharpest mercenary instincts. Even a modest success, say a production which runs in a mainstream London theatre for six months, can bring a healthy return on time and talent. The big subsidized companies pay the best rates. A production at, say, the Lyttleton Theatre at the National which is playing to 70 per cent capacity at an average ticket price of £10 (all conservative estimates) should bring the author something of the order of £700 a night.

The money continues to roll in with repeat productions around the country, the sale of subsidiary rights and royalties from the published text. This last is a fast-expanding source of income as publishers like Methuen and Faber make strong efforts to promote their drama lists. Last year John Osborne's *Look Back in Anger*, first produced in 1956, sold 20,000 copies, a figure matched by Tom Stoppard's *Rosencrantz and Guildenstern Are Dead* (1967) and closely approached by Harold Pinter's *The Caretaker* (1960).

Then there are the amateur, provincial and overseas productions, which can bring in income for years ahead. A popular play with universal appeal, such as *Private Lives* or *A Chorus of Disapproval*, is on somewhere every evening of the week. And it is not only the West End legends who make the money. Judged by number of performances, the fourth most popular playwright (after Shakespeare, Ayckbourn and Arthur Miller) is John Godber, who is best known in his native Yorkshire and in the North East where he is artistic director of the Hull Truck Theatre Company.

The West End still holds some magnetism but with the ubiquitous musical squeezing out the straight play and the price of seats accelerating faster than Concorde, much of the excitement of contemporary theatre is to be found far away from the bright lights of Shaftesbury Avenue.

A *Writer's Companion*

SAMPLE SURVEY OF THEATRE COMPANIES INTERESTED IN NEW WRITING

THEATRE COMPANY	NEW PLAYS RECEIVED	NUMBER THAT SHOW PROMISE	NEW PLAYS PRODUCED ANNUALLY	TIME TAKEN TO RESPOND TO PLAY SUBMISSIONS
GREENWICH THEATRE LONDON	30–40	5%	2 or 3	Anything up to 12 months
THE GATE THEATRE, LONDON	10–20	Perhaps 10%	On average, 2–4	Approximately 2 months
ORANGE TREE THEATRE, LONDON	25	Few	1–3	3–4 months
BUSH THEATRE, LONDON	40–50	3–4	6	Aim to respond within 3 months
CONTACT THEATRE MANCHESTER	20	Very few unsolicited ones not via agents 1 or 2 via agents	2–3	Immediate acknowledgements then 2–3 months as play is read and considered before a definite no or maybe is given
BELGRADE THEATRE COVENTRY	5	None are produceable, a small number generate real interest	1–4	6–12 months

THEATRE COMPANY	NEW PLAYS RECEIVED	NUMBER THAT SHOW PROMISE	NEW PLAYS PRODUCED ANNUALLY	TIME TAKEN TO RESPOND TO PLAY SUBMISSIONS
WEST YORKSHIRE PLAYHOUSE, LEEDS	50	30%	4–6	2–6 months if rejected. If we like a play it usually takes longer
COLISEUM THEATRE, OLDHAM	4	3 annually	1–3	4–8 weeks
NUFFIELD THEATRE, SOUTHAMPTON	20–25	perhaps 1 a month is worth serious encouragement	4–6	Approximately 2 months
ROYAL SHAKESPEARE COMPANY, LONDON	30–50	Maybe 5%	4–6	Less than 3 months
ROYAL COURT THEATRE, LONDON	30	5	12–15 (Theatre Upstairs); 6–8 (Downstairs)	From a week to a year in some cases
SOHO THEATRE COMPANY, LONDON	100	12	4	6–8 weeks
HAMPSTEAD THEATRE, LONDON	104	Serious interest in 3–4; less strong interest in 8–10	5–6	2–3 months, perhaps a little longer if the play is having more than one reading
ROYAL EXCHANGE MANCHESTER	1000–2000	10%	2–3	2–3 months
TRICYCLE THEATRE, LONDON	30	3–5	2–3 inhouse; 3 in association with touring companies	2 months

THEATRE COMPANY	How Do You Judge New Material?	Do You Offer Writers Constructive Criticism?
GREENWICH THEATRE, LONDON	We have *very* few readers and no reading budget. We tend to concentrate on scripts that come from agents and directors	If the play is one of the 5% that show promise
THE GATE THEATRE, LONDON	A team of readers submits reports to the literary manager. Rarely hold workshops	Always
ORANGE TREE THEATRE, LONDON	Mostly by readers – but there are readings and workshops for works with promise	Yes – depending also on the quality of the play
BUSH THEATRE, LONDON	Do not hold workshops. Plays are chosen by a process of readership	Yes
CONTACT THEATRE, MANCHESTER	Script panel. Artistic director reads likely scripts.	If it seems worthwhile. We don't consider ourselves obliged (or funded) to
BELGRADE THEATRE, COVENTRY	Unsolicited mss are seen by a panel of readers, occasional mss are workshopped. The Belgrade participates in the Stagecoach Regional Writers workshop scheme. Also supports local Coventry Playwrights Group	Yes – each reader writes a report for submission to the writer
WEST YORKSHIRE PLAYHOUSE, LEEDS	Script-reading panel, then hothouse internal new writing group, then readings/ workshop/production	Yes, if considered useful – in the form of a readers' report or directly from the Literary Coordinator
COLISEUM THEATRE, OLDHAM	Full script consideration followed by personal discussion with writer	Yes

THEATRE COMPANY	*How Do You Judge New Material?*	*Do You Offer Writers Constructive Criticism?*
NUFFIELD THEATRE, SOUTHAMPTON	I, as 'Script Executive' read them (we also have outside freelance readers) and either return with a letter or sometimes meet writer or pass script to artistic director. Run regular writers' workshops for local writers and so an average of eight rehearsed readings a year	Yes
ROYAL SHAKESPEARE COMPANY, LONDON	Unsolicited mss read and reported on by freelance readers, then passed to literary department. Very occasional workshops	Depends on the quality of work – sometimes
ROYAL COURT THEATRE, LONDON	Readers: weekly script meeting; workshops (readings of various kinds)	Yes
SOHO THEATRE COMPANY, LONDON	Readers panel considers material. Extensive workshop programme for beginners to advanced writers	A reader's report and a reply from the Literary Manager are sent to all writers who have submitted a play
HAMPSTEAD THEATRE, LONDON	All mss are read and reported on (synopsis and comments) in person at monthly script meetings by our script associates (actors, writers, directors who read for us). On these occasions other/ previous work of the writer may also be discussed. Recommended mss are then read by the Literary Manager and/or Artistic Director and/or Associate Directors. Frequently meet with writers whose work is of particular interest to us and work on these mss in detail. We may then pass some of this work to other theatres. Mount rehearsed readings of work-in-progress from time to time	If at all possible, yes. (In relatively few cases where *constructive* criticism is not possible, a simple and straightforward rejection is preferable in our view)

THEATRE COMPANY	How Do You Judge New Material?	Do You Offer Writers Constructive Criticism?
ROYAL EXCHANGE MANCHESTER	New plays are, almost without exception, commissions or prize winners from the Mobil Playwriting Competition	Where appropriate
TRICYCLE THEATRE, LONDON	We do have a weekly writer's workshop	No

THEATRE COMPANY	Lines of Best Advice to New Writers
GREENWICH THEATRE, LONDON	Get an agent. Get a director interested in your work. Offer all the support you can for a staged reading. Remember that unsolicited scripts are legion. They are a source of guilt and alarm for most theatres. Most are terrible and it is difficult to find the good ones amongst the mass of bad ones.
ORANGE TREE THEATRE, LONDON	Keep the cast to a maximum of six. Don't ape the televisual style of jumping from scene to scene. Don't try to cram in too much.
BUSH THEATRE, LONDON	See as much new work as you can but write from your own personal interests.
CONTACT THEATRE, MANCHESTER	Go and see lots of theatre. Know a theatre's interests and limitations before sending a script.
BELGRADE THEATRE, COVENTRY	Sending unsolicited scripts is not generally productive. It is much better to get involved in a workshop programme such as Stagecoach and Northwest Playwrights Scheme, both initiated by writers working together; this is an opportunity to form relationships with theatres and directors and experience the support of other writers.
WEST YORKSHIRE PLAYHOUSE, LEEDS	Find out about how different theatres operate before sending material in – be realistic about the process. Think carefully about the kind of work each theatre produces.

THEATRE COMPANY	Lines of Best Advice to New Writers
COLISEUM THEATRE, OLDHAM	Research the venues. Get to know the programming policy of venues. Understand theatre economics. Understand that *titles* help sell plays.
NUFFIELD THEATRE, SOUTHAMPTON	Go to the theatre a lot, read as many plays as you can, but don't be too influenced by them. They can suggest possibilities to your, not often a blueprint. Tell your own truth.
ROYAL SHAKESPEARE COMPANY, LONDON	The RSC is rarely the best place to submit your first play. Try Soho Theatre, New Play Festival, New Playwrights' Trust, etc.
ROYAL COURT THEATRE, LONDON	Go to the theatre. Get your work produced. Learn what space/ director suits your work.
SOHO THEATRE COMPANY, LONDON	Go and see as many plays as you can physically and financially manage.
HAMPSTEAD THEATRE, LONDON	Visit the theatre as much as poossible. Try (it is difficult) to develop the skill of differentiating between advice which is useful to you and that which is not – it is a crucial skill. Send out only clean and legible copies of your script (we suggest A4 one-sided double-spaced) – *never* the original, of course. Send only one example of your work in the first instance. Bear in mind that modern trends in theatregoing suggest that an audience expects of a full-length play an evening no longer than 165 minutes, no shorter than 75 (with interval), therefore one-act plays are read by this theatre for interest only.
ROYAL EXCHANGE, MANCHESTER	Always ask yourself 'Who might want to put on my play?', 'Who might want to watch it?'
TRICYCLE THEATRE, LONDON	Try to get an agent before submitting. Make sure the script is clearly and cleanly presented, and give a description and list of characters at the beginning of the play.

P.S. from Bill Alexander, Artistic Director of Birmingham Rep:

In our studio theatre, where we do *only* new plays, we have done five in the past year, and have announced plans to do a further six next year. The ones already performed have all been interesting pieces of work by developing new playwrights and have played to about 40 per cent capacity in the 100-seater studio. This disappointing level of interest won't change the policy, but it does give pause for thought.

Arts Council

THEATRE WRITING SCHEMES
AND AWARDS

THE ARTS COUNCIL has several Theatre Writing Schemes and Awards aimed at encouraging new work for the stage.

THEATRE WRITING BURSARIES

Bursaries are intended to provide experienced playwrights with an opportunity to research and develop their work for the theatre independently of financial pressures and free from the need to write for a particular market.

Bursaries are normally £3000 each, rising to a maximum of £5000 in exceptional circumstances.

Writers must apply to the Arts Council of the country in which they reside – England, Wales, Scotland or Northern Ireland. Bursaries are for stage plays only. The Theatre Writing Schemes do not provide money to help write radio, screen or television plays, poetry or opera libretti. Multidisciplinary work and adaptations for the stage *are* eligible but priority is given to original work. There is a separate scheme for theatre translations.

There is no standard application form. If you wish to apply, first telephone the Theatre Writing section (Tel: 0171–333 0100 ext. 431) for guidance. Once this has been done, write to the Drama Director at the Arts Council and outline the reasons why a bursary would be important to you. With your application you must submit copies of three full-length plays for theatre, whether produced or not, detailing the date and order in which they were written. An application should include an estimate of the sum of money you require for the project, and details of any other sources of income for the period, as well as the preferred date for the start of the bursary. Give the names of two referees in support of your application.

As the award requires the evaluation of writers' scripts, it can take up to four months to process an application.

COMMISSION OR OPTION AWARD SCHEME

Theatre companies and groups can apply for a grant of up to half the cost of paying a writer to write or translate a new play, to secure the rights to an unperformed play or to rewrite an unperformed play. Applicants must find at least half of the cost of the fee from their own resources.

THEATRE FOR YOUNG PEOPLE – COMMISSION BONUS SCHEME

A new play for young people will automatically be considered for a bonus of £500 payable to the writer. The bonus will only be given when the application for a Commission or Option Award is successful. Application forms are available from the Theatre Writing section (Tel: 0171–333 0100 ext. 431).

RESIDENT DRAMATIST ATTACHMENT AWARD

Under this scheme, theatre companies may apply for a grant towards the cost of having a playwright or theatre translator in residence for a continuous period of six months with the possibility of six months extension. Each award, for £4000, is made in the expectation of a new play. All companies, with the exception of the Royal National Theatre and Royal Shakespeare Company, are eligible to apply. The artistic director in charge of the residency and the playwright must present reasons why at this time they wish to work together during the term of the residency. The theatre company must undertake to pay at least £1000 to the playwright in respect of the residency in addition to any Arts Council award.

Telephone the Theatre Writing section for an application form in the case of a Commission or Option Award, the John Whiting Award or the Meyer–Whitworth Award. There are no formal application forms for other schemes, but it is wise in all cases to discuss your project with the Theatre Writing section before you apply.

For further advice, contact the Drama Officer for Theatre Writing at the Drama Department, The Arts Council of England, 14 Great Peter Street, London SW1P 3NQ (Tel: 0171–333 0100, ext. 431).

Making Pictures

THE SCREENWRITER IN SEARCH OF
AN IDENTITY

I AM WRITING this the day after Lindsay Anderson died. His *Independent* obituary encapsulated the man as 'difficult ... but intensely likeable and invigorating to be with', adding 'he may well have been the single most important individual in the post-war British cinema'. In a clutch of great films he directed at least one classic, *If . . .*, the story of an armed rebellion in an English public school. It appeared in 1968 at around the time of the student riots in Paris – a coincidence that put Anderson among the standard bearers of the radical left.

As I read on it occurred to me that Lindsay Anderson's career is an essential study for anyone who wants to make their way in films. This is what his life teaches us:

If it is recognition you are after, it is not enough to be brilliant and original.

Notwithstanding *If . . .*, *This Sporting Life* and other cinematic trailblazers, Anderson was never even nominated for a British Academy Film award.

You don't need huge money to make a great movie.

If . . . was completed in just ten weeks for £250,000.

But you do need patience.

The script for *If . . .* was put into first draft by David Sherwin and John Howlett when they were still at Oxford. It took them five years to interest a producer, Seth Holt, who then took another year to find Anderson, who took another year on revisions.

A strong nerve is a prerequisite for dealing with money men.

If . . . was turned down by every British distributor and financier.

Eventually, an offer came from America. The films division of CBS was ready to play white knight. A deal was struck, whereupon CBS decided to pull out. In the mere six weeks before shooting was due to begin an alternative package was agreed with Charles Bluhdorn, head of Paramount. 'Thus,' says David Robinson, 'it is only to an act of exceptional imagination by a Hollywood mogul that we owe a film that, in retrospect, must be acknowledged as a peak in British cinema history.'

The final lesson, which reinforces all the foregoing, is that to succeed in movies – as director, producer, writer, actor, second unit grip or whatever – you must have an eye to the main chance. In his last recorded interview, Lindsay Anderson said it all.

> I've been lucky but I've always used my luck. Successful people are the ones who know how to use their luck.

Those who are undeterred must also reckon with a singularity of the British film industry; nobody can be sure there is one. The problem is partly one of definition. Around fifty movies a year come out of British studios with credits that are predominantly UK-based. But at least half of these are initiated and partly financed by the film divisions of Channel 4, the BBC and the more enterprising of the regional television companies, notably Granada. The purists argue that television-sponsored movies are essentially for television, or as David Puttnam has it, 'they are imbued with the vision, traditions and limitations' of television. There are no big ideas, Hollywood-style. Blockbusters like *The Last Emperor*, and *Dances with Wolves*, although largely British financed, were bound to go West not just for the breadth of landscape but for a director with the necessary breadth of vision. David Lean could have met the challenge but since his death, five years ago, no obvious successor has emerged.

An envious gaze falls on France, where the film industry is the happy recipient of massive public handouts while benefiting from restrictions on television output. These go so far as to impose a ban on TV transmission of movies at peak cinema-going times. The message is to get out of the house on Saturday night and Sunday afternoon. What is on at the local Roxy has to be better than anything on television. The TV companies must also give 5 per cent of their profits to national film productions.

The contrast with Britain could not be more obvious. Here, state support is limited to the modestly financed British Screen (see Chapter 16). It was not exactly a major breakthrough when, recently, the Heritage Secretary promised an extra £80 million for film production – the industry's share of lottery money allocated to good causes. The divide is between France, where they can put together a bonanza budget to bring the Emile Zola classic *Germinal* to the big screen, and Britain, where reverence for a cultural milestone – *Middlemarch*, say, or *Martin Chuzzlewit* – is translated into a television mini-series. The pleasure quotient may be the same; who can tell? But what is indisputable is that the French think cinema while the British think television.

Indeed, television is the central training ground for writers and directors. The result, say the critics, is that on home ground they tend to choose parochial, introverted subjects with no pretension to mass appeal. According to Adrian Hodges, formerly head of British Screen, television is a place where 'the work that is remembered is always very serious work, so it's natural that most low-budget British films have a serious content to them'.

The only hope for British cinema, say the critics, is that we get away from the idea that film must, by definition, be 'profoundly worthy'.

Some observers put it more harshly. Nigel Andrews, who writes in *The Financial Times* denies the existence of a bankrupt native film industry: – 'there are merely native film makers bankrupt of commercial ideas.' He goes on to bemoan 'today's lack of any serial tradition' like the Ealing comedies or even the *Carry On* films and the Hammer horrors.

> But the problem is larger. The lack of self-confidence that has our producers weeping on the doorstep of Number Ten is part of the same failure of confidence that caused the crisis in the first place. We live in a Britain uncertain of its own identity. Caught in a cultural squeeze between America and Europe, and a historical squeeze between Empire and decline, we feel we must look in tiny, cobwebbed corners to find any indigenous popular culture at all. Hence films about Old Ireland like *The Field* or Old Gangsterdom like *The Krays* or Old London like *Little Dorrit*.

Where does this leave the home-grown screenwriter who has ideas but not the power to change British film culture? It leaves him on a 707 bound for Los Angeles. Hollywood beckons. Every year some 30,000 screenplays, television dramas, concepts and story treatments are registered with the Writers' Guild of America. An increasing proportion of this mighty output is born of the word processors of young expats who have caught on to the American dream – that talent and hard graft equals a million dollars. And it is not all fantasy. There are well-publicized leaps from back-street poverty to Sunset Boulevard. 'One day I was a struggling student,' a happy mould-breaker told the *Mail on Sunday*, 'the next I had an agent, a manager, two lawyers and an accountant.'

Or how about this for a wish come true?

June Roberts was a British TV drama producer when David Puttnam persuaded her to try her hand at writing one of the films in his *First Love* series for Channel 4. The result – *Experience Preferred, But Not Essential* – was picked up for American distribution and became an art-house hit. Douglas Kennedy takes up the story:

> The next thing Roberts knew, she was approached by a heavyweight Los Angeles agent wanting to represent her; she was brought out to the West Coast, where she 'took' a dozen or so meetings with studio executives and had a dozen or so writing offers, all of which she turned down. Then, after working on several projects which ended up in turnaround (one of which was for Michael Shamberg, producer of *The Big Chill*), she accepted a producer/writer deal with MGM and moved to LA, pitching them the idea of adapting Patty Dann's acclaimed coming-of-age novel, *Mermaids*.
>
> But MGM wasn't interested, and when that studio went through a traumatic series of corporate upheavals she simply decided to go ahead and write the first 30 pages of the screenplay on spec.
>
> 'Somehow, those pages got to Cher,' Roberts says, 'and when she committed to the project, it propelled me into meetings with every other star in Cher's age range.' What's more, Roberts suddenly received 50 writing offers within a five-week period.

A vital step in June Roberts' progress was attracting an agent. Hollywood is mesmerized by agents. The three largest – CAA (Creative Artists), ICM (International Creative Management) and the William Morris Agency – dominate the talent-handling business.

As Nigel Andrews tells it:

The people running studios now change rapidly, whereas the agencies have an awesome consistency of top personnel – and of personality too, handed down from men such as the CAA boss, Michael Ovitz, obsessed with Oriental disciplines and near-religious team spirit.

The studios are like British soccer clubs. They reel from one whizz-kid manager to the next. And when a new whizz kid comes in, where does he turn for ready-made ideas and projects to jump-start his production schedule? Why, to the agents. And what is the agent's main interest? To get more money for his client.

This may not be healthy for the film industry as a whole but the aspiring screenwriter can work the system to his advantage. Robin Lister, a London chartered surveyor before he migrated to Los Angeles, became a client of ICM on the back of his second screenplay. 'Once you get an agent and once you become however minor a player, you get in the loop. I'm now in the loop and I'm up for a writing assignment at Disney.'

Attracting an agent may not depend simply on producing a marketable script. Some sort of backup is needed to inspire confidence. It may be, as with June Roberts, a track record in another part of the business, in her case as a TV producer. But more probably, it will be a qualification. Hollywood is strong on diplomas. It is said that you won't get a job in a studio mailroom without at least an MBA. For screenwriters, authenticity is bestowed by graduation from a top film school – New York University, the University of Southern California (USC), or, best of all, the University of California at Los Angeles (UCLA). This last is under constant assault from agents looking for fresh talent. From the lecture halls of UCLA have come treatments for *Lethal Weapon*, *RoboCop*, and *Repo Man*, not to mention hundreds of television scripts for the likes of *Miami Vice*, *Cheers*, *LA Law* and *Star Trek, The Second Generation*. Students have been known to drop out because they have been too successful, too early. Their agents have told them they cannot afford the time for classwork when there are six-figure assignments to finish on a tight deadline.

Miles Millar was a film-school product who got himself a tough agent – David Warden who handled *Batman* and *Sleepless in Seattle*. When he signed up, Millar was a twenty-six-year-old Cambridge graduate who was at USC. He handed over to Warden a screenplay called *Mango*, 'an action comedy' based on the 'cop-buddy genre'. Warden sold it for $1 million.

Predictably, the fight for admission to a film school is intense and ruthless. At UCLA they get hundreds of applicants for an annual intake of just fifteen students. It is no deterrent that tuition fees are close to $30,000 a year.

Success brings huge rewards. Forget the millionaires. What about $50,000 for a first draft screenplay? It may not get to production – nine out of ten scripts end up on the junk heap. But there are writers in Hollywood who can make a good living out of failure and a very good living out of modest achievement. At the top end, fees of $600,000 for a screenplay plus a percentage of the profits and $300,000 for a rewrite are not unusual.

There are penalties. The most trying is the Hollywood work ethic which requires writers (by nature an independent and idiosyncratic breed) to submerge their identities. As pointed out by William Boyd, a British author through and through with several screen credits on his c.v., it is the director who collects the praise while the screenwriter gets the blame. The American Writers' Guild recorded what it saw as a major triumph last year when it persuaded the studios to raise the credit ranking of the writer above that of the producer. Still, it is the director who commands. For a writer to claim proprietorial rights over a page of golden prose is to jump the queue for the exit.

In Hollywood, it is rare for a project to be translated into celluloid without the assistance of at least three writers. Often the renovation is so extensive as to lose the original work altogether. Faced with demands to amend and adapt, sensitive writers can be forgiven their occasional outbursts. There is the story of Dorothy Parker throwing a typewriter through her office window. It crashed at the feet of a party of tourists on their round of the Paramount Studios. They looked up to see a distraught Miss Parker peering through the broken glass. 'Let us out,' she shrieked. 'We're as sane as you are!' That was in 1938 and though writers are no longer herded together and told to get on with it, nothing else has changed. During his days in Writers' Block, David Mamet commented that 'film is a collaborative business; bend over'.

Movie-writing takes time, which is the other big drawback to the screen trade. While a typical author might expect to spend a year on a novel, a screenwriter should not be too surprised if his words are still unspoken after a decade of toing and froing. He will be on to other work by then but the frustration of non-fulfilment can be hard. By way of an example, David Thomson has traced the gestation of *Tootsie*, a movie hit of 1982 starring Dustin Hoffman. It took seven years and ten people working on the script to bring it to the screen.

The treatment: In 1975, Don McGuire did a 30-page treatment, and then a full script. No one wanted to make it.

The rewrite: In 1978, Robert Kaufman added a rewrite. Again nothing, except that Dustin Hoffman became interested.

The reshape: Dustin Hoffman asked a friend, Murray Schisgal, to reshape the old material for him, but there was still no breakthrough.

The rework: Director Sydney Pollack (director of *They Shoot Horses, Don't They?*) then thought he might like to do it, and another writer, Larry Gelbart (creator of the *M.A.S.H.* television series), came in to do his bidding. It now became a 'go project', if not quite 'right'.

The doctors: Three more writers were called in to do further doctoring: Elaine May (one-time cabaret partner of Mike Nichols and now a specialist in uncredited script rewrites); Bob Garland, and long-time partners Barry Levinson and Valerie Curtin. (Levinson was the writer-director of *Diner* and *Tin Men*.)

The final tune: And, of course, when it came to production, Dustin Hoffman himself changed some of the lines.

Writers who are not great team players or who resent being screwed (even if paid handsomely for the experience) may prefer to stay at home where there is at least a chance of keeping a hold on one's own work. It then comes back to the question of financial backing – either from British Screen finance or the European Script Fund (see Chapter 16), both of which offer development loans on strictly commercial terms, or from the media giants.

The power of television notwithstanding, there are reasons for optimism. British cinema has advanced from the dull days of the late 1980s, when desperation was a small ad in the national press.

> Innovative writer needs £1 million. Major feature-length script completed. UK film industry out to lunch.

Paradoxically, one hopeful indicator is the cynical reaction of many young producers to any proposal for reintroducing subsidies such as the recent IMPACT initiative, which rests on government approval for a levy on distributors in return for tax breaks on reinvestment in UK productions. Stewart Till, head of Polygram, currently the largest investor in UK feature films, albeit Dutch owned, speaks for many of his contemporaries when he expresses nervousness 'about putting a levy on some films to reinvest in others that would otherwise not be made – probably for good reason'.

The young turks would like to see tax incentives and to enjoy the concession to write off production costs in one year, but they accept there is no alternative to strict commercialism. This does not assume a sheer drop downmarket. It does require an understanding of what sells in the States (witness the success of *Four Weddings and a Funeral*, an all-British movie which actually had its first showings in America) and a close correlation between marketable scripts and young bankable British actors – Liam Neeson, Daniel Day Lewis, Hugh Grant, Ralph Fiennes, Gary Oldman, Elizabeth Hurley, Helena Bonham Carter, Miranda Richardson, Emma Thompson, Natasha Richardson.

But if British screenwriters do manage to shake off their art-house image, part of the change will be a move towards screenwriting as a service industry – American-style. *Four Weddings* took three years to come to screen. In the wake of the film's success, Richard Curtis, its creator, offered *Independent* readers four rules and a suggestion on screenwriting. His first rule is to let things stew. Give time to find out if you really care.

> I've twice written films straight after I thought up the idea, and they were both disastrous. In 1989, I thought of a complete idea for a film about dreams at a petrol station on the A40. I drove home and started writing frantically. Six weeks later it was finished. Six weeks and one

day later it was in the dustbin. I re-read it and I realised it was well-constructed twaddle, it meant absolutely nothing to me.

On the other occasion, I wrote a film for America, to please Americans, which I made up on the way to a 'pitch-meeting'. Two whole years of writing later, I attended another meeting at MGM – they told me they absolutely loved the film, provided I could change the character of the leading man, the second lead, the cameos, the dialogue and the jokes. I said that only left the title. They said they wanted to change the title too.

Next, try not to pitch. Getting a commission may please the bank manager but, with screenwriting, the idea seldom relates to the final product.

As the writer writes, the film comes to life and changes. It's no longer, say, a social satire, it's a dead serious state-of-the-nation film, moved from the original Westminster location to the brooding Shetland Islands.

So you deliver your film, and the person who commissioned it is, *inevitably*, disappointed.

Rule three: take criticism from someone you love. Richard Curtis has shamelessly exploited his girlfriends.

My first film, called *The Tall Guy* was a four-hour muddle before my best friend, Helen, got her hands on it. Five different times she read it and cut it down. The film that was finally accepted was the fifth draft by both of us.

Four Weddings is a co-operation between me and my girl Emma. She read every draft from beginning to end. For a year I lived in terror of the fatal initials 'CDB' scattered throughout every draft she read. 'CDB' stands for 'Could Do Better'.

Last rule: don't count the rewrites. *Four Weddings* had at least seventeen, including one after the read-through and one during rehearsal. Rewrites are maddening but they invariably lead to a better script.

And then there is the suggestion, one that writers are bound to resist – for a while.

I suggest that – after you have let an idea stew, written the film you wanted without the compromises of a commission, let it be brutally edited by someone you love and who loves you, and then rewritten it 15 times – you cast Hugh Grant as the lead. It doesn't matter what the character is. If he's a middle-aged cop on the verge of retiring, Hugh will be perfect. If he's an Eskimo schoolboy – Hugh is exactly what you are looking for. This weekend, *Four Weddings* may pass the $30 million (£20 million) mark in America, and relatives in New York tell me that it's all down to Hugh. If we'd been canny, and cast him in the Andie MacDowell, Simon Callow and Rowan Atkinson roles as well, it could have passed $50 million by now. That's the hell of it. Whatever your script is like, no matter how much rewriting you do, if the punters don't want to sleep with the star, you may never be asked to write another one.

Valuable supplementary advice comes from David Puttnam, who reminds would-be screenwriters that 'the filmscripts of twenty years ago would, by and large, fail to satisfy modern audiences. Today's cinema-goers pick up hints and allusions with almost frightening speed. Indeed, they *resent* having a plot set out too plainly. They like to make the links, to interpret the hints, to engage with the story as they would with an inter-active game.'

It is a view endorsed by John Hodge, who wrote the script, his first, for *Shallow Grave*.

I realised how little you need to write into the dialogue and how few pointers you need to give for the modern audience.

The result was backing from the Scottish Film Production Fund, the Glasgow Film Fund and Channel 4 – and enthusiastic reviews for the finished product.

The great gurus of screenwriting are, surprise, surprise, two Americans – Robert McKee and Danny Simon. Danny is brother of Neil and is credited with having taught his sibling all he knows about pulling in Broadway audiences. Among fans of McKee, who offers a three-day Story Structure course, are John Cleese, who dismisses criticism of McKee's limited success in applying his own axioms (the odd TV credit)

with the traditional pedagogic argument that 'the ability to teach
something well is totally unconnected with being able to do it well'.
Anyone wishing to test the validity of his thesis will need to fork out
around £300. McKee and Simon visitations are signalled in the media
pages of the national press and in *Sight and Sound*.

SOURCES, on the other hand, is a wholly European initiative. The
aim is 'to contribute to a higher standard of European film and television
production by means of script-development workshops'. Based in
Amsterdam, the SOURCES workshops consist of two week-long group
sessions with an intermediate period for rewrites. The working language
is English. Participants are selected on quality of submission (script or
treatment), the track record of the writer and the European appeal of the
project. The fee is 1000 ECUs, including accommodation and meals.
Further information from: SOURCES, Jan Luykenstraat 92, 1071 CT
Amsterdam, The Netherlands, (Tel: 00 31 20 6720801; Fax: 00 31 20
6720399).

Anyone setting off on this experience and in need of confidence
should carry with them the image of the great Alfred Hitchcock, who
had one guiding principle:

> To make a fine film, you need three things: a great script, a great
> script and a great script.

Financing

FILMS

SUPPORT FOR BRITISH FILMMAKERS, including screenwriters and writers new to the cinema, is provided by British Screen, a commercial company backed by government grant. In the last four years some forty movies have attracted British Screen finance, among them *The Crying Game, Orlando, Damage, Tom and Viv* and *Widow's Peak*.

The financial muscle belongs to four major shareholders – Rank, Pathé, Granada and Channel 4 – whose input is topped up by £2 million a year from the taxpayer. This allows for an annual dispersal of £4–5 million to projects which 'explore British themes, cultural values or current concerns ... involve new talent ... and which would not otherwise proceed to production'.

The guiding principal of British Screen is that while it exists 'to take risks which the commercial sector ordinarily eschews, by backing inexperienced filmmakers and innovative ideas, its financial support should be provided on a strictly commercial basis'. The soft money of old-fashioned subsidy can 'all too easily have the effect of inflating production budgets and devaluing product in the marketplace'.

Typically, a producer who shows he is in fair sight of making a profit can expect a loan that will account for about 20 per cent of his budget. But of some 300 applications a year, only ten or eleven hit the jackpot.

A screenwriter can make his own bid for a development loan. His application will be considered if:

(i) The writer (in the case of a team, at least half the team) resides in the European Community.

(ii) The material submitted to British Screen constitutes the entire
      extant written development of the idea by the writer . . ..

(iii) In the case of an adaptation of a copyright work written by an
      author other than the writer, either (a) the underlying rights have
      already been obtained by or on behalf of the writer, or (b) a two-
      year option on the underlying rights has recently been obtained
      by or on behalf of the writer, or (c) a two-year option is available
      at a cost such that the total of option payments over two years will
      not exceed 50 per cent of the amount loaned to the writer.

(iv) In the case of an adaptation where the writer is the author of the
      original work, a one-year option on the underlying rights is
      available for £1.

For a successful application, British Screen offers the writer a loan
equivalent to half the amount currently agreed with the Writers' Guild as
the minimum payable for a treatment and first draft screenplay.

Screenplay Loans are intended to enable writers to set aside time to
write for the cinema: the transaction is not a commission. Copyright
in all material created as a direct result of a Screenplay Loan remains
with the writer, subject only to a contractual obligation to repay
British Screen the amount of the Screenplay Loan in specific
circumstances and on standard terms.

While there are no absolute criteria by which applications are assessed,
British Screen must be convinced that:

the eventual film, as envisaged by the writer, is likely to appeal to a
wide paying audience in cinemas throughout the world, both in its
original language and in other language versions; the story of the film
is inherently dramatic and cinematic by virtue of its potential to
stimulate powerfully the emotions and visual senses of an audience,
and that the writer is capable of realising that potential; either the
concept of the film, or the intention of the writer in developing the
concept into a screenplay, is in some identifiable way original.

Applications for Screenplay Loans can be made by writers of any level of experience, and there are no limitations as to subject matter or setting. However, the overall spread of Screenplay Loans favours:

> writers yet to achieve feature film credits; contemporary stories; stories which in character, setting or perspective are identifiably British.

A screenwriter may also join with a producer to make a bid for a development loan. If successful, 'the Loan will consist initially of an agreed amount up to [£5000] to cover costs incurred by the producer up to the point of delivery of the first draft of the screenplay. 'At British Screen's discretion, based on an assessment of the first draft of the screenplay . . . the Loan may be increased . . .' to allow for a second draft. Further increases may follow up to a limit of £10,000. Thereafter, application may be made for a 'preparation' loan to enable the producer to finance the final development of the screenplay before pre-production of the film begins.

EUROPEAN SCRIPT FUND

An alternative source of development finance is the European Script Fund, known to its friends as Script. Funded by Brussels as part of the Media Programme aimed at stimulating the European audio-visual industry, Script makes loans to producers, directors and writers to cover the costs of film and television projects at any stage of development up to pre-production. The value of the loans varies with circumstances but a writer's loan will not normally exceed 5000 ECUs. Funds are set aside solely for writer awards and there is a special writer's application form, which is a model of clarity.

Here is the checklist which accompanies the application form.

> Short films and documentaries will not be considered.
> Submissions must be typed.
> If you are applying with an adaptation you must submit evidence of rights to source material.
> We will consider no more than one application from each applicant per funding session.

Presentation is very important. If possible your application should be bound. Unbound and uncollated sheets can easily get lost. Incomplete applications will not be considered.

You may submit your project in any language of the European Community or of the other Script states. You do not need to translate your project material into English. Applications are read in the language of submission. A poor translation can hinder a project and is unlikely to help its chances of being funded. The European Script Fund does not normally use translators.

In the case of a successful application Script will make an assessment, based on the format of your application, as to how much it is prepared to loan. The Script Loan will be for the writing of the script and the securing of a producer. When you secure a producer for your project they will then be liable to repay the Writer Loan should the project go into production. Your producer will be eligible to apply to the European Script Fund for a Team Loan for the same project.

Please type your application and include all of the following in duplicate. If any of the following are not included your application will not be considered.

A **Script** – please state which draft you are submitting; A **Statement** as to how you see the work progressing to future drafts or a **Treatment** of not less than 10 pages along with at least **Two Sample Scenes** from the intended film/TV project or a **Previously Completed Sample** of the writer's work. A **Two Line Pitch** encapsulating the story; **Biographies** of all writers involved with the application; **Source Material Statement** – please state if the story is an original work or an adaptation of an existing work. In the case of adaptations, applicants must supply satisfactory evidence that rights in the underlying works are available to you. You should provide a statement detailing what has been done to secure the option or rights; **Nationality/Residence** – in the form of a copy of your national identity card or residency; **Documents** – permit or copy of your passport establishing residency in a Script state.

You may also include any or all of the following with your application:

Letters of Support – including any letters of intent or interest from producers/directors/cast/creative team, etc.; **Showreels** – any relevant footage from the creative team would be welcome. We would prefer showreels to be submitted on VHS tape; **Other Supporting Material** – including completed screenplays, source material, research documents, etc.

In addition to loans, Script's development support includes

The evaluation of delivered scripts by experienced and suitable experts. Script pays for an initial script analysis and report, which is then made available to the producer/writer team. The promotion of funded projects to potential partners/investors, capitalising on the Fund's extensive network of European TV and film industry contacts. As part of this effort to tap other sources of finance, Script organises translations of supported scripts, further enabling Script-backed projects to find partners across European borders.

Guiding funded applicants towards other suitable Media initiatives and European schemes, such as Eurimages.

For British writers, further information on Script is available from:

MEDIA Desk United Kingdom, Louise Casey, British Film Institute, 21 Stephen Street, London WIP IPL (Tel: 0171–255 1444; Fax: 0171–636 6568);

MEDIA Antenna Cardiff, Robin Hughes, c/o Screen Wales, Screen Centre, Llantrisant Road, Llandaf, Cardiff CF5 2PU (Tel: 01222 578370; Fax: 01222 578654);

MEDIA Antenna Glasgow, Margaret O'Connor, Scottish Film Council, 74 Victoria Crescent Road, Glasgow G12 9JN (Tel: 0141–334 4445; Fax: 0141–334 8132).

Ever Shifting Images
WRITING FOR TELEVISION

FOR A WRITER who is not already on the inside track, television can be the maddest of markets. In theory, the breaking of the BBC–TV duopoly to allow independent production companies a 25 per cent share of their output and the technological advances which have led to a multiplicity of channels should open up opportunities for newcomers. In fact, the reverse seems to have been the case. Why?

The introduction of market forces has put pressure on programme-makers to think big. To fill an hour of prime-time television it is no longer enough to come up with an idea capable of pulling a fair to middling domestic audience. A harder sell is demanded. What will it do to the opposition? (Wipe the floor with them, is the desired answer.) Is there potential for overseas sales and for video spinoffs? There was a time when BBC Enterprises and the marketing sections of ITV accepted what was handed to them; now they are in at the planning stage with their forecasts of add-on sales, which can make or break a production budget. And there is no denying the potential for exploiting the popularity of a programme beyond domestic transmission. Recently, Channel 4 declared its aim of doubling its international turnover within three years on the back of its own video label. Meanwhile, the BBC has linked up with the Pearson Group, owner of *The Financial Times*, and Thames Television (one-time London weekday franchise holder and now a highly successful production company), to launch two European satellite channels, one carrying news, the other entertainment.

Today, Europe; tomorrow, the world. Global television demands global products, as Rupert Murdoch, who controls more channels than the BBC and ITV put together, sussed out long ago. Announcing its first drama commissions BSkyB led with a thirteen-part co-production with Yorkshire Television, German broadcaster ZDE and Spanish broadcaster Antena 3. No shortage of international sales there.

Television is getting more like the American film industry and, as in Hollywood, the money men come into their own. With every market expansion, the media moguls try to limit the risk by investing in what they see as safe (famous) names tied to safe (solidly established) products. Hence film producers' devotion to the star system and to the reworking of familiar themes either as sequels or remakes. Hence, too, British television's fondness for lavish classic revivals which portray the old country not so much as it was as how foreigners like to imagine it used to be and for adaptations of the work of writers whose work is instantly recognizable to an international audience.

No wonder there is a growing overlap between film and television. With Film on 4 having set the pace with memorable entertainments such as *Mona Lisa*, *Hear My Song*, *Prospero's Books* and *The Crying Game*, other major producers are beginning to catch up. At the BBC the Films department under Mark Shivas invests in five feature films a year.

The loser in this game plan is the single drama – once the testing ground of new writing and acting talent. It is hard to imagine now but in the 1960s and 1970s there were opportunities galore for aspiring writers. As Alan Bleasdale readily concedes, 'doors opened even before we had knocked on them'. Festivals and fringe theatres were scoured for writers with original ideas who could meet the demanding standards of the Wednesday Play, Play for Today, Centreplay and Second City Firsts. In Manchester, Granada TV maintained its own small theatre as a tryout venue for talented unknowns.

The brave days for writers came to an end in the early 1980s when, in the dash for ratings, serials and soaps began to take over the schedules. The move to blockbuster productions was a natural progression in a highly competitive industry facing up to the challenge of the satellite dish and the all-pervading power of American popular culture. Nowhere is this more apparent than on ITV, where a marked decline towards the lowest common denominator followed the last reshuffle of the power pack.

Much of the blame is put on the Network Centre, which is supposed
to bring a sense of order to a channel divided between fifteen franchised
holders. It has the power to accept or reject submissions for national
viewing and those it accepts it slots into the schedule at a time of its own
choice. There is a single criterion for successful peak viewing – a
programme must be able to command a mass audience. For drama there
is the added requirement that it should be part of a long-running
recommissionable series. Alan Plater, prolific scriptwriter and President of
the Writers' Guild, calls the Network Centre 'the temple of doom',
which it most certainly is for serious writers with an upmarket image.
Last year, the Network collection of rejects included new works by
Michael Frayn and Peter Nichols. What chance a newcomer?

But maybe – just maybe – there is a reaction setting in. The problem
of Big is Beautiful is that not everyone thinks it is. Set aside the famous
mega-budget disasters – *Eldorado, Trainer, A Year in Provence, Lady
Chatterley* – and look instead at the general surveys of viewing habits.
Television remains dominant, that's for sure. On average, the British
spend more than half their free time fixated by the small screen. According
to NOP, for 5 million people, television is the *only* leisure activity.

And yet. A closer examination of the figures shows a decline in
viewing in the younger age sector (25–44) which is accentuated for the
AB social group. More worrying still for the programme makers is their
decline in public esteem. Not long ago, a Mori survey for the National
Consumer Council found that television was the lowest rated public
service, down further even than British Rail. Reconciling the appeal of
television as a medium with the apparent dissatisfaction with its output
has so far defied sociological inquiry though a fruitful line of research
opens with the National Opinion Poll revelation that 2 million Britons
are in the habit of making love in front of the television.

Putting sex back on the screen where it belongs may not be the
foremost consideration of the television planners but regaining audiences
has certainly motivated the BBC's revival of the single-drama. Heading a
recently created single-drama department, George Faber is spending over
£50 million on the 1996/7 season. That this is by no means a throwback
to Play for Today is pointed up by the grants of up to £100,000 he is
making to independent filmmakers, whose work may earn a cinema as

well as a television showing. But there is also a commitment to nurturing talent. The single drama has recovered its role as 'an invaluable training ground for new writers', who are headhunted from the fringe theatre and from film schools such as the National Film and Television School, the Royal College of Art and Bournemouth University. The message to the writer seems to be: Television still needs you. Confirmation comes from Faber's boss, George Denton, head of BBC TV Drama (his budget is £200 million for 400 hours of programmes), who strenuously denies that he is wedded to the star system – unlike ITV.

> ITV will simply take off a drama if it doesn't have an audience of more than 10 million. I will have some dramas on BBC2 with audiences of not much more than one million.

But this is not to backtrack on earlier arguments by suggesting that a writer's life is a happy one. The BBC has to go a long way before it persuades Alan Plater of the return of the Golden Age. For him, television is a world where writers

> are surrounded by batteries of producers, executive producers, asso-
> ciate producers, script editors and consultants, all demanding changes
> to script and finished film with no purpose other than to justify their
> professional existence. It is a world where the first run of a major
> drama series, Granada's Maigret, was produced without any rehearsal
> time; where one highly-praised series had three directors in 12 weeks;
> where another had two directors in 24 hours; where there are dark
> tales of programmes being road-tested, American-style, with a 'typical'
> audience, and re-edited in accordance with their 'typical' reaction;
> where BBC Drama has more departmental heads than it has depart-
> ments; where the ITV Network Centre not only demands an
> audience of eight million but needs to know who they are, where
> they live and how much money they have to spend.

It was not long after Alan Plater had his say that Nick Elliott, head of BBC Drama Series, decamped to the ITV Network Centre after only ten months in his job. For Plater this might seem like a case of out of the frying pan, but the buzz from the BBC was of a senior man so hemmed in by politics that even Network Centre came as a happy release. His departure, said a senior insider, 'is obviously due in part to the purgatory of the BBC's bureaucracy and accounting'.

In this tightly controlled set-up, the writer's best chance of break-through is to jump aboard a bandwagon – in other words to write for an established series. Contributing to *Writers' Newsletter* (the journal of the Writers' Guild) in Autumn 1994, Christopher Penfold, editor of *The Bill*, put out the welcome mat for writers new to television:

> *The Bill* . . . requires of its writers recognition of the few absolutes of its successful format, some knowledge of the Metropolitan Police and, most of all, it requires perceptive understanding of the regular characters . . . The commissioning process here can be harsh . . . It can also be immensely rewarding for a new writer. There are no serial elements to contend with, no pre-determined storylines to follow. Every episode starts with a clean sheet and the question 'what do you want to write?' Within three months, you could see it on the screen – a quick turnaround which gives real meaning to 'learning by experience'.

The Bill is exceptional. The risk of attaching to a long-running series with a narrow format – an unashamedly predictable soap opera, for example – is of losing out on opportunities to test the imagination. Ming Ho, Script Executive for Zenith Productions, warns writers who are sending a script as an introduction to their work:

> A completely original piece is more constructive than an attempt at an episode of e.g. detective drama, as it gives a better indication of the writer's strengths, weaknesses and interests. We may then want to find out if he can write to a format, but in the first instance, we want to know what's special about that writer's approach. By original, I don't mean something which strives to be 'different', but something the writer really wants to write, rather than something he perceives to be commercial. It's a common misconception among first-time writers that you only want to see a script which proves its professional credentials by being like an extant series, whereas a solidly executed script of this nature can tell you nothing more than that the writer – like hundreds of others – has a basic level of technical competence.

This is, of course, important, but won't make you any more interested in that writer in preference to another.

This year, Christopher Penfold has been given a wider brief, to nurture new writers for Thames TV as a whole. But he is no easy touch.

I shall be looking for writers who have already attained a level of achievement with playscripts or filmscripts and who seriously want to write television drama – writers who perceive the format of the series as a framework for freedom rather than as a statute of limitations.

That said, all the long-running series – *EastEnders, Casualty, Brookside* – have provided new writers with a launch pad. Rona Munro, who wrote the screenplay for Ken Loach's movie *Ladybird, Ladybird*, started on *Dr Who* and moved on to *Casualty* before writing *Men of the Month* for Screen Two.

Interestingly, *The Bill* was itself the creation of a newcomer to television. Geoff McQueen was a young carpenter and joiner when he decided he wanted to write. Encouraged by his wife, he took part-time work and wrote a still unpublished novel. The bailiff, who made frequent calls, was 'a good old boy when he could have been hard'. The underlying lesson, as in all writing, is that dedicated, almost obsessional effort is a corollary of success.

Jimmy McGovern, the creator of *Cracker* and widely acknowledged to be on the crest of the new wave of television writers, gave up a job in the building trade to go to college and become a teacher. By then he was already in his late twenties. Married with three children, he held on to his writing vocation by his fingertips until his television début as a contributor to *Brookside*. He went on to win the Samuel Beckett Award for *Needle*, a drama about drug abuse in Liverpool on BBC1 and the Writers' Guild Award and Broadcasting Press Guild Award for the series *Cracker*.

Knowing the right people – or getting to know them – helps. A proposal to a named producer or commissioning editor stands more of a chance than one sent to a 'Dear Sir' of a drama department. It is not simply that a name will feel bound to reply, if only with an acknowledgement. Finding out who is the most suitable recipient for an idea, either by watching the credits or by telephoning a company, shows that the writer is doing his homework. Even so, do not expect an immediate response. Bob Flynn, a screenwriter with a track record, had to wait nearly two years for a reaction to a sample script.

> It was a jolly little letter from someone I had never heard of informing me that she had found my script – which took over a year to research and write – due solely to the fact that they were having a clean-out before moving offices and thanks for sending it in. I actually laughed. What's two years between friends and the script mountains in the labyrinths of the Beeb? The fact that it wasn't even a rejection had me in hysterics.

One way of getting known is to take a job – any job – within the industry. That is how they used to do it in newspapers when every messenger boy was an editor in the making. The modern counterpart is someone like John Sullivan. He was a brewery labourer in 1966 when he sent in his first script. Then he got a job as a BBC sceneshifter. Eight years on he convinced a producer that a series about an angry young misfit might appeal. As it turned out, *Citizen Smith* did have a following, though not as great as John Sullivan's next effort, *Only Fools and Horses*.

A characteristic of both series, and one deserving general application, is that they were right for their time. *Citizen Smith* hit the period in the 1980s when the loony left was much in the news, while *Only Fools and Horses* (like *Minder*) reflected the dodgy, get-rich-quick attitudes of the late 1980s. A frequent trigger for rejection of an otherwise competent and imaginative proposal is its failure to relate to contemporary interests.

Occasionally a writer is ahead of his time; more frequently he is way behind it, busily recycling ideas that might have passed muster ten years ago but now do no more than bring on a weary sensation of *déjà vu*.

Competitions are strong draws for talented newcomers (why otherwise would they be mounted?) but, however well organized, they are not a guarantee of recognition. Just think of all those literary prizes that go to the wrong people! Still, the odds are better than the National Lottery and, once noticed, a participant can generally rely on active encouragement. When *Rag Doll*, a tragi-comedy about incest, won an HTV playwriting competition, its author was a single mother on the dole. Now

Catherine Johnson is hard put to it to keep up with the demand for her services. Her output ranges from episodes for *Casualty* and *Love Hurts* to *Sin Bin*, a much-acclaimed BBC single drama.

Schools' programmes are traditionally hospitable to newcomers. Even allowing for frequent repeats cutting back on the amount of original output, up to 1000 hours a year transmitted by BBC and ITV suggest a wealth of opportunities. Drama especially. This is confirmed by, among others, Howard Schuman, himself a highly experienced and proficient writer whose credits include *Selling Hitler*. After the success of this screenplay his television career stalled until he met Richard Langridge, executive producer of Scene, the drama division of BBC Educational Television.

> Richard asked if I'd be interested in writing a studio play. He seemed to be offering me the chance to have some fun – and 'fun' is not something normally associated with working in modern television. I cautiously proposed *Young Jung*, in which 14-year-old Rosa Rosenband, granddaughter of an eminent psychiatrist, sets up as a Jungian analyst to treat her wingeing classmates. Richard Langridge then did a very strange thing: he immediately commissioned me. Having learned to look any television gift horse not only in the mouth but in every other orifice as well, I was still suspicious. But when the script for *Young Jung* was finished, Langridge confounded my suspicions and gave it the green light. Cas Lester booked the very sharp Juliet May to direct. Between them, they gathered performers and a design team who shared the conviction that video studio drama can create a magical, slightly unreal world. Rosa's school, Hammersmith streets, a bohemian household and a key dream sequence were meshed into an imaginative visual world by the direction, sets, lighting, costumes, music and sound design.

Producers rarely respond constructively to an out-of-the-blue telephoned pitch, or a suggestion for an open-ended meeting – and who can blame them? 'I prefer it on paper before I meet and talk,' says Brenda Reid, head of drama at Anglia, 'because some people are really good at pitching and some are not so good and it's hard to separate the idea from the personality.'

She is being polite, of course. Producers do not want to talk directly to unknowns for the simple reason that they do not want to encourage the nutcases. Letters are bad enough.

Adrian Mourby, a drama producer for BBC Wales, has an antipathy for the 'closely typed missive in which the "banned" author explains that the Arts Council, BBC and government have hitherto conspired to intimidate producers into rejecting this work' and describes it as 'a significant augury'.

> One author actually wrote and asked me to pick his play up in person because many years ago he'd sent a script through the post and it had gone astray; John Cleese had found it, he claimed, altered the names and called it *Fawlty Towers*. Another explained that he scanned *Radio Times* each week because the London Drama Department sent him coded messages in the programme billings while another booby-trapped the pages with thin cotton so that each page would tear slightly when prised apart. That way he intended to prove his theory that over the last 20 years the BBC had simply rejected all his scripts on receipt. Many playwrights are paranoid but only the truly bad ones fail to recognise it.

For newcomers out to prove their talent, the only way forward is to show what they can do. Tony Charles, head of drama at Meridian, has sound advice on discovering the truth.

> All the would-be writers sitting out there thinking of doing it would have far more chance if they wrote on spec an episode of *Birds Of A Feather*, or *Lovejoy*, or whatever show that we're doing. It's a very good way of seeing if somebody can actually write . . . because you have a yard-stick, comparisons with other writers' dialogue.

And the emphasis on 'showing' is important. This is television, remember. Too many words spoil the pictures; just as too many characters spoil the plot.

One way on to the network is via the independent production companies, who, benefiting from the Government's desire to break the cosy TV duopoly, are on course to provide at least 25 per cent of BBC and ITV programmes. If it seems, thereby, that running a production company is an easy way to make a million, forget it. This is a highly competitive market in which profit margins are razor thin. Appearances can be deceptive. Absolutely Stupendous Productions Ltd is as likely as not a back room off Tooting Broadway managed by a telephone answering machine. The producer who heads up ASP will be out lobbying commissioning editors. He knows only too well that few of his treatments will be taken up and that those which do get into the schedules are unlikely to last more than a season. There are now more than 1000 independent producers, their numbers swollen recently by redundancies at the BBC and ITV. Channel 4 is their clearest target, while the murkiest is the BBC. Nicholas Fraser, for ten years an independent producer until he became commissioning editor for religion at Channel 4, argues that the BBC is the worst place to sell programmes.

> Despite the innumerable Task Forces, the management has yet to find a system of incentives for its executives encouraging them to commission independent producers. Giving work to an independent means less money for your own staff and less work; it involves creating redundancies. No wonder cautious and loyal BBC department heads, trained in the old paternalistic tradition, have taken to change reluctantly, leaving the corporation far behind its antiquated planning quotas.

Still, it is the independents who are doing the most to nurture the latest generation of screenwriters. Even if they do not provide an entrée to the screen networks, contacts with independent producers can bring dividends in the shape of offers to write for corporate television. This refers to videos and films made for commercial, industrial and government organizations. They can range from training programmes and the video equivalent of house magazines to prestige propaganda and advertising features. The market is difficult to assess but estimates go as high as an annual expenditure of £300 million, which translates into at least 6000 productions.

The problem for writers involved in corporate television is the absence of any guidelines on payment. The market is too diffuse for the Writers' Guild or other professional associations to negotiate a standard agreement.

Writers must fend for themselves. Since they are working to a tight brief, usually with material supplied by the client, they are expected to surrender copyright. There is therefore no question of repeat fees or royalties. But if the production company is honest and the client is sensible enough to want a professional writer, the rewards can be up to the level of network television and far beyond that of radio.

A guess at standard rate would be £2000 plus for an hour-long programme. Some writers prefer to value their time on a daily rate which allows for the probability of numerous rewrites.

If a writer and production company have not previously worked together it is as well to ask for an advance on payment to show goodwill. Some production companies with respectable client lists are none the less run on a shoestring. They are not above telling their accounts departments that when it comes to payments writers are last in the pecking order. Whereas, if there was any justice in the world they would be first.

When it comes to mainstream television, the independents win or lose on the strength of their ideas. They therefore have a vested interest in taking seriously any writer who puts up a realistic proposal. And they are likely to respond more quickly than network producers and editors, who can take up to three months to deliver a judgement. Even so, it is a naïvely optimistic writer who sticks to the convention of submitting a script or outline to one company at a time. If the idea is any good, there is no harm in encouraging a little competition. The knowledge that others could be interested may stimulate a producer to put in a pre-emptive bid.

There is disagreement among independents as to whether it is best to send in a synopsis or a full script. Of the twenty production companies we approached, twelve come down in favour of synopses, though invariably with qualifications.

> If the synopsis interests me I then ask for a script as a further example of the writer's work and then a meeting might follow.

> Sample writing is essential if nothing is known about the writer.

> Synopses are useful for evaluating novels for adaptation, or factual material on which a film or series is to be based – but then only as a

first step, to weed out unsuitable material without wasting too much time on either side.

If a writer submits a series plot, we advise sending synopses of further episodes, rather than full scripts.

Of the eight production companies who prefer full scripts, the common experience seems to be that synopses are unreliable indicators of talent.

Synopses rarely show the quality of writing.

Synopses rarely capture the flavour of the script and its characters.

The problem, of course, is how to cope with the sheer weight of material.

Synopses from new writers are meaningless. How can we tell if they can actually write? Then again, we don't have time to read 300-page unsolicited scripts.

A sensible compromise, one calculated to be mutually beneficial, is suggested by Nic Phillips, Head of Comedy at Celador Productions:

I prefer a very short synopsis, a very brief outline of each main character and one full, well presented script with the minimum of stage directions.

From our survey, it seems that the independents with a television track record receive up to thirty or forty unsolicited scripts a month and try to respond, constructively or otherwise, in six to eight weeks. Asked how many unsolicited scripts show promise, the responses are too vague to be helpful. This is explained by Ming Ho of Zenith Productions.

While it's relatively rare to option a script which has come in unsolicited, there are many cases when we might take an interest in the writer's future work, or commission him to write an episode of a series or another original project.

So I interpret 'promise', not in terms of whether we decide to produce or develop the script in question, but in terms of whether the writer is of interest to us – either for this project, or for something else.

She adds:

I also think it would be helpful to define what we mean by 'new' writers, as the term can cover a variety of different situations – e.g. people who have never written anything before; people who have been writing for some time but have never had anything produced; novelists or journalists who have never written drama before; writers who have had stage or radio plays produced but have not previously written for the screen; writers who have had a short, or perhaps, even a Screen Two produced but who have not yet created or written for a series or serial.

Within the television industry, the latter two categories would be referred to as 'new writers', although they might already be quite established in other media.

Asked for a few lines of best advice to writers, this is how our sample of independent producers responded:

Know your market, know what you're writing for (TV or film, long-running series or mini-series, etc.), know who you're writing to and what they are looking for.

Keep the story line simple and work on well-delineated, rounded characters.

If a script has typos, spelling mistakes and is presented in an unprofessional manner, the creative quality of the script normally follows suit.

Don't send more than one project to a company at a time. One is enough to give an idea of your writing, and a script executive bogged down by multiple submissions from the same writer will be less keen to read the work.

Try and get a script report done for you by a professional (pay for it, if necessary) to assess its chances and your skill before sending it out to production companies.

(a) Study the schedules and don't pitch things that don't have a prayer; (b) Don't send your script to more than two or three production companies at once; (c) Chase for a response to your script after three to four weeks. If you want it back, send an s.a.e. within six weeks.

Be aware of what the television networks are interested in re. length or format of projects but without losing the individuality of the idea and project.

You must get an agent but be warned that agents who stay in business are very choosy about their clients.

Do not ask for a critique; it's a wholly unrealistic expectation.

Be professional. Read books like *The Writer's Handbook* to help you *become* professional.

Watch television.

Study the genre. Examine and understand structure; if you're writing comedy, be funny. Surprise me!

If you have talent someone will eventually spot it. So don't give up!

Keep writing and keep rewriting. Too many give up too early if they don't get a quick sale. The only way to learn your craft is to keep at it. Learn about the business side – find out who the buyers are and what they want. Watch their shows. Read the trades.

Words into Pictures

AN AUTHOR'S BRUSH WITH TV

THERE COMES A TIME in every author's life when a television producer calls.

> Hi there. You don't know me. My name is J.J. Fastbuck. I make programmes for Channel 4. Anyway, I wanted to say, I've read your book. And you know what? I think it's great. Just great. Maybe we should meet?

Pause. The wise virgin does not respond with gurgles of happy anticipation at the coming seduction. Television can spell wealth and fame beyond the dreams of Jeffrey Archer. It can also mean a load of trouble with no reward to show for it. The throwaway reference to Channel 4 is suspect.

Everyone in television production has a line open to Channel 4, which relies exclusively on independents to fill its schedule. But for every thousand ideas put up to commissioning editors only one or two achieve screen time. Thus 'making a programme for Channel 4' can be interpreted literally but is more likely to mean that a proposal is floating up and down the corridors of Horseferry Road with as much chance of coming to fruition as a love thy neighbour campaign in Bosnia.

A gentle interrogation of Mr Fastbuck will clarify matters. If the name of his company is not immediately recognizable it helps to be able to identify his offspring. No need to overdo it. It is enough at this stage to establish that Fastbuck has some sort of track record. How audiences and critics judge his creativity can be researched at leisure.

Assuming your latest fan can prove his credentials, the next step is to decide where to meet. The initiative is with Fastbuck. He has three options. He can suggest that you come to him, that he comes to you, or that you meet on neutral ground for lunch or a drink. The first is the likeliest. A producer enjoys the power of drawing writers towards him, like supplicants at a rich man's feast. Anyway, he feels safer on home ground. But that is his problem, not yours. A moment's reflection will show that if you do the travelling, even if it is just across town, you will be clocking up the hours on what may well be a total waste of time. Resist. And remain strong when the producer throws an inducement: 'You can see how we operate here. I'm sure you'll be interested.'

No you won't. The typical producer works in a dingy room in a dingy office block. When he is in active business he hires all the services he wants for a particular project but you will not see any of this. The best you can hope for is a video player showing extracts from past triumphs. The most advanced piece of equipment on view is liable to be the water cooler.

The assumption holds true for the producer who can add BBC or ITV after his name. There is nowhere quite so depressing as the sanctum of a BBC staffer. Even the newish offices at White City lack visitor appeal, a fact tacitly confirmed by the number of meetings held in the canteen.

Thus, both on grounds of economy and mental stability, the aim should be to tempt the producer out of his lair. You have to be a hot prospect indeed for him to venture far. But a midway restaurant or bar will, by his choice, indicate your rank in the pecking order. A health food salad or a pub lunch are equally bad news.

The meeting opens with the usual civilities. You hear of the trouble the producer has had with his new car, the details of his affair with a continuity lady and unconfirmed gossip of a rival who is said to be under investigation by the Serious Fraud Squad. He will then say, 'But enough of me. Tell me about yourself. Given a free hand, what would you really want to do for television?' The urge now is to throw in every idea you've ever had. A career-load of accumulated intellectual baggage is dumped on the table. In the next hour, the producer will sift the items of interest, murmuring appreciative comments the while. Only later will dawn the realization that there is no onus on Fastbuck to involve you in his plans.

Maybe he will but, then again, maybe one of your pet projects will be farmed out for adoption, without consent. You could try claiming copyright but just see how far that will get you. Unless fully documented, an idea shared is common property.

The consolation is in knowing that Fastbuck is primarily interested in your latest book, the pride of the literary circuit. And, indeed, the centre point of the meeting is an exchange of views on how best to translate your work into a televisual commodity.

This is the moment to strike a deal. OK, so you acknowledge that Fastbuck is still at the exploratory stage but assuming – just assuming – that something does come of his wildest dreams, what's in it for you? A fee for research or scripting, perhaps? Maybe Fastbuck should talk to your agent to work out, in broad principle, what you would expect to gain from repeats and residuals. At the very least you should be hired as a programme consultant. After all, this is *your* book.

But it rarely happens like this. Producers are as adept at avoiding financial commitments as they are skilled in flattering their victims into working for nothing. So, over handshakes of good intent you are invited to go off and detail a proposal which Fastbuck can use in his negotiations with commissioning editors. This may take a week or two in which you might otherwise be earning a living but it is hard to resist the challenge.

And then? Well, then, you join the multitude of television writers in waiting. You, or rather Fastbuck, could strike lucky or you could live in hope for years on end or you could die and be forgotten until one of a new generation of television executives decides you are ripe for revival and hires an adaptor. At which point your grandchildren cash in.

Assessing the Situation Comedy

NO PART OF TELEVISION has a claim to exclusivity, least of all situation comedy. The genre has interbred with comedy drama and with shows for stand-up comics. Result, uncertainty and confusion all round. Whole seminars are taken up with the question, 'What is situation comedy?' without arriving at any clear answers.

For what it is worth, received wisdom starts with the *Guinness Book of Sitcoms* and a quotation from an article *circa* 1948 about *Band Waggon*, a show that ran throughout the war. It starred Arthur Askey and Richard Murdoch, who were supposed to share a flat at the top of Broadcasting House. Their weekly misadventures were said to exploit 'situation comedy' in the style of *The Jack Benny Show*, the darling of the American airwaves in the 1940s and 1950s. The *Jack Benny Show* was essentially a radio comedy about putting on a radio comedy, an introspective format which allowed the star full reign in exploiting his trademark for tight-fistedness.

What *Band Waggon* and *The Jack Benny Show* had in common, apart from famous comics who were playing themselves, was a half-hour slot, a fixed location, a small number of players and a central theme that could bear frequent repetition. But it does not take more than a random sample of the sitcoms we have known and loved to realize that this framework is very loose indeed. Ask the experts.

'Sitcoms need to have a link with reality,' says John Sullivan (*Citizen Smith, Only Fools and Horses*). As an example, he cites *Yes, Minister* and *Yes, Prime Minister*. These were extremely good because of the dialogue. It confirmed everything we had always thought about politicians. From the first episode I realised that I was watching something very clever. It gave out so much qualified information about the civil service. And it was this information – the contorted civil service speak – that made the humour. I didn't need to understand what they were talking about. In fact, the less I understood, the better.

But if it is reality we are talking about, what of *Blackadder* or *Red Dwarf*, which have their comedy rooted in pure fantasy?

As a veteran sitcom performer, Richard Briers may be a little nearer the mark when he argues that 'you have to have the right thing at the right time'. He rests his case on *The Good Life* 'because twenty years ago people were turning green and were into DIY'. There are several other examples. *The Rag Trade*, which ran for three lengthy series in the 1960s, was revived in the 1970s and was voted by newspaper readers the most popular TV programme of all time, arrived just at a point when trade unions were losing their appeal and the obstreperous shop steward was becoming a figure of ridicule. More recently, *Absolutely Fabulous* caught on to the mega-hype of public relations, as seen in all tabloids, and *One Foot in the Grave* reflected concerns of and for an ageing population.

But then how do you explain the lasting popularity of *Dad's Army*, which came along nearly twenty-five years after the war ended? Hardly topical. The idea occurred to Jimmy Perry when he was a struggling actor on the edge of middle age. 'I had three characters, Captain Mainwaring, only he was a sergeant then, a soppy boy and an old man. I picked these from the Will Hay films like *Oh Mr Porter* – the pompous man, the fat boy and the old chap.'

There is a nugget of wisdom here. Could it be that successful situation comedy rests on enduring characters recognizable in some small way from our own lives? Eric Chappell (*Rising Damp, Only When I Laugh*) certainly believes so.

Most good comedy comes from character and from recognition of the weaknesses of each other. If you take yourself too seriously and can't laugh at yourself, I doubt you can write good comedy. It's not so much the situation that's important – if the characters are interesting enough, you can put them in a hole in the ground.

The argument is given a twist by veteran producer Dennis Main Wilson (*The Goon Show*, *Hancock's Half Hour* and *Til Death Us Do Part*):

Humour comes out of being confident in yourself, having the ability to see things dispassionately and when things get worse, being able to laugh at it. An utter hatred of the establishment is also useful.

But so also is producer sympathy. Instant success is a rarity in situation comedy. *Dad's Army*, *One Foot in the Grave*, *Hi-De-Hi* and *Are You Being Served?* needed two or three series to take off.

We could go on like this indefinitely. Let's face it, analysing situation comedy, or any sort of comedy, is like trying to pat a block of runny butter. The only valid test for comedy is the quota of laughs. You have to try it to see if it works. All else is subjective value.

It was easier to live with this uncertainty in the days when television was a cottage industry and the financial risk of taking a chance on untried talent was somewhat less than the national debt. Writers educated in radio comedy progressed to television along with producers who were already familiar with their work. One such was Dick Sharples.

Some of the best and most memorable sitcom series (many of which are still being repeated) were produced by what was really a simple double-act of writer plus producer/director acting on their gut instincts. After the Head of Department had made his decision to commission a pilot script – and on receipt of that script, decided to make a pilot – if that pilot showed the hoped-for potential, the writer and his or her producer/director were left alone to produce a series.

If that series did reasonably well on the network, then this double-act went on to produce a further series. If it didn't, the writer and producer/director were politely shown the door.

That was the BBC. For ITV there was a Networking Committee on which the big five companies wheeled and dealed their schedules. No one said it was easy to get an idea taken up but producers backed their judgement and the companies backed their producers, relying on talent and track record to see them through.

The system has changed in two ways, both for the bad according to old hands. There is now much greater centralization, with power concentrated on the big two – David Liddiment, the BBC's head of entertainment, and Vernon Lawrence, controller of drama and entertainment at ITV Network Centre, the organization that supplanted the Networking Committee after the last reallocation of franchises. With big money at stake, the emphasis is on mass-appeal sitcoms which can pull an audience of 10 million plus and show promise of longevity, maybe up to a hundred episodes.

In pursuit of this chimera – and this the second way in which the system has changed – producers have to justify their recommendation in what sounds like a parody of sociological jargon. There is, says Dick Sharples, much talk of 'audience identification', a script's 'aerodynamics' and its 'dramatic diagonal', whatever that means. It is no longer good enough to laugh out loud at a script, it has to be pre-researched with viewer panels deliberating on what sort of screen characters they would like to see. The decision-making process involves numerous creative committees (a contradiction in terms?) and can take up to eighteen months to complete.

This is all very frustrating for writers brought up on back-of-an-envelope proposals and handshake deals. But it is hard to avoid the belief that criticism of current practice is as much a feature of the generation gap as it is a genuine warning of falling standards. Writers whose credits filled the screen in the 1960s and 1970s now find themselves submerged under the comedy new wave. Their last gasp is to blame the system.

Greater centralization at the BBC and ITV may be regrettable but it is offset somewhat by the independently minded Channel 4, where Seamus Cassidy, commissioning editor for comedy, is by no means obsessed by mega-ratings. Once they are accepted there is now much greater effort put into nurturing scripts so that they live up to their potential. BBC2, for example, has its own Script Development Unit which oversees scripts from submission to eventual production.

The independent production companies bring another dimension to the commissioning process. The best known is Hat Trick (*Have I Got*

News For You, Whose Line Is It Anyway, Drop the Dead Donkey), where Denise O'Donoghue is reported to be able to reduce the interval between idea and go-ahead to mere days. Rowan Atkinson's company, Tiger Aspect, takes credit for *Mr Bean*, naturally, but also for *Harry Enfield and Chums*. And there are many others ready to push hard on behalf of sellable ideas. Meanwhile, individual producers who can boast a success or two are on a fast track to the decision-makers.

Writers who are ambitious to break into the sitcom market should know that it is no longer enough to send in a brief synopsis and a few jokes with an offer to talk. Those days have gone. Serious consideration begins with a full script and several story lines showing how the sitcom and its characters will develop. The writer is expected to understand the rudiments of television production such as using no more than three sets – the maximum number that can be fitted into a studio – and avoiding crowd scenes (too expensive).

At ITV they look for a realization that the half-hour is interrupted by ads. In other words, there must be a natural break with a strong opener for the second half. If viewers enjoy the commercials (made with much bigger budgets) more than the sitcom, it is the sitcom that will be dropped.

One of the singularities of situation comedy is that many of the best are written by couples – Jimmy Perry and David Croft (*Dad's Army, Hi-De-Hi, It Ain't Half Hot Mum*), Ben Elton and Richard Curtis (*The Young Ones, Blackadder*), Ronald Wolfe and Ronald Chesney (*The Rag Trade, On the Buses*), and Dick Clement and Ian Le Frenais (*The Likely Lads, Porridge*). Clearly there are advantages in working with someone who can react to jokes and build on ideas. All humour is a two-way process. The first sign of success is getting others to share a laugh.

Extracts from the Agreement between the Writers' Guild of Great Britain and Producers' Alliance for Cinema & Television (PACT)

THIS AGREEMENT ... sets out the minimum terms and conditions to be observed in contracts between Associates of the Producers' Alliance for Cinema & Television ... and members of the Writers' Guild ... The Agreement covers:

Feature films with a budget in excess of £2 million; feature films with a budget between £750,000 and £2 million; television films budgeted at £750,000 and above; films with a budget below £750,000; television series and serials with format provided other than by the writer.

The following is a summary of essential terms:

The writer ... undertakes

i   to attend meetings and conferences at the producer's offices or studios or elsewhere as the producer may reasonably require ... The writer shall receive an allowance of £75 for each day of attendance ... after acceptance of the final draft of the script.

ii   to carry out adequate research and preparation for the work ...

iii   to write the treatment, first draft, second draft and principal photography script of the work and to deliver each of them on the dates specified. . .

iv   make incidental and minor revisions as the producer shall reasonably require.

Undertakings by the Associate:

i   the writer ... shall be notified of the date time and venue of the showing of the 'rough cut' and shall be invited to attend.

Dispute Proc~~~~~

Any matt~~ ~~ ~~ispute ... shall be referred to a Standing Joint Committee consisting of not more than three representatives of the Guild and three representatives of the Association . . .

Rights

Full copyright in the work for which the writer is engaged shall vest in and be the sole property of the associate for all media.

In the event of any writer's work being used wholly or partly in any book, journal or other publication, the associate and the writer shall negotiate terms for such uses as may be utilized as required.

. . . The extent of the interest or any financial participation in merchandising shall be the subject of mutual agreement between the writer and the producer.

Travel and Subsistence

Where a writer is required to travel more than thirty miles . . ., the producer shall reimburse the costs of travel. . .

Where a writer is required to travel by air the producer shall only make bookings on either an airline operating scheduled passenger services, or on charter flights having safety standards acceptable to the British Civil Aviation Authorities.

Collecting Societies

The producer will lay no claim to any monies payable to the writer via foreign or domestic collecting societies ... The writer shall have no claim to payment by the company in respect of rights collectively licensed.

Passing of Copyright

Copyright in products of the writer's services shall pass to the producer as payment is made for that stage in respect of which the services were rendered.

Videotape

On completion, the producer shall provide a domestic copy of the production to the writer.

SCHEDULE OF MINIMUM FEES AND USE PAYMENTS

Feature Films Budgeted at £2 Million and Over:

Treatment

Commencement Payment	2500
Acceptance Payment	1500

First Draft

Commencement Payment	4800
Delivery Payment	4800

Second Draft

Commencement Payment	2400
Delivery Payment	2400
Principal Photography Payment	4800
Total Minimum Payment	23,200
Additional Use Pre-Payment	8000
Total Guaranteed Payment	31,200

Payments for Uses

UK TV, including European Cable Television Transmission:

£2000 per transmission limited to seven years and subject to a minimum payment of	6000
US Network TV Prime Time	13,000
US Network TV Non-Prime Time	2000
PBS	1500
US other TV	1500
Rest of the World Free TV	6000
US Major Pay TV	5500
Other US and Rest of the World Pay TV	2000
Video	3000

Feature Films Budgeted at £750,000 Up to £2 Million:

Television Films Budgeted at £750,000 and Above and Not Subject to Any Budget Ceiling Figures refer to television productions of ninety minutes duration. For television productions of more or less than ninety minutes the script fee shall be pro-rated.

Treatment

Commencement Payment	1000
Acceptance Payment	1000

First Draft

Commencement Payment	3500
Delivery Payment	3500

Second Draft

Commencement Payment	1200
Delivery Payment	1200
Principal Photography Payment	2600
Total Minimum Payment	14,000
Additional Use Pre-Payment	5000
Total Guaranteed Payment	19,000

Payment for Uses

The producer opts before the first day of principal photography to take within the total minimum payment either worldwide theatrical rights or two UK network TV transmissions and a limited cinema release in the UK over a period of three months ... This limited theatrical release may take place within a period commencing nine months before the first television transmission in the UK and terminating three months after.

If the theatrical rights are taken:

UK TV, including simultaneous European Cable transmission, £1250 per transmission, limited to seven years and a payment of £3750.

If two UK television transmissions are taken:

Additional UK Television transmission within seven years, per transmission:	2000
UK (Full) theatrical	subject to negotiation
US theatrical	subject to negotiation
Rest of the World theatrical	1200

Whatever the option taken up the following residuals apply:

US Network TV Prime Time	9750
US Network TV Non-Prime Time	1800

PBS	1000
US Other TV	1000
Rest of the World Free TV	2500
US Major Pay TV	2750
US and Rest of World Pay TV	1250
Video	1200

Films Budgeted Below £750,000:

The terms for films in this category tend to be exactly the same as for films budgeted at £750,000 and up to £2 million, except that the producer is not required to make the £5000 advance payment against additional uses.

The total guaranteed payment is therefore £14,000.

Payments at all the stages from treatment to completion are negotiable above the minimum.

Once UK television uses purchased over a period of seven years from the date of first transmission have elapsed each further transmission on UK television may be purchased by payment of 20 per cent of the current scale fee for that use.

How To Publish Your Poetry

BY PETER FINCH

THERE IS PROBABLY no one at all in Britain, Ireland or America who earns his or her living just from the *writing* of verse. Tennyson might have sold 60,000 copies a year of *In Memoriam A.H.H.* in the 1850s but a poet today is doing wonderfully well to sell one-tenth of that. The Poet Laureate gets a nominal stipend and a gift of wine, the total value of which is less than £100. It is a mark of the commercial esteem in which poets are held. My son, by doing two paper-rounds, can earn more than that.

Yet poetry appears never to have been so popular. There were 40,000 entries to the last Arvon Foundation competition and almost as many to the Poetry Society for its annual national contest. Hundreds of thousands of people enter poetry competitions, further thousands then send their poems to the poetry magazines. It is a paradox which resists probing. Poetry is an esteemed art of impeccable pedigree with a commercial status of nil.

Is that it, then? You might feel inclined now to throw your poems in the bin and have done with it. Yet you can improve things; there *is* an audience, a large one, reluctant but tappable – the poets, the people doing this versifying, even you. You can buy books, you can read magazines. In fact if you've any inclination at all to write and publish contemporary poetry you must do this.

Poetry has a widespread but very thin market – invisible when viewed for profit – but it's there.

Many thousands of novice poets in this country suffer the grand delusion that once they've actually written something this act alone makes

them important. They imagine it turns them overnight into vital creators
with something to say. Poetry is at first a matter of apprenticeship and
hard work. They ignore this. They insist that what they've scribbled is
enough, they want it published. I just cannot imagine similar people
buying a violin, scratching a few notes and then applying to join the
London Symphony Orchestra. Ah, but poetry is different – yes: it does
different things.

   Much poetry gets written for personal reasons – exorcising emotions,
depleting desperations, dealing with love and coping with despair. This
kind of writing is therapeutic and should be left in the drawer. If you feel
what you've written goes beyond that, persevere.

→   *Think*

→   *Read*

→   *Write*

And if you are certain that poetry is more important to you than simply a
romantic attachment to the idea of 'being a bit of a writer' – then keep
on.

SENDING IT IN

Your first attempts at publication – getting a poem 'accepted' – should be
directed at magazines. Start where you'll have the best chance and then
move on. When submitting work the following points should all be
borne in mind:

→   *Research your market.*   Do not simply send your work to the first
apparently suitable address you find. Read widely, actually support the
magazines you've picked. Be perfectly clear about the kind of thing
they print and assure yourself that you will fit in.

→   *Keep a record book.*   List the name and address of magazine, date
of submission, titles of poems sent and then leave a space where you
can record reaction.

→   *Send around six poems at a time.*   Short to medium length if
you've got them and avoiding epics. Show a range of subject matter

and style. Give the editor as much variety as possible to increase your chance of acceptance.

→ *Do not go overboard.*   In no circumstances submit your life's work. There is nothing more likely to put an editor off than a bulky parcel enmeshed with rubber bands and string accompanied by a letter beginning: 'I enclose 300 poems written over the past few months . . .'

Some things you shouldn't do:

→ *Don't bribe.*   Don't offer to subscribe *if* your poems are accepted (an editor would like you to subscribe anyway). Don't say you'll buy dozens of copies of the issue you're in to sell to your friends. Don't mention how much bad luck you've had, how long you've been hunting for publication, your lack of success. Don't plead, suggest how desperate, depressed or deranged you are.

→ *Enclose a stamped addressed envelope*   large enough to accommodate your submission and with enough stamps on it to pay for their weight. THIS IS VITAL. If you don't pay in advance for the return of your mss it is unlikely that you'll see them again.

→ *After you've mailed your envelope, expect to wait.*   You may hear after a few days, but usually it takes weeks. There is no hard-and-fast rule – surveyed magazines quoted 'report times' (the gap between receiving a submission and sending a reply) varying between two weeks and three months. A lot will depend on the time of year, if the editor is on holiday, or if an issue has just been published, which means the editor will be in the middle of a lot of extra work. In my experience, three weeks is about average. There are some magazines, however, who don't reply at all until they are just about to go to press, at which stage they send back everything which is not required. The rule is patience, hold on.

→ *Finally, don't complain.*   Your poems may be new and vital, and it is certainly unreasonable for some editor to keep them dark and unread for month after month, but *you* chose to submit them. *The editor didn't ask.* It will do you no good writing, it will be embarrassing if you phone and in no circumstances whatsoever turn up in person to find out what's going on.

The information I've left out so far concerns what happens when you get a result. How are you told? No fanfares, it slides in via a brief letter, sometimes on a reversed rejection slip attached to the returned part of your originally submitted batch. There is nothing too formal about it – editors may be renowned for sending curt rejection slips but they mail brief acceptances too.

REJECTION

The most usual result of sending your poems is to have them sent back again. Rejection. It comes like a slap in the face, you don't expect it, don't deserve it. Why you? The common reaction is to blame the editor, the magazine, the system, anything bar the poems.

But let's put this in perspective. Does rejection mean that the work is inferior? Are the poems really not up to scratch? In many cases, unfortunately so. Many poets submit work that they know is unfinished, that is weak, unexciting, that they recognize as flawed, sometimes that they do not themselves even like. They imagine, I suppose, that someone else will find their second-rate creations worthwhile. It doesn't happen, of course. Only famous poets can get by on bad poems and even there the fame eventually wears out.

It is worth looking at exactly what standard is aimed for. The only specific, often quoted by editors when defining their needs, is the phrase 'good poetry' – and what is that? There is no unassailable standard of quality; the term changes according to fashion and to the recommendations and predilections of those poets who sell more than others at any specific time. Good poetry – you cannot even look back through literary history to find it. That, too, changes in importance, according to the whims of the age which does the judging. So what does it mean, this subjective average? What the editor likes, I suppose, what he or she decides to use.

There are many reasons why rejection takes place, and the sheer volume of poetry received by poetry magazines is undoubtedly high on the list. At its height, *Outposts* received 83,000 poems a year, *Poetry*

Review gets 30,000 and even much smaller magazines can manage to see 4000–5000. Out of this huge input of verse as few as 120 are printed by *Outposts*, 130 in *Poetry Review* and perhaps only 60 in a smaller journal such as *Iota*. This is less than $\frac{1}{2}$ a per cent.

Some editors send everything back once they've got enough in hand for a specific issue. Others clear the decks periodically – even sending back good work – in order to give themselves space to breathe. Generally, though, the main reason is incorrect submission. You haven't studied the magazine, you've sent in the wrong kind of stuff.

In a survey I carried out among a good cross-section of British poets I discovered that everyone had suffered rejection at some time and no one had regarded a poem's return as reason for giving up on it. Most agreed that a rejected poem should be tried again elsewhere, repeatedly, until it became boring or new work had taken its place.

If your poems come back in batches one after another try not to get paranoid. Don't worry about what the postman may think. He doesn't care. Think of it like juggling; as poems return, pack them up again and send them out elsewhere. Do remember to remove the rejection slip – it's been known for poets to forget. If the manuscript becomes tatty or overfolded, retype it. Keep it looking new.

Reputations are fragile things. They don't come easily and they don't come overnight. Build yours by perseverance and determination and, most importantly, by creating competent work. Rejections never stop but they can be encouraged to slow down.

THE BOOK-LENGTH MANUSCRIPT

You are ready for your first slim volume. Poetry collections are habitually slim, sometimes too thin to have the title printed on their spines. If you imagined a fat book – hundreds of pages – it won't turn out like that.

Presentation for submission to a publisher is not complicated. Avoid being fussy. Prepare each poem as if for magazine submission, omitting your name and address from each sheet. Give some thought to order, particularly the final poem. This should give a kind of completeness to the selection, a rounding-off rather than a stopping in mid-air. Groups of short poems dispersed among longer pieces will assist the flow. Divide the selection thematically if you can. If that won't work, run the poems sequentially, in order of date of composition. If you've employed similar images in different poems put them at opposite ends of the collection or leave one out altogether. Don't be afraid to rearrange the contents a number of times until you get it right. A lot of readers won't follow your order anyway – they'll dip and skip. Ignore them. Prepare your selection in the best shape you can.

TITLE

And the title. What have you called your selection? Sometimes this is obvious, it will leap at you. More often though it is a problem. Booksellers will tell you that titles are important, they help the impulse purchase, and anything that encourages people actually to pick up a book is worth serious consideration. It may be that a single poem in the collection has a gripping title. If so, use that. Perhaps there is a thematic connection you can embroider. Do not take the obvious and easy way out. Your title has a job to do.

The best titles are individual, unorthodox, apposite for their content yet unexpected labelling for a book of poems.

MARKETS – THE BOOK

Commercially it is a small one. Despite what you may read in the Sunday papers and allowing for a few notable exceptions – Phillip Larkin, Carol Ann Duffy, Wendy Cope, Roger McGough, Ted Hughes, Seamus Heaney – poetry does not sell in large quantities. Compared to books on gardening, cookery or romantic novels it is a non-starter. Its continuing attraction for a small number of British publishers remains a mystery.

The main output comes traditionally from Faber & Faber (an influence of T.S. Eliot's) and here only one new, untried poet – if that – is taken on each year. The other principal publishing houses are Jonathan Cape and the Oxford University Press, both with active lists, both taking on first-time poets – but never those without a reputation. Other important companies include the Harvill Press, Gomer Press, Chatto & Windus, Edinburgh University Press, Blackstaff Press, and Hutchinson, all with poetry in their catalogues – although new names do not get added that often.

Other publishing houses do publish poetry: Macmillan, Dent, André Deutsch, Michael Joseph, etc. – although their lists have been so reduced in recent years that their interest could now be said to be in retreat. The recent trend has been for a revival of interest by mass-market paperback houses – notably Penguin – in putting well-produced and competitively priced volumes before the general public. As well as having a long-standing interest in anthologies – *The Penguin Book of Victorian Verse*, *The Penguin Book of Zen Poetry*, *The Penguin Book of Contemporary British Poetry*, etc. – Penguin have also expanded their list of classic poets – Wordsworth, Betjeman, Whitman – to include a series of comprehensive selections from the output of contemporary writers like Peter Redgrove, U.A. Fanthorpe, Carol Ann Duffy, Roger McGough, Andrew Motion, James Fenton and Jeremy Reed. In addition, they produce an extensive range of anthologies and collections for children and have recently revised their classic series of poetry trios from the 1960s – *Penguin Modern Poets*. This is no arena for beginners, however; almost everyone published has established themselves previously elsewhere.

Both the Women's Press and Virago, keen to be seen as publishers of work from all genres, have also dabbled with poetry, as have the Gay Men's Press, but as yet no concerted policy has emerged.

The real growth during the past decade has been among the specialists – Bloodaxe, Dedalus, Salmon, Carcanet, Seren Books (formerly Poetry Wales Press), Littlewood Arc, Enitharmon, Stride, Gallery Press, Peterloo Poets, Anvil Press – indeed Bloodaxe probably publishes more new poetry per year than all the commercial companies put together. Often begun by one person, these enterprises have developed with the help of public subsidy and managerial flair to fill the middle ground between part-time pamphleteering and full-scale commercial publishing at a national level. Some of them – notably Carcanet – already operate with commerce in mind if not exactly in response to market forces. A number use professional warehousing, representation and have national distribution. Their books are first class, rivalling the best productions of their more commercial counterparts. Their motivation is what drives them, often with missionary zeal, putting poetry before profit. They are accordingly much more open to the newcomer, to the less tried poet with a good collection to hand.

The small presses – 500 or more in the UK – spread out across the base of the pyramid. It is here where the real risks – creative rather than commercial – are run. Little presses cover, like little magazines, the full spectrum of production quality and content. Many are spinoffs from magazines following a particular predilection in more specialist form. Others exist to further the editor's interests or the work of a founding group. They are basically open but if you mail poetry to them do not expect regular commercial practice to hold sway. Manuscripts get considered but the procedure is haphazard. Write first to check out the ground.

It would be little use for me to recommend the best publishers to receive the manuscript of your first volume. Fashions change, considerations shift. Small presses alter from day to day. In any event, one or two recommended publishers would receive so many manuscripts that they would be swamped. Spread the market, stretch out as far as you can. Don't necessarily try the obvious. New publishers who have never touched poetry before may be interested – be persistent, try them. The worst that can happen is for your book to get sent back.

But remember, *don't submit blindly*. Always find out first what a particular publisher's books are actually like. Read widely. Know what's going on. It is the only way.

Peter Finch is a poet, former small publisher, magazine editor and a bookseller. His best sellers include the recent The Poetry Business *from Seren Books, which includes an extensive magazine and small press address listing,* Poems For Ghosts, *also Seren Books, and* How To Publish Your Poetry *from Allison & Busby.*

What Are They Talking About?

AN IRREVERENT GUIDE TO PUBLISHING TERMS

Acknowledgements Names of those an author wishes to thank for help in research or permission to quote.

addendum Correction slip. Now very rare. Publishers generally prefer to ignore mistakes.

advance Money paid to an author on signature of contract in anticipation of expected royalties. Begrudging recognition by the publisher that an author has to live while writing.

AFC Association for Colleges.

A-format Normal-format paperback.

agent Friend, counsellor, front man and beneficiary of 10–15 per cent of his clients' earnings. A good agent is a salesman, accountant and lawyer rolled into one.

ALCS Authors' Licensing and Collecting Society (see page 236)

ALPSP Association of Learned and Professional Society Publishers.

appendix Afterthought and supplementary material following the main text.

APVIC Association for Principals of Sixth Form Colleges.

ARELS Association of Recognised English Language Services.

artwork Illustrative copy ready for reproduction.

BA Booksellers' Association of Great Britain & Ireland.

BAC British Accreditation Council.

backlist Old books that continue to sell. Often the most valuable part of a publisher's output.

bibliography List of secondary sources used by an author to support his own interpretation of events.

binding The spine of a book or magazine which is perfect bound (glued as in paperbacks), stapled or sewn (pages sewn together and glued).

B-format Slightly larger paperback.

bleed The process whereby illustrations or a printed image can run off the edge of a page.

blurb Short summary of a book to catch the eye on its cover or in a catalogue.

book club A mail order business selling to members at a discount price.

bromide A photographic positive print.

bulk The thickness of paper or (as in 'bulking') the padding out of a book to make it look bigger than the sum total of its words.

b/w Abbreviation for black and white.

CAL Copyright Agency Limited (of Australia).

camera-ready copy (CRC) Final text with artwork ready for reproduction by photographing, usually by litho.

caption A line or two explaining an illustration.

case Hard-cover binding.

cast off Word count.

C-format Glossy paperback, the same size as hardbacks.

character Letter, symbol or punctuation mark.

circa Indicates approximate dates.

CISAC Confédération Internationale d'Auteurs et de Compositeurs.

CLA Copyright Licensing Agency.

cloth Another term for hardcover.

co-edition A publication produced in an identical format in a number of countries or languages.

coffee table book Large book with lots of illustrations. More for dipping into than a solid read.

commissioning editor Commander of the purse strings who stands between an author and his pet project.

copy Typescript and illustrations; a publisher's raw material.

copy-edited A manuscript after a copy editor has worked on it. Said to remove errors but few authors would agree.

copyright The claim to ownership by the creator of a work and his heirs.

Copyright Licensing Agency(CLA) An organization that collects photocopying fees on behalf of authors.

credit Printed acknowledgement of copyright or of quotation sources or of assistance to the author.

CSA Computer Software Association.

dedication An author's declaration of love, invariably for a partner who has had to suffer a creative temperament.

delivery date Date for handing over the manuscript to a publisher, otherwise known as the author's nightmare.

discounts Trade discounts to booksellers are typically around 40 per cent but the chains like Dillons and Waterstones can command up to 50 or 55 per cent.

drop of shelves A floor-to-ceiling display of books on a wall of shelves.

dummy A mock-up of a few pages to sell an idea for a book before it is actually worked and produced.

dump bin Bookshop display unit promoting a particular book or several books by the same author or books by several authors on the same or connected topics.

dust jacket Single loose sheet of paper used to cover a hardback book. Often carries an illustration which bears little relationship to the contents of the book.

edition The publication of a work printed from one setting of type. Hardback and paperback publications of the same work are different editions, whether issued simultaneously or not.

electronic publishing Images reproduced through television, video devices, disks, tapes, cassettes, closed-circuit broadcasts, cable broadcasts – anything that is not print.

ELT English language teaching.

embargo Date before which information supplied to the media should not be printed or screened. Rarely deters a good journalist.

end flaps The narrow ends of the dust jacket which are tucked over the boards of the book to hold the dust jacket in place. This, if anywhere, is the place for the author's photograph.

endpaper The double-page spread at the front and back of a book which holds the bound text to its covers.

erratum See *addendum*

extent The length of a book in number of pages or words.

facsimile Exact copy.

footnotes Explanatory notes to the main text appearing at the bottom of a page or at the end of a chapter. The greater the number of footnotes, the more incompetent the author.

foreign rights Translation or reproduction rights sold to an overseas publisher.

foreword Introductory comments, often a plug for the book by someone more famous than the author.

format The size and shape of a book. A-format is the standard mass-market paperback format; standard hardback size is 'Royal', approximately 234 x 156 mm.

frontispiece Picture or plate facing the title page of a book.

front cover The outside of the binding. The first thing you see on picking up a book and thus the main selling point.

FSDU Free-standing display unit.

gatefold A page in a book which folds out.

gross and net sales Gross sales are sales before returns (see below), after allowance for which the publisher is left with a net sales figure.

gross profit margin Net revenue minus manufacturing costs and royalties.

hard back Stiff board binding.

hard copy Written, typed or printed copy as opposed to copy on disk which is soft.

hardware Computer equipment.

house style Editorial rules on spelling, punctuation and grammar.

IFRRO International Federation of Reprographic Rights Organisations.

impression Number of copies of a book printed at any one time. Several impressions can equal one edition.

imprint A publisher's name or symbol. One publisher can have several imprints.

in-house Carried out by staffers.

indent Space at the beginning of line or paragraph.

insert Loose card or leaflet.

IPRs Intellectual Property Rights.

ISBN International Standard Book Number; a numbering system used to identify titles.

island ends The prominent end of shelves, perfect for posters.

ISO International Standards Organisation.

justified type Type set so that margins are aligned vertically.

layout Pattern of text and illustrations on a page.

logo Identifying symbol or trademark.

lower case Small letters, unlike upper case.

lunch The means by which a publisher softens up an author before persuading him to agree to something which may well be against his own best interests.

merchandising Product spinoffs from a media event – games, sweatshirts, disks, toys.

mock-up Rough artwork.

monograph Treatise on a single specialist topic.

moral right The right of an author to be identified as the creator of a work.

ms./mss Abbreviation for manuscript/manuscripts.

MTA Minimum Terms Agreement between the Society of Authors, the Writers' Guild and certain enlightened publishers.

Net Book Agreement A restrictive practice approved by publishers and booksellers whereby books are sold at prices fixed by the publishers. This is supposed to deter discounting and most other forms of innovative marketing.

NUJ National Union of Journalists.

NWU National Writers' Union.

odd pages The right-hand or recto pages.

offprint A printed copy of a single extract from a book or journal.

origination Reproduction of original material such as typesetting and platemaking.

out of stock Frequent response from bookseller or publisher to any customer eager to part with money for a particular title.

PA Publishers' Association.

packager One who puts together a book then sells it on to a publisher.

PACT Producers' Alliance for Cinema & Television.

pagination Page numbering.

paper The most common mass-market paperback paper is 'bulky news'. This differs from newsprint in that it is, as the name implies, bulkier

and it also has a less grey colour. A much wider variety of papers is
used for hardbacks. The figures which follow the name of the paper
are, first, its weight in grams per square metre (gsm) and, second, its
bulk in microns.

permissions Rights to quote from copyright material, usually for a fee.

plant costs This is the term used rather loosely in the industry to describe
all start-up manufacturing costs, as opposed to 'run-on costs'.

PLR Public Lending Right.

PLS Publishers' Licensing Society; the organization that takes the
publishers' share of photocopying fees.

point of sale Promotional displays in bookshops.

PPA Periodical Publishers Association.

preface Author's justification for writing.

prelims Preliminary editorial, including title page and contents.

print run The number of copies to be printed and published.

proof A roughly printed copy intended for checking and correction.

publication date Widely ignored by bookshops and reviewers.

remainders Dud titles which are shifted on to the discount market after a
year of gathering dust in conventional bookshops.

rep An upmarket travelling salesman who carries a publisher's new titles
to the bookshops.

returns/frees A proportion of each book's print run is given away free to
literary editors and reviewers, while another slab, having been
distributed to booksellers, will be returned unsold. Publishers estimate
about 15 per cent returns/frees for hardbacks and 25 per cent returns/
frees for paperbacks. There is wide variation in the returns/frees
performance of individual titles.

reversion Return of rights to an author once his book goes out of print.

review copy Sent to literary editors more in hope than anticipation of a
review. Review copies usually end up in second-hand bookshops,
a handy secondary source of income for impecunious journalists.

royalties The percentage of the price of a book paid to the author,
generally at yearly or half-yearly intervals. What the author expects
and what he actually gets is never the same figure. Royalty statements
explain why this is so but since no one except publishers' accountants
understands royalty statements, the discrepancy remains a mystery.

RRO Reprographic Rights Organisation.

run on An additional print immediately following a first print run.

search fee Charge for picture research.

serialization Gutting of a book for extracts in a newspaper, usually before the official publication date.

showcard Bookshop display promoting adjoining pile of new titles.

signature Group of sixteen or thirty-two pages.

software Computer programmes.

STM Scientific, technical and medical publishing.

subscriptions (subs) Orders for books placed by bookshops.

subsidiary rights The potential for a book's spinoff earnings – translation, serialization, film or TV adaptation, etc.

synopsis Author's summary of what he hopes to write.

teleordering Sophisticated system for bookshops to order copies through a central computer. Falls foul of publishers with mediocre distribution.

title page Page at or near the beginning of a book which bears the title, and generally the names of author and publisher.

trade book Book specifically designed for general retail distribution.

TRIPS Trade Related Aspects of Intellectual Property.

typeface Description of print style, e.g. Times, Roman.

typescript Hard copy ready to be printed.

typo Typographical error.

unjustified With a ragged margin.

upper case Characters or capitals, unlike lower case.

visual Rough layout of artwork.

WAG Writers' Action Group.

WIPO World Intellectual Property Organisation.

wobblers Promotional devices dangled from the shelf to attract the browser's attention.

Indexing

IT MAY BE TRUE, as many professional indexers concede, that the best person to compile an index is the author. But for any book worthy of an index, the labour can be long and hard. Moreover, it takes a really dedicated author to go back over his own work, sentence by sentence, to winkle out all the references that might be of value to his readers.

According to Douglas Matthews, whose indexing triumphs include the *Alan Clark Diaries*, the *Frank Muir Book* and an English translation of *Mein Kampf*, 'The function of an index is not to be a précis or abstract of a book, but to signpost particulars within the text, concisely, comprehensively and accurately. It points out where to look for all names, terms and topics of relevance by listing them, usually alphabetically, wherever they occur within the book, and then by referring to a page or column number, though sometimes even more precisely to a defined position on a page, or to a paragraph number.'

Some readers use indexes only occasionally, simply looking for a single entry, going directly to a specified page to begin their reading. Others – students engaged in research, for example – may be more rigorous, noting several entries on a piece of paper, perhaps following up some cross-references. The way the book and its index are to be used must influence the choice of entries.

If the book is substantial and the index runs to several pages, author and indexer may like to exploit the index in educating the reader. This raises the possibility of comparisons or juxtapositions that do not occur in the text. An author-cum-indexer who is new to the craft should begin by looking through the indexes of several comparable books. Try to recall indexes you have found useful in your own work, and what you liked or disliked about them.

Most books have only one index; a few, though, have one or more small specialist indexes, each dealing exclusively with some principal aspect of the book. Thus a history book might list the names of people mentioned, and a book on war might have a simple index of battles. A legal text would almost certainly have a separate index of cases, and a poetry book would probably index poems by their first lines.

Unless there is a special reason for multiple indexes a single index serving all purposes seems preferable: it is simpler to locate and the reader need look through only one sequence of entries.

Compiling an index depends on knowing the numbers of the pages on which the entries will fall. But you can make a start as soon as the typescript is finalized. At this stage, begin to think about the kinds of entries your index will contain.

Try to put yourself in the position of your readers.

Who are they? Are they professionals? Postgraduates? Undergraduates? Or school pupils? Upper or lower secondary, or primary? The complexity and language level of the index should match those of the book.

Why does the book need an index? In what way will it differ from the contents list? What level of detail will the reader want from it? A reference to the single page where Keynesian economics is actually defined? A note of all the pages where Simon de Montfort is mentioned? Or a list tracing the developing explanation of desertification, the countries it affects and the problems that it brings?

An understanding of the readers' needs will help determine what to put in and what to leave out; and for the items that are included, what words to use and what cross-references to add.

In some books there is a limit to the space available for the index – it may have to fit on one page, for instance. If so, the editor will say how many entries the space is likely to allow.

But often there is no definite limit and the length is up to you. In practice each index seems to have a natural length, but it is useful to have a friendly critic to tell you if the index seems too sparse or too cumbersome.

COLLECTING POSSIBLE ENTRIES

Write entries on separate pieces of paper

Use a different piece of paper for each entry. This enables you to sort the entries later. Cards are usually easier to work with but also more expensive.

Record references in the right form

If a topic is discussed continually over two or more pages, record the reference as a range: 34–5. If it merely receives isolated mentions, record individual pages, even if they are consecutive: 34, 35.

Think about meanings, not just the words

A good index includes not just the terms, events and people in the book but the concepts, ideas and relationships. Some words in the index may not appear in the body of the text at all.

Don't record every mention

In general, include references only to those pages where there is a fairly substantial treatment of the subject. Omit casual and irrelevant mentions – for instance, a phrase such as 'towns the size of Manchester' would probably not merit a reference under 'Manchester'.

Record doubtful entries

Always record doubtful entries for later consideration. It doesn't matter at the outset if there are too many entries – too many is better than too few. You can always leave some out later but you cannot easily go back and look for something you decided against and then regretted.

Don't worry about the final structure

At this stage keep a fairly open mind about the final organization and grouping of the entries. Early decisions about the structure of the final index may interfere with the selection of entries. It may be easier to divide references into sub-headings even at this stage, but be prepared to change the groupings or to split main entries if they become too big.

Sorting your entries

Whilst still collecting entries, pause every so often and sort the ones you've got into alphabetical order. (The order at this point need not correspond to the final order, but sorting makes the work simpler.)

SELECTING ENTRIES

The main basis for the inclusion or omission of possible entries must be common sense and a close understanding of the needs of readers. So, sift through the possible entries. Will they help the reader? One useful guide is evenness: whether the book is indexed lightly or heavily, coverage of different topics and parts of the book should be at about the same level.

STRUCTURING ENTRIES

By this stage you will probably find that there is a natural pattern of main entries and sub-entries. Only occasionally is it appropriate to have sub-sub-entries. In grouping entries, as in selecting them, evenness and consistency are good guides. Is this to be an analytic index, with many short individual entries, or a synthetic index, with groupings chosen to show associations or make comparisons?

analytic		synthetic	
archery,	56–7	sports,	11–19
bowls,	45–6	archery,	56–7
croquet,	62	bowls,	45–6
. . .		croquet,	62
sports,	11–19		
see under individual sports			

If any one entry or sub-entry seems disproportionately long (more than five or six references, perhaps) consider dividing it into smaller parts. In the case of long entries it might be wise to promote the sub-entries to main entries in their own right.

WORDING ENTRIES

Keep trying to put yourself in the place of your readers. What will they want to find? How will they look for it, what words will they try?

For example, the obvious first try for an ecologist interested in recycling is under 'recycling', but 'energy conservation' or 'conservation of energy' are reasonable alternatives. A philosopher researching the writings of Ludwig Wittgenstein is quite likely to try 'Wittgenstein, Ludwig' or an individual title, such as '*Tractatus Logico-Philosophicus*', so both should be included. A photographer may well look for 'photograph' but is unlikely to try 'image'. A geneticist is more likely to look for '*Drosophila melanogaster*' than for 'fruit fly', because it is customary and the designation is more precise; but to allow for the reader forgetting the species name the index could usefully include 'fruit fly, *see Drosophila melanogaster*'.

Trust your instinct. If still uncertain, always include doubtful entries and seek a second opinion.

Wording of headings

In general, prefer specific concrete headings (such as 'inflation rate, rise in') to abstract general ones (such as 'rise in inflation rate'). Aim to begin with nouns ('clothing, protective') rather than adjectives ('protective clothing'). Avoid adjectives, including nouns used as adjectives, as headings – if necessary, repeat the word:

avoid	use
safety	safety belt
belt	safety curtain
curtain	safety match
match	

Headings often work better when in the plural. Thus in the following entry 'trees' seems preferable to 'tree':

trees
age of
deciduous
diseases of
evergreen
see also under individual names

Wording of sub-headings

Adjectives may make useful sub-headings. If you include words such as 'of', 'and' or 'for' in sub-entries, do so consistently:

lifting	lifting
of patient with	blanket
spinal injury	
on to a stretcher	spinal injury
with a blanket	stretcher
with webbing	webbing bands
bands	

Split entries

Avoid having two entries for the same topic, such as 'angling' and 'fishing', with overlapping references. Collate all the references under one heading, and if necessary direct the reader to this heading from the other.

Double entries

If you list the same references under two headings, make sure that the lists are identical. It is easy to overlook anomalies such as this:

> Brunel, Isambard Kingdom (1806–59)
> SS *Great Britain*, 82, 93
>
> ships, development of
> SS *Great Britain* 82, 87

Clearly both entries should read:

> SS *Great Britain*, 82, 87, 93

CROSS-REFERENCES

Will the home plumber with a blocked pipe try under 'plumbing' or 'pipes' or 'central heating system' or 'blockages'? Faced with a problem such as this, one solution is to cater for all contingencies by means of cross-references. These can be extremely useful to the reader – but be sparing with them, especially if the book and index are short.

'See'

Suppose for the above that the best heading is 'plumbing'. You could list the appropriate pages, perhaps with sub-entries:

> plumbing, 26–41
>   blockages, 38
>   lagging, 29
>   pipes, material of, 27

And provide cross-references to this entry, such as:

> blockages, *see* plumbing
> pipes, *see* plumbing

'*See*' can also assist when the book uses precise terms to make distinctions new to the reader. So a book on cybernetics might speak of the operating part of a computer as 'the processor', whereas the reader, not realizing this, might think of it simply as 'the computer'. Again the index can help: pages may be listed under the more formal word, 'processor', and a cross-reference under 'computer' can be used to make this clear:

> computer, *see* backing store; operating system; processor

'*See under*'

You may wish to redirect the reader not just to one entry but to a *range* of entries scattered through the index. For this '*see under*' may be preferable. Thus in a book about mountaineering you would not want to collect under 'mountain' a single list of all the pages that mention mountains:

> mountains, *see under individual names*

'*See also*' and '*compare*'

Bearing in mind the length and complexity of a book and the way it is likely to be used, consider the pros and cons of using the index to make links between topics. Would such cross-references be genuinely useful or superfluous?

For example, the indexer may draw attention to related aspects of the same subject. So the index of a book on politics might contain an entry such as

> elections
>   *see also* electoral reform

Or the indexer may suggest contrasts, especially where the related term is not an obvious one. So, a biochemistry text might have

> oxidation
> *compare* reduction

REPEATED ENTRIES

In some circumstances, index entries may be virtual duplicates of each other. Consider an entry such as this:

> public transport
> > buses 7, 22, 34–8, 63
> > railways, 7, 22, 41–55, 64, 66, 92
> > taxis, 7, 23, 67
> > *see also* self-drive hire cars

Each of the sub-entries – 'buses', 'railways' and 'taxis' – may need to be indexed in its own right. Is it better to list all the references once only, against the one main entry ('public transport'), and to direct the reader to this composite list; or to repeat the relevant page numbers against the sub-headings (such as 'railways') where these are given as main headings?

The best guide is often the length of the list. If it is long, it is probably wise to put it in one place only and refer the reader to this:

> railways, *see* public transport

But if it is short – only two or three page numbers – it is usually kinder to repeat it:

> taxis, 7, 23, 67

The reader may otherwise be irritated at having to leaf through the index to find the second entry, then discover that it cites perhaps one page number only.

As author-indexer you may want your reader to see 'taxis' in the context of the whole 'public transport' list. You can force this by putting a '*see*' reference, irrespective of the number of references:

> taxis, *see* public transport

or invite it with a '*see also*':

> taxis, 7, 23, 67
>   *see also* public transport

It is helpful to the reader to include a note explaining any conventions adopted in the index – for example, that references to illustrations rather than text are printed in bold:

> plate tectonics, 67, 69, **69**, 81

ORDER OF ENTRIES

Index entries are usually arranged in alphabetical order. This can be letter-by-letter or word-by-word:

letter-by-letter	word-by-word
grey	grey
Grey, Lady Jane	Grey, Lady Jane
grey area	grey area
greybeard	grey matter
greylag goose	grey wolf
grey matter	greybeard
greywacke	greylag goose
grey wolf	greywacke

The letter-by-letter form is generally recommended. Whichever system you choose, be consistent. It two headings differ *only* in that one has an initial capital – as 'grey' and 'Grey' in the example above – put the capitalized form second.

Names of people

Give names in full. Provide further information, such as dates of birth and death, titles, and posts held, if this is helpful to the reader.

The position of the entry in the index is determined by the surname and then by the forename if two or more entries share the surname. More unusual names are positioned according to usage: thus in 'W. Somerset

Maugham' the surname is 'Maugham', whereas in 'Ralph Vaughan Williams' it is 'Vaughan Williams'. 'Walter de la Mare' is treated as 'de la Mare'; 'Guy de Maupassant' as 'Maupassant'. Names beginning 'Mac' or 'Mc' are positioned according to the spelling: if the two groups are widely separated it may be helpful to add a cross-reference, such as 'Mac-, *see also* Mc-'.

Titles of publications

Cite and position titles according to the first 'significant' word, as with '*The Times*'.

Saint

If 'Saint' is abbreviated to 'St' in the text, follow this convention in the index. Position names as if 'Saint' were spelled out in full. If you think it necessary, add a cross-reference under 'St'.

Accents

Treat accented and unaccented letters as equivalent – collate 'ê' with 'e', 'ü' with 'u', and so on.

Cross-references

Any cross-reference should be the last item in an entry, and all words other than quoted index headings should be printed in italic:

> prime ministers
>> appointment of, 91
>> constitutional function of, 89
>> *compare* presidents; *see also under individual names*

Initials

Each entry and sub-entry should have a lower-case initial unless the word is a proper noun:

> industrial archaeology
> industrial relations
> Industrial Revolution

Indentation

Begin each entry and each sub-entry on a fresh line, and indent the sub-entries:

> Bach, Johann Sebastian (1685–1750), 43–67
>> compositions of, 51–65
>> instruments played by, 48–9
>> posts held by, 44–6

If you have sub-sub-entries, run these on from the sub-entry, following a colon and separated by semicolons:

> Bach, Johann Sebastian (1685–1750), 43–67
>> sons: Wilhelm Friedmann, 72–3; Karl (or Carl) Philipp Emanuel, 73–5; Johann Christoph Friedrich, 76; Johann Christian, 77–9.

In this example the sub-sub-entries are not alphabetized but are listed in order of age.

Page numbers

Use the fewest possible digits: 32–3, 124–7, 132–48, 160–3, 200–5. The '1' is repeated in '-teen' numbers: 14–15, 113–14.

Italics

The words 'see', 'see under', 'see also' and 'compare' will be printed in italic, as will all words other than the actual headings and sub-headings. Titles of publications also will be in italic. Please underline the relevant words in the typescript.

> paper-folding, see origami

REVISING THE INDEX

As a last stage, leave the index for a day and then return to it afresh. Read through the index as a user rather than an author. Ask yourself these questions:

→ Are all the entries really necessary? (If you remove some, don't destroy them in case you change your mind later. And be sure that there are no cross-references to the deleted entries!)

→ Is the wording right?

➜ Are any entries or sub-entries too long?

➜ If there are duplicate entries, are the lists of page references under the corresponding headings identical?

➜ Should you add or delete any cross-references?

➜ Are the entries in order?

If, as an author, the prospect of compiling an index still attracts, pin to the wall the essential characteristics of a professional job, courtesy Douglas Matthews:

> It should be comprehensive, that is, include everything that a reader may need to consult (though not a loose, free-floating abstraction like 'arrogance'). It should be precise, every entry being specific, so that all identifications are distinct. In this way the index becomes a self-contained reference work within the covers of the book. It should be accurate in its locations, so that when the reader is directed to page 54 for something, he will actually find it there. I recognise a disturbing condition which I call 'indexer's drag', particularly with dense and detailed books, where, if I concentrate on page 54, making the entries and the page reference, and then move on to page 55, I find myself mistakenly writing '54' until my mind catches up. There is a corresponding condition, 'indexer's leap', looking forward to the next page so much as to anticipate the number before getting there.

He goes on:

> Finally, to the most practical consideration of all: who pays for the index? Rarely is it the publisher, more usually the author, often by having the fee deducted from royalties. Publishers will hate me for suggesting that, as authors, you request better terms in your contract, ideally shifting the responsibility for payment to the publisher, either in whole or in part (in the Minimum Terms Agreement, the cost of the index is split 50:50 between author and publisher). The index seems so remote and abstract when drawing up a contract, and the cost implications so unknown. The price of a good index may be several hundred pounds, which is a consideration well worth pondering.

Someone to Watch Over You

THE HARD PART IS FINDING AN AGENT

IT CANNOT BE SAID TOO OFTEN: 10 per cent of nothing is nothing. Unpublished writers are mortified when an agent declines to represent them. But like everyone else, agents do what they do to make a living.

A typical agency is a one- or two-person operation with occasional secretarial help. If all goes well it has on its books a core of writers whose combined royalties keep the business running. But bearing in mind what it costs to maintain an office and personnel, the client list has to contain some strong sellers to make the agent's 10 per cent worth having. Trouble is, there are not enough rich authors to go round. And if an agency is strapped for profitable authors it is unlikely to take on an unprofitable one.

The image of the hard-pressed agent is at odds with his portrayal by the popular press, where multi-million-pound deals make the headlines. At the last count there were four mega-wheeler-dealers – Ed Victor, Giles Gordon, Andrew Wylie and Andrew Nurnberg. Ed Victor and Andrew Nurnberg are their own men, while the other two share the glory – Giles Gordon, formerly with Sheil Land Associates, now with Curtis Brown, and Andrew Wylie with Aitken, Stone & Wylie Ltd. They are contrasting characters – Giles Gordon is the artist-in-waiting who spends as much time writing books and articles as he does agenting other writers; Ed Victor is a great entertainer, inordinately proud of his three homes (Long Island, Regents Park and Sissinghurst) and his collection of vintage cars. Andrew Wylie is the man behind the mask, the camera-shy fixer who is said to enjoy reading a balance sheet more than a novel. Last year, when he was in London on a flying visit, his press pictures were twenty years out of date. Andrew Nurnberg is the intellectual, a brilliant linguist who might well have become an academic.

Both Ed Victor and Andrew Wylie are as well known in New York as in London (Wylie is American director of Aitken, Stone & Wylie), Andrew Nurnberg takes the whole of Europe as his home ground, while Giles Gordon is more the British or, as he would prefer to say, Scottish, gentleman. He lunches at the Garrick Club, Ed Victor at Groucho's, Andrew Nurnberg at the best restaurant in whatever capital he is visiting. Andrew Wylie doesn't lunch.

What they have in common is their capacity to add zeros to their clients' advances. It was Giles Gordon who scored a £5 million eight-book deal for Peter Ackroyd; Ed Victor who clinched £100,000 plus for Barry Humphries' first novel before a word was written; Andrew Nurnberg who gathered in close to £250,000 for Boris Yeltsin's memoirs, and Andrew Wylie who satisfied Martin Amis's ambition to hit the half-million (almost) for his novel *The Information* and a book of short stories.

There are other newsworthy agents with marketable clients, and not a few who profit from the law of copyright by administering literary estates (who was it who said that the only good author is a dead author?). There are also agencies that employ more staff and have higher overheads than many publishers. But this does not detract from the opening premise, that literary agencies are characteristically small businesses in need of a friendly bank manager. To get on the list of one of the hundred best agencies, the fledgling writer must be able to show that he is capable of paying his way. He can do this by coming up with the big idea (Carole Blake of Blake Friedmann discovered Michael Ridpath's thriller *Free to Trade* on her slush pile, a chance find that made Mr Ridpath's fortune) or, more probably, by showing a body of work in evidence of talent that is bursting to take off. Neither the one-book writer nor the occasional writer ('I like to keep my hand in') is welcome.

It works both ways. If it is economically unsound for an agent to sign up a writer who is unable or unwilling to aim high, it makes even less sense for an author to give up part of a modest income when he could just as easily handle his own affairs. It would be like hiring a top lawyer to negotiate a simple letter of agreement. For this reason, few agents are interested in academic, technical or educational works.

An agent comes into his own when he really has something to sell. Once he is convinced of the value of a product – a novel, a play, a biography or whatever – he will set his mind to gaining the best possible terms for his client. Finance will be his foremost interest. And why not? Writers are generally inhibited when it comes to arguing money. It is a brave man who can say, 'This is the figure I want because this is what I believe I am worth'. The agent, on the other hand, can attack the market with unashamed enthusiasm for an author's talents. He will be after a substantial advance of course, but cash up front is by no means the sole consideration. Long-term commitment and readiness to invest in promotion and marketing will affect thinking as, too, will the reputation of the publisher for paying royalties on time and without spurious reductions.

The agent to do without is one who always takes the line of least resistance, grabbing the first offer that comes along. A quick deal may satisfy the ego but is rarely in accord with long-term interests.

When it comes to signing a contract, a good agent will have studied the small print, correcting omissions such as the failure to allow for higher royalties beyond a certain minimum scale and cutting out offending clauses. For example, a publisher will usually try for world rights whereas an agent will hold back on the US market and on translation, both of which need to be negotiated separately. A book does not have to be a bestseller to earn advances and royalties in several countries, languages and formats, sums which in themselves may be quite small but which can add up to a healthy income. A writer acting on his own behalf is unlikely to realize all the possibilities.

By the same token, a skilled agent will demand for his client a say in a mind-boggling array of other subsidiary rights – film and television adaptations, talking books, video, multimedia, serialization and book club.

What, then, of the practicalities of bringing writer and agent together in happy alliance? This is the difficult bit.

The Writer's Companion Survey of Agents

Most agents actively seek new writers but few sign up clients as a result of receiving unsolicited material. Rather they exercise their skills in talent spotting by reading first novels, literary magazines and review sections of the national press, or rely on word of mouth recommendations from social and professional contacts.

This fact of life, which emerges from a *Writer's Companion* survey of a dozen leading agents, goes unrecognized by budding authors. Unsolicited manuscripts clog the agents' post. An average intake is thirty to fifty packages a month but two respondents are in the eighty to a hundred category and one agent tops 150. Of these, less than 2 per cent show real promise. An agent who receives twenty to thirty unsolicited manuscripts a month reports 'less than five strong leads in fourteen years'.

Ten out of the twelve respondents prefer to see synopses rather than completed manuscripts, and of the ten, two are happiest with synopses and sample chapters.

> I ask for a synopsis to begin with as that tells you something about the author. Besides, it can be a subject matter that is of no interest to me or something that I would not wish to try and market.

Anyone sending material to an agent can expect to wait a minimum of two to three weeks for a response but 'it depends on how good the manuscript is. If it is hopeless it goes back more quickly'.

Constructive criticism is reserved for submissions that hint at potential or, as one agent concedes, 'when the writer is a friend of an existing client'.

We asked our cross-section of agents for a few lines of best advice to writers in search of representation. Here is a selection of their replies:

> It's always worth attempting to get things published in literary magazines, read on the radio, or entering respected writing competitions. Anything published should be mentioned in the covering letter. Also, avoid long, boring synopses and always send some sample chapters but never the whole script unless asked for. Also, just keep trying if you are determined. Agents are just as subjective, of necessity, and selective, as individual publishers.

> To those who think they can jump on the band-wagon of such subjects as political thrillers, horror, or whatever happens to be in vogue, don't do it. Write about something that matters to you and on subjects that you genuinely care about.

Present material clearly and neatly. Submit only what is asked for. Know who your market may be (especially in non-fiction). Only ever submit a finished piece, be it a story, synopsis or sample chapter, *never* a draft.

Don't alienate oversubscribed agents with boastful or gimmicky letters. Make sure your opening and first chapter are as good as you can make them and send a few pages with your synopsis. When asked to send several more chapters, send consecutive ones and *not* picked from here and there (unless it is a practical non-fiction book).

First-time writers should ensure that their submissions to agents include a full c.v. of writer and a properly presented synopsis. The completed manuscript must be typed, double-spaced and properly formatted (especially important with illustrated books, children's). Do not try to submit to publishers first and then decide to use an agent without admitting to rejections. Either write direct to publisher or use an agent from the outset. Some market research on overlap with other books is always useful.

Make sure that the material is clearly presented: typed in double-spacing and on one side of the paper only. NEVER submit random chapters as they do not give a good overall impression. Be honest if you have submitted the material to publishers or other agents. Return postage is always appreciated.

Study the market – talk to booksellers, libraries – look at catalogues, go to trade fairs. Persist, persist, persist.

P.S., from Carole Blake of Blake Friedmann:

We get an enormous number of unsolicited submissions, averaging twenty a day. I am unable to take on 99.75 per cent of them so this is the method I use to sift them, and to prevent ourselves being buried by them.

Everything is logged in by a member of staff the day it is received. I am given a pile every morning which I look at for half an hour once I've dealt with my mail. The reason that I do this myself is because when I used to pass them around the office, I found that young assistants enthusiastic and eager to discover something wonderful, erred on the side of generosity and would spend valuable hours (of their time and mine!) reading whole mss and writing detailed readers reports for me. I can't afford this much time when I know, harsh as it seems, that my agency couldn't cope with taking on new clients every month, let alone every week.

So, I do the initial sifting. Letters written in green capitals; letters from obvious 'odd sorts'; manuscripts in handwriting; people who send random pages ('I thought you would like to see a sample of my writing so I am enclosing pages 27, 54, 69, 320 and 651.' It happens. Honestly.); manuscripts on subjects I know nothing about and therefore don't handle; manuscripts on subjects that clash with those I am already representing; manuscripts on subjects that I know, from my knowledge of the trade, just aren't selling; manuscripts on subjects that have 12 forthcoming books already announced; manuscripts which have covering letters without vowels in the sentences; all these are easy to say no to within a minute of my laying eyes upon them.

Any that I think show promise are then distributed among my staff for preliminary reading. Anything that passes that sifting comes to me for reading.

This is where it is likely to get held up. My reading priorities have to be as follows:

1   Delivered mss, part-mss, by authors who are already commissioned by publishers. These must be read by me before being delivered to the publisher who already owns them. They are always top priority, and often go through several drafts, and are often edited by me and my partner.

2   Speculative work by my published authors – mss, part-mss, sample chapters, synopses. All these go through many drafts too, and often require extensive editing.

3   Speculative work by my unpublished authors. Material as listed in 2, and with the same last sentence only more so!

4   Unsolicited material from authors who would like to join us.

You can see why it can take a time. If I think I can see a huge reading pile ahead of me, I will often write to a promising unsolicited to warn them of the expected length of the delay, and will offer to return the material to them immediately if they don't feel they want to wait. This particularly happens around the time of a trade fair (you can imagine how the reading pile builds up around Frankfurt, say!), or a month when eight of my published writers have all delivered a manuscript, or when I'm taking a holiday (I know the working week for an agent is pure holiday, but I do like to go away occasionally).

I think this is a pretty fair and honest way of dealing with material we haven't asked for in the first place. But we still get castigated on a regular basis.

Example: We used to return material that had fallen at the first hurdle pretty quickly, say within three days. Were we thanked for not holding on to material we knew we couldn't handle? Not at all. We've had furious and angry accusations of wasting people's time and postage, because we obviously haven't read every word of a 600-page manuscript on ancient Egyptian history, with the letter ending with an invitation for me to try to exonerate myself! I write back to these people explaining that a 10-people agency can only handle a certain number of clients, so knowing that their material was in an area we never handle, we courteously returned it quickly so they could send it off to someone more likely to be useful to them.

We now return this material after a pause of, say, ten days. You should see the piles in my office . . .

Example: If something goes through several readings here, then has to queue up for my time, shows some promise so I perhaps read it twice, put it to one side for a few days to think it through carefully, then decide that it's just not quite good enough so return it, I often receive rude replies, with accusations of wasting time with the manuscript when the author could have sent it on to someone more likely to be useful to them, if only I'd said no more quickly.

Do you see the pattern here? I'm not asking for a huge amount of sympathy, because new authors are the industry's lifeblood, but it does sometimes get a bit Catch 22-ish at this end of the game.

If only authors would realise that running an agency is a *business*, in some cases pretty big and sophisticated businesses, then I think they would have more understanding of what the parameters are.

What all agents love are short, sane informative covering letters telling a little about the author and the material. A synopsis and two chapters, and a respectful pause while it's dealt with! This is how Michael Ridpath sent in his unsolicited material to me in September 1993. I wrote and told him I liked it and would like to see the whole manuscript, but not for a month because of Frankfurt. After that period of time, he sent in the manuscript with a short note saying he quite understood about the delay. His manuscript, *Free To Trade*, auctioned to UK publishers in December 1993, was published on 15 January 1995 by Heinemann in the UK and HarperCollins in the States with enormous publicity campaigns and author tours. Fourteen weeks in the bestseller list in the UK and twenty-nine other languages have so far been contracted. We have several film offers on the table. Not a bad slush-pile find.

It helps of course to have enormous talent!

A writer in need of an agent can narrow the field by identifying those agents who cover a particular interest. Some agencies do not deal with plays or television scripts, for example, though they may have outside associates who handle this side of the business for their established clients.

The famous names exercise the heaviest clout, of course, but the most powerful agencies are not necessarily suitable for a beginner who may feel the need for the close personal contact offered by a smaller agency. On the other hand, the smaller agency may already have taken on its full quota of newcomers.

There are writers and publishers who swear by the Association of Authors' Agents. To qualify, an agent must have been in business for three or more years and bring in average commissions totalling not less than £25,000 a year. The Association's code of practice rules that all monies due to clients should be paid within twenty-one days of cheques being cleared.

Agents who specialize in representing playwrights and screenwriters (not to mention directors, producers and actors) are likely to belong to the Personal Managers' Association. Where a client's interests overlap (a playwright may turn to novel-writing, or a novelist may become a top-flight television dramatist), two or more specialist agencies may cooperate on a shared-commission basis. These interlocked deals are on the increase. Andrew Nurnberg, one of the big names mentioned earlier, makes most of his income by handling foreign-language rights for authors on other agents' books.

Advice frequently given by the agented to the agentless is to seek out the opinion of authors who have been through the mill and learn from their experiences. Writers' circles and seminars organized by the Society of Authors and the Writers' Guild are fruitful sources of gossip.

It is useful to know from the start what agents charge for their services. Ten per cent is standard but an increasing number go for 15 per cent and a few pitch as high as 17½ or 20 per cent – plus VAT. A VATable author can reclaim the tax. Others must add 17½ per cent to the commission to calculate the agent's deduction from earnings. Reading fees are condemned by writers' associations and spurned by leading agents. It has been argued, by writers as well as agents, that a reading fee is a guarantee of serious intent; that if an agent is paid to assess the value of a manuscript, he is bound to give it professional attention. Sadly, this is not necessarily the case. While there are respectable agents who deserve a reading fee, the regular charging of fees can too easily end up as a means of exploiting the naive. But some agents do invoice certain administrative costs such as photocopying.

Do not be disappointed if an agent, or even several agents, gives the thumbs down. They may be overloaded with clients. But even if this is not so, remember that all writing is in the realm of value judgement. Where one agent fails to see talent, another may be more perceptive. The best advice is to keep trying.

When a writer does strike lucky, the first priority is to arrive at a clear understanding as to the scope of mutual commitment. Will the agent handle all freelance work – including, for example, journalism, personal appearances on radio and television, lecturing – or just plays and scripts, or books? Will the agent take a percentage of all earnings including those he does not negotiate? This is a touchy subject. Some writers think of their agency as an employment exchange. Any work they find themselves should not be subject to commission. But this is to assume a clear dividing line between what the agent does and what the writer achieves on his own account. In reality the distinction is not always apparent.

Understanding the market: what's needed, by whom, in what form, and in which media, is all part of an agent's job. Once he knows what his client can do, he is able to promote his talents to the people most likely to want to buy. Eventually, offers come out of the blue – an invitation to write for a newspaper, say, an editing job or a chance to present a television programme. It is at this point that the writer is tempted to bypass his agent. 'Why should I pay him, he didn't get me the work?' But the chances are that he did, by making the author a saleable property in the first place.

If a writer is persuaded that his agent is no good, or no good for him, he should look elsewhere. Actors do it all the time but writers seem curiously reluctant to jump from one agency to another. The distinction may have less to do with degrees of apathy or generosity of spirit than with the competitive nature of the agency business. Theatrical agents are by and large a tougher breed. They have to be because there are so many of them chasing a limited amount of business. Literary agents are altogether a more gentlemanly crowd. Since they rarely go in for poaching each other's clients, there is little incentive for authors to switch allegiance. But times are changing. With the rise of the transatlantic publisher, American agents are showing a greater interest in writers whose appeal extends beyond the domestic market. Their eagerness to compete for top-flight clients is already having an impact, with certain high-profile authors making it known that they would not be averse to a move.

A writer who has yet to make his reputation and is thus unlikely to be head-hunted needs to think carefully before dumping his agent. It is one thing if the agent is incompetent (and in a profession without qualifications or necessary training there are bound to be duds) but quite another if the writer is expecting too much, too quickly.

An agent combines the skills of a salesman, an accountant and a lawyer. If asked to provide his own job definition, he would probably call himself a professional adviser. (Not, he would hasten to add, a teacher. An agent does not expect to tell anyone *how* to write.)

Yet another way of defining an agent is to think of him as a partner.

The relationship between writer and agent, assuming they get on well together, invariably lasts longer than any connection with individual editors, publishers, producers or directors.

To a confused world, the agent brings a welcome note of stability.

Copyright and Wrong

COPYRIGHT IS A MESS, a sprawling, shifting mess which defies rational analysis. For once, the lawyers are not entirely to blame. The chief culprit is the new technology which has made it easier to duplicate material without acknowledgement or payment. The problems mounted when every office, school and college acquired its own photocopier. Hardly anyone thought twice before reproducing articles, chapters from books or even whole books. Savings showed up on library budgets. Why buy six or sixty copies of a publication when you can make do with one? The irony, as noted by Mark Rose (*Authors and Owners: The Invention of Copyright*), was that the photocopier was a direct descendent of the printing press, the starting point for copyright law. Thus, copyright's 'technological foundation has turned, like a vital organ grown cancerous, into an enemy'.

But now we have the new new technology – Internet – and, before long, the information highways which have no clear ownership and are almost impossible to police.

Here is Nicholas Negroponte, the media guru at Massachusetts Institute of Technology, pitching just a short way into the future.

> Most people worry about copyright in terms of the ease of making copies. In the digital world, not only the ease is at issue, but also the fact that the digital copy is as perfect as the original and, with some fancy computing, even better. In the same way that bit strings can be error-corrected, a copy can be cleaned up, enhanced, and have noise removed. The copy is perfect.

But, in the digital world it is not just a matter of copying being easier and copies more faithful.

We see a new a new kind of fraud, which may not be fraud at all. When I read something on the Internet and, like a clipping from a newspaper, wish to send a copy of it to somebody else or to a mailing list of people, this seems harmless. But, with less than a dozen keystrokes, I could redeliver that material to literally thousands of people all over the world (unlike a newspaper clipping). Clipping bits is very different from clipping atoms.

Internet duplication is not only efficient, it is incredibly easy.

Nobody has a clear idea of who pays for what on the Internet, but it appears to be free to most users. Even if this changes in the future and some rational economic model is laid on top of the Internet, it may cost a penny or two to distribute a million bits to a million people. It certainly will not cost anything like postage.

Negroponte concludes: 'Copyright law is totally out of date. It is a Gutenberg artefact. Since it is a reactive process, it will probably have to break down completely before it is corrected.'

There is no shortage of statistics to underline his message. In the Far East it is reckoned that over 90 per cent of all video cassettes sold are pirated. Unauthorized printing of books in China, Russia and a motley of smaller nations is said to be depriving British publishers and their authors of £200 million a year. As for the dear old photocopier, a luxury product just ten years ago, it is now responsible for some 300 billion pages of illegally reproduced material.

What is to be done? On one side are those who argue for abandoning traditional ideas of copyright. Rather than try to tighten up the current law (which may, in any case, be impracticable) they would introduce a more liberal regime which would serve the interests of education, economic growth and civilization. Their case is illustrated by the long running dispute between America and China. It may be galling for the US to have its finest brains picked clean by a repressive regime but if we want to bring the Chinese into the family of democracies, should we not be delighted by their enthusiasm for Western technology and culture?

So what that they lift ideas that should be making money for their originators. Owners of intellectual property could look to other sources of income. This is how publishers reacted to the photocopying threat, by hiking up the price of academic and reference books and journals. In this way, the cost of illicit copying was built into the overheads.

Owners of electronic rights are beginning to think the same way. Francis Pritchard, an academic specializing in computer law suggests:

> Maybe the price of software will reduce and the price of manuals increase. People who create works must find other ways of earning money from their creations than simply by charging for copies. Take the 'shareware' business as an example; software developers make their products freely available, and ask people who use it regularly to send them a small fee. Shareware might not make developers multi-billionaires, like Bill Gates, the Microsoft founder. Yet some earn comfortable livings, even when only five per cent of users pay up.

Naturally this is not a strategy that appeals to writers who want to hold their market value. After all, it is only recently that the potential for making money from copyright has taken off. As Michael Sissons, writing in the *Author* points out:

> A generation ago the main constraint on the earnings of writers was in fact the inhibition on the transmission of the written word to the consumer. Paperbacks were in their infancy, bookshops were still, in the main, Dickensian shambles, the processes of production, distribution, reprinting and marketing were antique. Today the book is a more attractive and desirable object for the consumer, it can be produced and reprinted far quicker, and the computer has revolutionised the distributive and retail processes. The bookshop is at last a place to enjoy.

But that is only part of the story. The time has long since gone when authors had to rely exclusively on royalties from their books in print. Nowadays there is a kaleidoscope of revenue-earning opportunities – translation rights, serial rights, rights of quotation, anthology, merchandising, book-club rights, film and TV adaptation rights, dramatization rights, and, potentially, photocopying and electronic publishing.

Of the organizations representing writers' interests, the Copyright Licensing Agency (CLA), is closest to the computer terminal. Set up in 1982 as the negotiating arm of the Authors' Licensing and Collecting Society (ALCS) and the Publishers' Licensing Society (PLS), the CLA first got to grips with education to produce a licensing scheme for reprographic rights which brings in over £2 million a year.

As a follow up, the CLA made agreements with several foreign reprographic rights bodies, boosting yearly income by another £1 million. The latest advance is a deal with the Confederation of British Industry on licensing industrial users of copyright material. The licence allows for up to nine copies of extracts from books and journals published in the UK. Above this level, fees are payable on a case by case basis. Licence fees are adjusted to the number of 'professional employees' within a company; that is, all staff except clerical personnel and apprentices.

Whether or not a similar scheme can be applied to electronic rights depends largely on developing an effective policing system. If Negroponte is right in believing that the superhighway is also a freeway, then a large area of copyright will be unenforceable. But reports are already filtering through the technological grapevine of new metering systems which will allow publishers to monitor and record the use of their information on Internet and other networks. The digital debate is set to run and run.

Meanwhile, back on earth, there is much that the individual writer can do to guard against the pirating of what is, or what might turn out to be, a valuable property. The best advice is always to check the small print.

Any publisher who offers a deal that is dependent on exclusive rights must be regarded with suspicion. The chances are that he has in mind a nice little earner that does not require him to pay the author a single penny beyond a basic fee or royalty. This is what happens to contributors to academic and specialist journals, who are invariably asked to assign their copyright as a condition of publication. The reasons given are wildly imaginative, ranging from conditions in the US where a publisher must assert copyright over a whole journal to prevent pirating (not true) to the need to regularize applications to reproduce. The latter is a real cheek, since under the current CLA rules all the money collected for the photocopying of articles from British journals and periodicals is taken by the publishers. Yet more outrageously, money set aside specifically for British authors by overseas collecting societies, including those of Norway, the Netherlands and Germany, is purloined along the way by the publishers.

The response is to argue that authors receive all that they are entitled to under contracts freely entered into but this is to subscribe to the naive view that academic writers are in any position to argue. In reality, their need to publish is closely linked to career advancement. When an offer comes they jump at it. But this does not excuse the injustice of having the ownership of their intellectual property taken from them at the earliest possible stage of publication. The ALCS, the Society of Authors and the Writers' Guild are united in their efforts to secure a remedy.

It is not only contributors to journals who suffer. As Michael Ryder discovered:

> Publishers of multi-author volumes also take copyright. I have a chapter in a book just published by a supposedly very reputable academic publisher and I discovered that it takes copyright unless you write to say otherwise. I wrote back to say that it could not do so without a written assignment but I am the only person to have retained the copyright in his chapter, my name being specifically listed on the appropriate prelim page!

Even those who make a living out of writing and are skilled in the devious ways of publishing can lose out simply by ignoring the subsidiary clauses of a contract or, if reading them, by not realizing the long-term implications. Imagine, for example, the frustration of a contributor to the part-work boom of the late 1960s who even now can see his work reproduced in a dozen languages – without recognition or reward. Or the predicament of the ghostwriter who finds that the celebrity whose life he has portrayed adopts the written word as his very own – the ideal material for a profitable one-man show. The sad litany of rights carelessly discarded would make a sizable volume in itself.

A popular ruse is to invite the surrender of copyright as a condition for entering a competition. TV-am went one further in setting up a book based on a poetry competition. Here is the letter that was sent out to the chosen few:

You will recall that some time ago you entered the above poem(s) in our poetry competition. We are pleased to advise you that your poem(s) has been selected to be included in a TV-am poetry book ... In order to proceed with the publishing of this book, TV-am now wish to acquire all copyright and any other rights in your poem(s) in all media world wide for the full period of copyright and any extensions and renewals thereof ... In consideration of you assigning to TV-am all the above rights, TV-am shall pay to you the sum of £10.'

Every writer is grateful for recognition but there is a limit.

The struggle for ownership of copyright is particularly acute in film and television. Leading an attack by the Writers' Guild, writer and director Bryan Forbes relates how he was forced into waiving copyright under threat of discontinuing work on a film that had already started. Copyright consultant Geoffrey Adams adds: 'if someone with as much clout as Bryan Forbes cannot enforce the rights given him by law, what hope have less famous owners.'

And once surrendered, there is no going back. As Nicola Solomon, a lawyer specializing in copyright law, warns, 'an assignment of copyright is binding ... it is not contingent on an agreed fee or royalties being paid. If a publisher fails to pay, your only remedy ... is to sue for the unpaid debt but you will not be able to regain copyright.'

Never say never. There must be occasions when the surrender of copyright is justified. A writer who works to order, adapting material provided for a company training course, say, or a sponsored history to be used as a promotional tool, would be pushing his luck to argue for more than a set fee.

Another moot point arises when it is not altogether clear who it is that has first claim to copyright. The most obvious example is the journalist – say, a columnist whose by-line appears twice weekly in a national newspaper. If he is on the payroll, with all the rights and responsibilities of an employee, then copyright on his articles is assumed to belong to his employer – 'unless otherwise agreed'. In other words, if the journalist is a self-assertive type who is ready to bargain with his editor he may well emerge with a contract which secures his copyright beyond the first printing. A scribe with less muscle might prefer to rely on his editor's sense of decency in handing over a share of any supplementary fees. It does happen on most national papers, but over the rest of the printed media those who commission work invariably demand exclusive copyright, including syndication rights. This applies to freelancers, who, technically speaking, are entitled to copyright, as well as to regular employees. The journalists' unions urge members to resist but the need to make a living in a highly competitive market weakens the resolve of all but the star turns.

Recently, sound and fury broke over *The Telegraph* when its editorial director, Jeremy Deedes, circulated freelancers with the unwelcome news that henceforth the acceptance of work would be dependent on handing over all copyright, including electronic rights. Reactions from contributors were immediate, with the NUJ leading a campaign for a retraction. There followed some furious backpeddling by Deedes, who insisted that he was merely trying to ensure that his group had rights to publish *The Telegraph* in its latest forms – the *Weekly Telegraph* and the *Electronic Telegraph*. In this case, said the Society of Authors, 'Seeking a total assignment of copyright was unnecessary and therefore objectionable. One can understand that a freelance journalist contributing an occasional news item may not want to seem to be difficult over what may appear a minor issue. On the other hand authors (particularly those contributing poems, short stories and reviews) almost invariably retain copyright and are wise to do so.'

Mr Deedes accepted the point and agreed that individual arrangements would need to be worked out.

Others have not submitted quite so gallantly. Currently, the NUJ is hot in pursuit of Reed Business Publishing and Reuters over demands to secure copyright on freelance material. Meanwhile, in the States, ten members of the National Writers' Union are squaring up in court against the *New York Times* and Time Inc., among others, accusing them of the unauthorized sell-on of their articles to computer data services. The result will have an impact wherever the media barons rule.

The individual writer may feel dwarfed by the battles. But advice stands on reading the small print. And, given half a chance, holding on to those electronic rights.

British copyright is enshrined in the 1988 Copyright Designs and Patents Act, an updating which almost immediately became outdated as European legislators got to work. Having reaffirmed the Berne Convention rule that copyright protection lasts for fifty years from the author's death, the Government is now trying to fall in line with a Community directive extending copyright to seventy years. There is no inherent logic to this figure. It is merely part of a general tidying-up process in which the highest figure on offer (in this case, for German copyright) is judged to be the common standard. By the same reasoning, the Italians are having to change their copyright on musical recordings from thirty to fifty years to match the British law.

There is something wonderfully ironic, not to say typically bureaucratic, in adding on to copyright at a time when the information revolution is putting the whole concept under threat. But the immediate concern is the confusion caused by the prospect of works that have recently entered the public domain going back into copyright.

> Thus, through no fault of their own, unlicensed publishers of James Joyce and Virginia Woolf may find themselves in court, under what is effectively retrospective legislation. Alternatively, while recent editions may be allowed free of copyright, new editions may have to pay royalties, thereby distorting the market. The cost to publishers is unknown; the cost of the legal battles will be passed on to the public, who will also be robbed of some of their common property and intellectual inheritance. And once again law will be made in remote, unaccountable courts.

To the concerns of Jim McCue (writing in the *Spectator*) must be added two particular worries that are occupying the Society of Authors and other writers' associations. First, who precisely owns the extra twenty years? Hugh Jones, a lawyer member of the Publishers' Association's Publishing Law and Copyright Committee, advises a close look 'at the terms of each publishing contract, the true intention of the parties at the time they entered into it'. He goes on:

Where the grant of rights to the publisher is for the full term of copyright 'including all renewals, reversions, and extensions thereof', the publisher would certainly benefit from any 20-year extension. But these words are by no means always present: the most common phrase in publishing contracts refers simply to 'the full legal term of copyright'. Arguably, what the parties meant by this was no more than the current term at the time the contract was signed, almost certainly life plus 50 years . . . In the absence of any hard evidence of what the parties actually meant, it may well be that the present publisher cannot simply assume that his licence will continue, and will have to revert to the copyright owner to agree an extension and, if necessary settle new terms.

The Draft Statutory Document issued by the Board of Trade is ambiguous on these points, asserting merely that where 'the work was subject to an exclusive licence, ownership of the revived copyright in it belongs to the exclusive licensee'.

The heirs of several famous authors could be in line for the equivalent of a lottery win. Of course, no one speaks in those gross materialistic terms. When Ian Weekly, the eldest grandson of D.H. Lawrence's wife Frieda, was asked to justify renewed royalties, he said they would go some way to compensate for Lawrence running off with his (Weekly's) grandmother. 'My grandfather Ernest would see it as justice.'

More ominously, James Joyce's grandson Stephen regards the extension of copyright as an opportunity to tighten his protection of 'the spirit and the letter' of his grandfather's work. This connects in to a second worry of the Society of Authors, that copyright will be used to restrict legitimate research and creative enterprise. Historians and biographers are most at risk. Examples are already cropping up of studies cut short or circum-scribed by the reassertion of copyright. Here is Dr Martin Stannard writing in the *Author*.

Two years ago, a major American publisher commissioned a critical edition of a twentieth-century novel. The contract was for worldwide distribution. As far as the publisher was concerned, the novel was out of copyright in both the USA and Europe. The editor began work in good faith, submitting his mss this summer. Then the publisher's lawyers became nervous. Although the book could be published well before the 30 June 'deadline', the major sales would not come until the autumn when the universities and colleges stock up for their courses. Since it seemed probable that a licence fee would be payable after 30 June, and since no one knew how much an estate might be allowed to charge, the publisher was unwilling to put its head in that noose and cancelled the European printing.

The implications are far-reaching.

Everyman, Penguin and Oxford *World's Classics* all have similar texts on the UK market. There may be a chance, unless licence fees are kept within reasonable limits, that these books will go out of print. If the paperback market starts to drop titles of 'classic' twentieth-century works now published cheaply, this will seriously affect the teaching of literature in this country.

Penguin and others have large programmes of commissioned titles, revising the 'corrupt' texts of earlier printings and adding an editor's preface and footnotes. Where will the new legislation leave these ongoing projects?

Where, indeed. A suitable cooling-off period in which work in progress might be completed without hindrance or charge might serve the cause of natural justice. A complimentary amendment, recommended by the Society of Authors, is for the restoration of copyright to be limited to an equitable fee for material used. For the add-on period of twenty years, copyright holders would not be able to withhold rights of access or permission to quote. The government seems to have accepted this. The Draft Statutory Document appears to suggest (the wording is convoluted) that if you signed a contract last year to write a biography of an author who was going to be out of copyright when your book was published, you will still be able to quote freely in spite of any revival of copyright. Moreover, the owner of the revived copyright will not be able to prevent publication or grant exclusive licence. The only condition of publication will be the payment of whatever royalty or fee is reasonable. Many writers feel that this concession should apply across the board. Even if it is accepted that an author's beneficiaries should enjoy an unearned income for half a century after the funeral, it is not at all clear that they are necessarily suitable guardians of the literary estate. Copyright, of whatever duration, can be an oppressive law used to stifle debate and to block the spread of knowledge.

To take a personal example, some time ago I wrote . . . *And the Policeman Smiled – ten thousand children escape from Nazi Europe* (friendly reviews and respectable sales, thank you for asking). The book contained a great many reminiscences – chiefly edited extracts from tape-recorded interviews. In the weeks before publication letters went out to contributors asking for corrections on matters of fact. No problem.

Less than a week after publication, I heard from a solicitor representing an author who was working on but had not yet produced a book on the same subject. The claim was that I had breached copyright in just about every particular known to law. It was tempting, but too easy, to counter the charge with a cry of sour grapes. My rival was naturally put out that I had beaten her to the finishing line but there was more to her case than that – or so it appeared from the claims listed by her solicitor.

The core of the dispute was our contrasting approach to interviewees. Whereas I had asked simply for permission to quote, subject to the usual safeguards, she had drawn up an agreement which assigned copyright. The result was that where we overlapped, which was quite often, she claimed precedence even in cases where I had been first on the scene. That was not all. I was accused of exceeding the limits of propriety in quoting from various books and articles. Notwithstanding my full and often fulsome acknowledgements, I began to fear a whole army of complainants lining up against me. My supposed literary transgressions were likely to occupy the courts for as long as the Guinness trial.

Enter my white knight – a lawyer who, in checking out the references, soon put paid to the suggestion that I had infringed copyright of published writers. The extracts I had used all fell within the bounds of 'fair dealing'.

The second part of the case against me related to copyright on interview material. My complainant had tried to stitch up her informants with an agreement of exclusivity. But this applied only to the words spoken to her. It could not stop interviewees from talking on the same subject to me or to anyone else they felt like inviting in for a chat. The case collapsed, though for weeks afterwards I had a recurring nightmare of a black-robed lawyer bearing over me, preparing to strike me down with a rolled summons.

Unjust charges of appropriation are nothing new, though nowadays we are spared the outrageous claims pursued for the sole purpose of making a fast buck. R.C. Sherriff, he of *Journey's End*, the war drama which made his fortune in the West End and on Broadway, was one of many who got caught up in a plagiarism racket, as he recorded in his autobiography *No Leading Lady*.

> You first had to write a play. You brought into it every possible idea and situation that you could think of. You then registered it, established your copyright, and sent it to every worthwhile manager on Broadway. As the play was usually rubbish the copies soon came back. Some managers didn't even bother to return it, and that was all to the good. You kept copies of the letters you sent, with the registered postal receipts, as evidence that the play had been submitted.
>
> You then sat back and waited for the plays that the managers produced. Sooner or later a money-spinner would come along. Having packed your play with an infinite variety of situations, it was not difficult to discover points of similarity with the one you had decided to go for.
>
> You then drew up a damning list of similarities, and began proceedings against the manager and the author. It didn't cost you anything to take legal proceedings. There were lawyers on hand who would do the work for nothing, and go fifty-fifty on the proceeds.

Like others before him, Sherriff saved himself the cost of a lengthy court action by paying off the racketeers.

Nowadays, it is not individuals but the media corporations who try it on and who exercise the roughest clout when it comes to arguments about copyright. And here the contention stretches way beyond the written word to take in the whole range of audio-visual and computer programmes.

FILM AND TELEVISION

Again there is discord between British and European law, though, in this context, writers are unanimous in their praise of Brussels.

In late 1992 the European Commission's Rental and Lending Directive declared the 'author' of a film to have the right to sanction (or stop) rental and to be paid 'equitable' remuneration'. But who is the 'author'? Under British law, he is generally assumed to be the producers, an interpretation which naturally offends writers and directors. The European Community, on the other hand, takes its lead from France where the primary author of a film is the director but others, including the scriptwriter, can also be named as co-author. As can be imagined, producers are not accepting the directive as gospel. Their first reaction was to threaten a deluge of legal paperwork and a bare-knuckle fight on the shareout of copyright for every new production. Their second thought was to seek loopholes in the directive. Inevitably, they found room to manoeuvre in and around a batch of clauses that can be interpreted in ways that suit local conditions. Their resolve is strengthened by the knowledge that while writers, together with composers and performers, have the right to 'equitable remuneration' what this means in practice is not at all clear.

The ALCS sees two possible solutions. One is for a flat-rate payment to the writer. The other is for writers to agree to a collective administration of the sort already operating in Germany. In this case, the ALCS would presumably do for scriptwriters what it already does for print authors. Producers want none of this. Their remedy is to insert into contracts a clause which disposes of 'equitable remuneration' as 'deemed to have been paid' under whatever financial arrangements are made for setting up a project. Incredibly, this may square with the letter of the directive though it most certainly does not accord with its spirit. Further clarification must wait on draft legislation, which should reveal where government sympathies lie.

Whatever the way forward, it must be accepted that lending is horrendously difficult to control. It has been known for years that the loss of income attributed to domestic sound and video recorders runs into billions. With the advance of technology, the problem is bound

to worsen. Before long we will have video on demand, an almost limit-
less choice of programming available to any home at a push of the
remote control. In some versions of this futuristic state, viewers will
rarely summon up a whole programme. Instead they will want segments
of programmes, selected from the whole menu and patched together by
the computer. Sailing enthusiasts could choose great sailing moments
from half a dozen programmes and English students could choose
the gravedigger scene from six different productions of *Hamlet*. The
entire system would be *à la carte*, says Chris Barlas in a recent ALCS
newsletter.

> We are at the threshold of something very new and very strange. The
> digital media will enable us to do things with other people's work
> that only a couple of years ago would have been quite impossible.
> I've seen programmes that let children incorporate clips of film into
> school essays, programmes that take dictation and print the words on
> a screen, programmes that electronically read books in a variety of
> voices. The technology is mind boggling.

So too is trying to evolve a method by which writers can receive their
just reward.

Copyright applies to all written work, unpublished as well as published.
For works not published during the author's lifetime, the period of
copyright runs from the date of publication. For a published work of
joint authorship, protection extends from the end of the year of the death
of the author who dies last.

In most books a copyright notice appears on one of the front pages. In
its simplest form this is the symbol © followed by the name of the
copyright owner and the year of first publication. The assertion of
copyright may be emphasized by the phrase 'All rights reserved', and in
case there are any lingering doubts the reader may be warned that 'No
part of this publication may be reproduced or transmitted in any form or
by any means without permission'.

But this is to overstate the case. It is perfectly legitimate for a writer to quote from someone else's work for 'purposes of criticism or review' as long as 'sufficient acknowledgement' is given. What he must not do is to lift 'a substantial part' of it. In one case, four lines from a thirty-two line poem were held to amount to 'a substantial part'. On the other hand, even a 'substantial' quotation from a copyright work may be acceptable if a student or critic is engaged in 'fair dealing with a literary work for the purposes of research or music study'.

Common sense suggests basing the assessment on the length and importance of the quotation; the amount quoted in relation to the text as a whole; the extent to which the work competes with the work quoted; and the extent to which the words quoted are saving a writer time and trouble.

Some years ago the Society of Authors and the Publishers' Association stated that they would usually regard as 'fair dealing' the use of a single extract of up to 400 words, or a series of extracts (of which none exceeds 300 words) to a total of 800 words from a prose work, or of extracts to a total of 40 lines from a poem, provided that this did not exceed a quarter of the poem.

In at least one respect the 1988 Copyright Act anticipated Brussels. For the first time the European concept of 'moral rights' was introduced into British law. The most basic is the right of paternity which entitles authors to be credited as the creators of their work. However, paternity must be asserted in writing and is not retrospective. No right of paternity attaches to authors of computer programmes or computer-generated works or typeface designs. Authors creating works in the course of their employment have no right of paternity where the copyright originally vested in the employer and the employer has authorized the publication complained of. Also, no right of paternity is infringed where the work was written specifically for publication in a newspaper, magazine or other periodical, or in a 'collective work' such as an encyclopedia, a dictionary or a yearbook.

A second moral right is that of integrity. In theory, this opens the way to forceful objections to any 'derogatory treatment' if derogatory amounts to 'distortion or mutilation . . . or is otherwise prejudicial to the honour or reputation of the author'. Mis-correction of grammar by an illiterate editor does not qualify. In the absence of test cases, all things are possible, but relying on lawyers' gossip it seems that a book would have to be savaged beyond recognition for an injunction to be granted.

Those most likely to have their right of integrity infringed are film directors (specifically mentioned in the 1988 Act) and visual artists, who might, for example, suffer the attentions of an airbrusher. For those in the writing trade, the Society of Authors urges 'locking the stable door before the horse bolts by ensuring that your contract does not permit the publishers to make significant editorial changes without your agreement'.

This is a genuine risk in that contracts can legitimately dispose of moral rights which may 'be waived by written agreement or with the consent of the author'. There are cases where the concession is reasonable. For example, a ghostwriter may reasonably be expected to waive moral rights. After all, the ghost has chosen to be anonymous or, more probably, to be relegated to the acknowledgements.

TITLES AND TRADEMARKS

Technically, there is no copyright in a title. But where a title is inseparable from the work of a particular author, proceedings for 'passing off' are likely to be successful. A purely descriptive title such as *London in the Nineteenth Century* may be used with impunity by another writer. But if you are planning to write the fictional diaries of a pimply teenager, a title like *The Secret Life of Adrian Pole* will almost certainly get you into trouble with Sue Townsend.

The risks of causing offence multiply when a unique image is involved. In a recent full-page advertisement promoting the services of the Patent Office the *Mr Men* characters created by Roger Hargreaves (60 million books sold to date) are offered as an example of a registered trademark that protects the author against literary and other predators. The interesting feature of trademarks is that, unlike copyright, they go on for ever. The Coca-Cola and Kodak marks, for example, are well over a hundred years old. Neither of these have close literary associations but what about Thomas the Tank Engine, who now has his own trademark, or Mickey Mouse? The official British artist of the Gulf war, John Keene, has faced legal threats from the Disney Corporation for having painted a picture of the devastation of a Kuwait beach which included a Mickey Mouse doll.

In theory it should be easier to preserve copyright in fictional characters than in titles. But in broadcasting, a frequent source of dispute is the lifting of characters from one series to another when there are two or more writers involved.

'TV people like to believe that the character becomes their own,' writes Kenneth Royce, creator of *The XYZ Man* and *Bulman*, 'forgetting that without the author's original, there would be no such character'. As a minimum precaution he urges a writer approaching a TV deal 'to resist strongly any attempt to change the names of his characters'. Why make stealing easier than it already is?'

THE SINGULARITY OF LETTERS

The copyright status of a letter is something of a curiosity. The actual document belongs to the recipient, but the copyright remains with the writer and, after his or her death, with the writer's estate. This has caused difficulty for some biographers who have assumed that it is the owners of letters who are empowered to give permission to quote from them. This only applies if the writer has assigned copyright. Even then, the way may not be smooth. Witness the frustration of Eric Jacobs, the biographer of Sir Kingsley Amis, who found himself unable to quote from letters written by the novelist because the Bodleian Library, which has the bulk of the Amis papers, would not concede any part of the copyright Sir Kingsley has invested in them. The matter was resolved only when the letter writer himself requested permission to quote from his own correspondence.

It is dangerous to assume that letters which are not in themselves of great intrinsic value are fair game for a biographer. Copyright owners do not have to look far for reasons to assert their rights and may not be swayed by appeals for liberality. The author Diana Souhami spent five years researching a book detailing the 'strange romance' of Greta Garbo and Cecil Beaton which fell victim to a failure to gain permission to use letters Garbo wrote to her friend Mimi Pollak. Cape had to pulp the entire hardback edition, a decision they described, not unreasonably, as 'just appalling'.

COPYRIGHT IN LECTURES AND SPEECHES

The pre-1988 rule was unnecessarily complicated and depended, for example, on whether the lecturer was speaking from prepared notes. Now, even if a speaker talks without notes, copyright exists in a lecture as soon as it is recorded (in writing or otherwise) but not until then. The copyright belongs to the person who spoke the words, whether or not the recording was made by, or with the permission of, the speaker.

This means that nobody may make substantial use of a transcript of a lecture without permission. The Act does, however, make one important exception: where a record of spoken words is made to report current events, it is not an infringement of copyright to use or copy the record for that purpose provided that the record is a direct record of the spoken words and the making of the record was not prohibited by the speaker.

COPYRIGHT ON IDEAS

Writers trying to sell ideas should start on the assumption that it is almost impossible to stake an exclusive claim. So much unsolicited material comes the way of publishers and script departments, duplication of ideas is inevitable.

Frequent complaints of plagiarism have led publishers and production companies to point out the risks whenever they acknowledge an unsolicited synopsis or script, warning correspondents, 'it is often the case that we are currently considering or have already considered ideas that may be similar to your own'.

That this is not a complete defence is suggested by the case brought by a London schoolteacher, Keith Wooldridge, against Radio 4. Mr Wooldridge asserted that the BBC had purloined his idea for a series about pets and their owners. A district judge at Bromley Crown Court agreed with him and ordered the BBC to pay damages and costs. One of the interesting features of the case is that it was brought under the Small Claims procedure which avoids the heavy legal fees associated with a High Court action.

Others have followed Mr Wooldridge's lead. We heard recently from Guy Lyon Playfair who has scored a triumph with a little help from Willesden County Court. His case related to a BBC programme called *Ghostwatch*, which, he argued, was inspired by and, to a significant extent, based on his book *This House is Haunted*. He listed twenty close similarities between book and film. The BBC offered an out-of-court settlement.

But there are signs that the BBC is toughening its stance. When *Black and Blue*, a Gordon Newman play about a black undercover policeman on a London estate, went out in September 1992, writer Jon Paul Morgan thought the plot and characters were remarkably similar to a play he had submitted to the corporation. With the assistance of the Legal Aid Board, he sued for breach of copyright. The BBC countered with a letter to the Board asking it to stop funding the author, who, it was claimed, was on a 'speculative mission'. The request was turned down but, whatever the outcome, it is clear that the BBC is worried at the prospect of a spate of copycat actions.

Writers who are nervous of the attention of rivals are best advised to maintain a certain reticence in dealings with the media. They should, for example, resist the urge to give out all their best ideas at an expensive lunch or in a brainstorming session with an ever so friendly producer who just might be able to slot their programme into his overcrowded schedule. It is flattering to be invited to hold forth but the experience can be costly unless there is an up-front fee. No less a writer than Frederic Raphael has been caught out in this way. Invited to develop a 'major series', he soon discovered that:

> I had been swindled into spending time and energy, without fee, on a project to which no one was committed at all. My ideas were now on file; my garrulous suggestions were lodged in the minds of those who might later, without acknowledgement, make use of them. I was not wholly shattered to be told eventually, on the telephone, by

the senior producer (who said that he had 'learned a lot' from 'our' experience), that the Department Head had decided to put the whole thing on ice.

The lesson was plain.

The way I feel about executives, the time is approaching when I shall charge a consultancy fee for saying hello. And another for goodbye.

The fact is that to succeed in an action for infringement of copyright on an idea or on the bare bones of a plot, the copying of 'a combination or series of dramatic events' must be very close indeed. Proceedings have failed because incidents common to two works have been stock incidents or have revolved around stock characters common to many works. Furthermore, as copyright is not a monopoly, it is a perfectly good defence if a later author can show that he had no knowledge of an earlier author's work.

The best way of protecting ideas, says solicitor Carolyn Jennings, is to 'get anyone who sees your work to sign a letter confirming that they will not disclose the ideas behind your work to anyone else, and will not use those ideas except by arrangement with you'. The catch, as Ms Jennings readily concedes, is that 'it is very difficult to get broadcasters or film companies to sign such a letter'. In a highly competitive, fast-moving industry, it is likely that many synopses or scripts based on similar ideas are floating around though created entirely independently.

Minimum security is in refusing to discuss ideas before they are written down. If there is still a worry that a proposal could end up in the wrong hands, copy the manuscript, send it to yourself by registered post, then deposit the package and dated receipt at a bank or other safe place. At least then no one can fault memory on essential details.

PERMISSIONS

A quotation of a 'substantial' extract from a copyright work or any quotation of copyright material, however short, for an anthology must be approved by the publishers of the original work.

It is in the author's interest to deal with permissions as early as possible. Last-minute requests just before a book goes to press can lead to embarrassing difficulties if fees are too high or if permission is refused.

Whenever copyright is an issue, a contract must specify the territory permissions should cover. The difference between British Commonwealth and the World can be a yawning gap in fees. Some publishers have a standard letter for clearing permissions which may help to speed up negotiations. But rights departments are notoriously slow in responding to requests from individuals who are unclear as to what they want or who give the impression of writing in on spec.

Difficulties can arise when the identity of a copyright holder is unclear. The publisher of the relevant book may have gone out of business or been absorbed into a conglomerate, leaving no records of the original imprint. Detective work can be yet more convoluted when it comes to unpublished works. When copyright holders are hard to trace, the likeliest source of help is the Writers and their Copyright Holders project, otherwise known as WATCH. A joint enterprise of the universities of Texas and Reading, WATCH has created a database of English-language authors whose papers are housed in archives and manuscript repositories. The database is available free of charge on the Internet.

If, despite best efforts, a copyright owner cannot be found, there are two options; either to cut the extract or to press ahead with publication in the hope that if the copyright holder does find out he will not object or will not demand an outrageous fee. The risk can be minimized by open acknowledgement that every effort to satisfy the law has been made.

ANTHOLOGY AND QUOTATION RATES

The Society of Authors and the Publishers' Association have recently revised their recommendations for 'basic *minimum* fees' for quotation and anthology use of copyright material.

PROSE

The suggested rate is £82–£96 per 1000 words for world rights. The rate for the UK and Commonwealth or the USA alone is usually half of the world rate. For an individual country (e.g. Canada, Australia or New Zealand): one quarter of the world rate.

Where an extract is complete in itself (e.g. a chapter or short story) publishers sometimes charge an additional fee at half the rate applicable for 1000 words.

This scale generally covers one edition only. An additional fee may be payable if the material is used in a reset or offset edition or in a new format or new binding (e.g. a paperback edition) and will certainly be required if the publisher of an anthology sub-licenses publication rights to another publisher.

Fees vary according to the importance of the author quoted, the proportion of the original work that the user intends to quote and its value to the author/publisher requesting permission. The expected size of the print run should also be taken into consideration and may affect the fee. It is usual to halve the fees for quotations to be used in scholarly works with print runs of under 1000 copies.

POETRY

For anthology publication in the UK and Commonwealth a minimum fee of £30 should be charged for the first ten lines; thereafter £1.50 per line for the next twenty lines and £1 a line subsequently. This rate may be reduced by one-third if the poem appears in a literary or scholarly journal or an anthology that contains more than forty poems in copyright or in a book with a print run of less than 1500 copies. The rates for established poets may well be significantly higher.

For any subsequent edition or for separate publication elsewhere (e.g. in the USA, Australia, Europe, Canada) it is recommended that a further fee be charged and that this could be reduced to not less than half the original fee – in order to encourage the wider sale of anthologies containing the work of new poets. Anthology fees for publication in the USA of established poets may well match the fees for anthology use in the UK.

There is pressure from some publishers and agents to increase permission rates by up to 50 per cent. Authors have mixed feelings. They like it when the money comes to them but they are less keen to pay out. The likely compromise is a 20 per cent increase.

US COPYRIGHT

The US Copyright Act of 1909 provided for two separate terms of copyright, a period of twenty-eight years from publication followed by a renewal period of a further twenty-eight years. A new copyright Act, which came into force in January 1978, made changes in the duration of copyright protection and set out rules for the transition of existing works.

Copyrights registered before 1950 and renewed before 1978 were automatically extended by the new act until December of the seventy-fifth year of the original date of registration. This meant that all copyrights in their second term were extended for nineteen years. But copyrights registered after 1950 and before December 1977 had to be renewed. Strictly speaking, this should no longer be necessary. Following a Congressional amendment, if copyright has already been secured, the period of protection is extended automatically. But there may still be advantages to renewing copyright protection in the work's twenty-eighth year (that is, by 31 December 1996 for works published in this country in 1968). It may help particularly for works that have gone out of print, because any legitimate enterprise would request a Copyright Office search in order to acquire rights. Renewal will vest copyright in the name of the renewal claimant (for example, if the original author is dead); it also provides prima facie evidence of the validity of facts stated in the renewal certificate.

Copyright renewal, along with registration (if the work was not registered with the Library of Congress in the first place) costs $20. Further information and the appropriate forms are available from the Copyright Office, Library of Congress, Washington, DC 20559, USA.

For queries on British copyright contact: The Intellectual Property Policy Directorate, Copyright Enquiries, Room 4/5, Hazlitt House, 45 Southampton Buildings, London WC2A 1AR (Tel: 0171–438 4778).

Reading Between the Lines or Looking for Libel

OF ALL THE FRIGHTFUL things that can happen to a writer, a lawyer's letter threatening libel proceedings ranks among the most horrific. As an experience to be earnestly abjured, it is not far short of leaving the only copy of a completed manuscript on the 77 bus and some way ahead of pretending to be out to the bailiffs.

What makes it so much worse is that libel has a way of creeping up on you unawares. Take the three-year saga initiated, wholly innocently, by David Lodge when, to demonstrate his arguments on plagiarism, he drew links between his book *Nice Work*, published in 1988 and a Harlequin Mills & Boon romance called *The Iron Master* which appeared in 1991. The idea that he might be libelling Pauline Harris, the author of *The Iron Master*, never entered his mind. Even the wide coverage stimulated by his article in the *Independent* did not alert him to the risks. As his publisher observed, 'It was a perfectly amiable article that David wrote. There was nothing malicious in it. It was inviting a response.'

He got more than he bargained for. Pauline Harris found that her work was no longer acceptable. She was, in effect, sacked by HMB, who, she said, 'would not accept my innocence'. So traumatized was she by a 'regrettable coincidence' (she had not read any of David Lodge's books) that she suffered writer's block. David Lodge readily accepted that Mrs Harris was 'completely innocent of plagiarism' and said so in an open letter published in the *Independent on Sunday* but the process of law lumbered on towards the High Court where eventually Pauline Harris was awarded 'substantial damages'.

The saddest aspect of the case is that it inhibited an otherwise timely debate on the validity of authors' claims to originality. The admission by both authors that *Nice Work* and *The Iron Master* owed a mighty debt to Elizabeth Gaskell's *North and South* passed by almost unnoticed.

The bigger the writing name the more likely it is to attract litigants. When Anthony Burgess published his novel *The Worm and the Ring*, a reader identified with a fictitious school secretary because her own doctor had the same name as the doctor of the secretary in the book. Burgess settled out of court with a large cheque.

Almost every established writer has a horror story to tell. When Graham Greene was trembling on the publication of his first success, *Stamboul Train*, a libel action was threatened by J.B. Priestley, who saw himself ridiculed in the book. Greene's biographer, Norman Sherry, reveals that Heinemann, who published both authors, made clear that if they were to lose one of their authors, it would be Greene who would have to go. But instead, 'Greene had to share the cost of the changes Priestley required and the changes had to be made immediately from a public telephone box without time for reflection'.

Failure to reach an early accommodation can lead to that particular form of lawyer's torture which consists in adding up the costs to a total not far short of the national debt.

The broadcaster Derek Jameson was brought to the edge of bankruptcy by an unsuccessful action against the BBC for what he regarded as damaging inferences. When Gillian Taylforth, the *EastEnders* star, lost her case against the *Sun* she faced a legal bill that was said to be around £500,000.

Success, on the other hand, can bring riches. For reasons lost in the deliberations of the jury rooms, awards are invariably out of all proportion to damage suffered. It used to be the rule that compensation for a serious libel should roughly correspond to the price of a good house. Now the guideline leads to a palace. Speaking up for press colleagues who have found themselves in the High Court, William Rees-Mogg points out that 'if newspaper vans ran amok in London and crashed freely into innocent pedestrians, that would cost their proprietors less than a few defamatory paragraphs'.

For those with the gambling instinct, the chance of jackpot winnings is a powerful draw. It may be a safe general rule, as the Book of Proverbs tells us, that 'A good name is rather to be chosen than great riches'. But, in the wonderful world of libel, lawyers are ready to admit that some plaintiffs go for the money. There is the story of a famous critic who was offered a settlement plus an apology or double the money and no apology. He decided he could live without the apology. Recent big awards include £300,000 to Koo Stark, £500,000 to Jeffrey Archer and £1 million to Elton John. No wonder Britain is known as the defamation capital of the western world.

But ending up on the winning side is no guarantee of a handsome windfall. By far the largest libel award to be given in a British court was the £1.5 million damages credited to Lord Aldington in his action against Count Tolstoy. Count Tolstoy could not afford to pay and for a time Lord Aldington faced the prospect of bankruptcy in his efforts to meet his own lawyers' bills. When, in 1988, Michael Meacher lost his case against *The Observer* and had to pay damages, the newspaper was still £40,000 down on the final reckoning. Top lawyers are very expensive.

If not money, what is the pull of a libel action? Setting the record straight may be a worthy motive but those who go to court to defend their reputations invariably find that the matter which offends them is publicized yet more heavily and stays longer in the public memory. A sexy case like that featuring Gillian Taylforth produces reams of detailed coverage. It has been argued that while the original story of an unconventional coupling on the A1, as published in the *Sun*, reached 25 per cent of the population, the court proceedings lifted that figure to more than 80 per cent.

Court 13 in the High Court is the source of much free entertainment. As John Mortimer, that liberal (former) lawyer has observed, 'Libel actions fulfil much the same function as the circus in the days of ancient Rome; the miseries of the masses are alleviated by the public suffering of the few, and there are a good many laughs to be got along the way.'

There are those, like Mathew Parris, the *Times* columnist, who would do away with libel altogether.

Imagine a world in which anyone could write or say anything they liked about another, true or false, with impunity. Some would do just that. Much that was published would be fanciful. It would quickly become common knowledge that the papers and airwaves were full of rubbish. The *Sunday Sport* is blazing a noble and unacknowledged trail in this respect.

More seriously, John Mortimer argues that there has to be some protection against 'falsehoods and rumours that might affect a victim's health or put his or her livelihood in peril'. Mortimer favours 'a proper retraction . . . boldly printed on the front page'.

This would take us closer to continental Europe, where defamation is a crime of the lowest category heard in a few minutes in the equivalent of a magistrates' court with a laid-down scale of fines. There is no immediate prospect of anything so radical but the need for reform is accepted by the Lord Chancellor. Four years ago he welcomed the recommendations of a working group, under the chairmanship of Lord Justice Neill. Since then, there has been a gradual move forward, led by the Court of Appeal. It is now able to substitute its own finding when it disagrees with a jury's estimate of damages. The first impact was on Teresa Gorman, MP, who had a £150,000 libel award cut to £50,000 by the Court of Appeal. It seems that the low circulation of the publication in which the libel appeared was an important factor in their lordships' thinking. A few months later Esther Rantzen saw her £250,000 libel damages reduced to £110,000. As an aside to the main judgement, Lord Justice Neill said that large awards should be subjected to 'more searching scrutiny' than had been customary. The warning had a dramatic effect on lawyers' workload. Libel writs were down by as much as 40 per cent in 1992, though since then the figures have jumped again.

In 1994, the court rules for defamation proceedings were tightened to give the defendant a better chance of responding constructively to an action against him. There is now a requirement on the plaintiff to give greater details of matters relating to a claim for damages and a new procedure whereby either party can obtain 'a ruling as to meaning' in advance of a trial. Are the words complained of capable of bearing a particular interpretation? It is up to the plaintiff to show clearly that they are.

Further change must wait on the government finding time to introduce legislation. While there is no great sense of urgency (MPs who love shouting off opponents are themselves none too keen on reforms that may encourage outsiders to be more outspoken), the Lord Chancellor is committed to encouraging 'sensible settlements, as well as providing a fast track for the disposal of straightforward claims'. The way forward, he believes, is to cut from three years to one the time limit for starting an action for defamation (this will curb the use of 'gagging writs' such as those used by the late Robert Maxwell to foil legitimate press investigation into his nefarious activities), and to introduce a new defence which will avoid the need for a trial if the defendant is prepared to offer amends and pay damages assessed by a judge. There will also be a new summary procedure under which every defamation claim will come before a judge at an early stage. The judge will assess whether the claim is suitable for summary disposal, or whether it should go for trial, with or without a jury. He will have power on summary disposal to award damages up to a fixed ceiling. This will make it easier for an ordinary citizen to seek redress against a rich opponent who, otherwise, is liable to keep a trial going as long as possible in the hope that a plaintiff will run out of patience and money. The High Court will lose its monopoly on libel. Straightforward and modest claims will be heard in the County Court.

The Lord Chancellor also promises that the Court of Appeal will clarify what is to be taken into account by juries when deciding damages. This holds open the possibility of extending the rule in Scotland, where the plaintiff has to prove a damaged reputation. Current English practice is far harsher in that once the words are shown to be libellous, hefty damages can be obtained even if no real harm has resulted.

Many reformers would go further. They want the responsibility of a jury to be limited to saying if damages should be substantial, moderate, nominal or contemptuous. The judge would then decide on the appropriate figure. A useful compromise would compel juries to explain their calculations. As Lord Donaldson has observed, 'having to give reasons puts a substantial premium on ensuring that the head rules the heart'.

Meanwhile, there are subtle ways in which the libel laws can be manipulated by imaginative lawyers. Recently, the statute books were raided for an action for malicious falsehood, the likes of which were outside the experience of contemporary proceedings. Linda Joyce, a former maid to the Princess Royal, was wrongly accused by *Today* newspaper of stealing letters from the Princess. She could not afford to go to court and since legal aid is not on offer for libel she assumed defeat. But then her lawyers realized that for an action for malicious falsehood, legal aid was available. Linda Joyce won her case and a reported £25,000 payment from *Today*.

The implications are far-reaching, as Geoffrey Wheatcroft points out:

> The law of malicious falsehood exactly reverses the law of libel. It *is* necessary to prove that the words complained of were untrue and malicious, as the very phrase 'malicious falsehood' suggests. And it *is* necessary to prove actual damage, as opposed to an amorphous hurt to someone's good name.

These are surely fair tests in whatever circumstances.

> Newspapers and publishers would be protected against gold-digging actions and gagging writs; poor and rich alike would be protected from the abuse of its power by the press.

The flip side to reforming the libel laws is that a simplified and, by definition, cheaper procedure may act as a stimulant to litigation. But this could be the modest price for silencing the caterwauls of wounded celebrities for a comprehensive privacy law; censorship by any other name. Some of the ideas mooted are terrifying in their scope. As Victoria Glendinning reported in her RSA lecture, serious consideration has even been given to the legal suppression of any information claimed to cause distress to the living, with no time limit. Such a move could put a stop to all serious biography.

The aim of reform should be to achieve more freedom, not less. Britain is already among the more secretive democracies, with obstacles to the truth at every turn. If we want seriously to save time and money on much-ado-about-nothing libel cases, we could make a start by curtailing the Official Secrets Act. Newspapers might then no longer fill their pages with trivia and, instead, write about things that really matter.

RULES OF THE GAME

The standard definition of libel is the publication of a statement which tends to lower a person's reputation in the estimation of 'right thinking

members of society'. Twenty years ago the Faulkes Committee on
Defamation suggested minimizing the value judgement implied by 'right
thinking' by relying instead on the estimation of 'reasonable people'. But
the arcane form of words survives, presumably on the assumption that in
our muddled world, and despite all contrary evidence, 'right thinking' is
still an identifiable attribute.

The distinction between libel and slander is explained by Peter Marsh,
a barrister specializing in defamation.

> Whether or not the publication is in a permanent form determines
> whether it is libel or slander. Films, broadcasting and matter published
> in newspapers falls into the category of libel. On the other hand, if I
> gossip with work colleagues about a person's sexual proclivities in
> derogatory terms that amounts to slander. In 1991, Dr Malcolm Smith
> was awarded £150,000 damages for slander in a case against a fellow
> general practitioner, Dr Alanah Houston, over allegations of sexual
> harassment. This was reduced to £50,000 on appeal.

Another important difference is that in libel there is no obligation to
prove that any actual damage as opposed to hurt to reputation has been
suffered, while in slander cases it is necessary to show that the plaintiff has
suffered material damage.

It may be that the defendant in a libel case did not intend harm. No
matter. All that the plaintiff need show is that the offending statement
would be understood by right-thinking people to refer to him. There is a
clear warning here for fiction writers not to venture too close to real life.
It may seem a neat idea to introduce friends and neighbours into a story
– it is so much easier to describe people you know – but if one of them
is cast as a villain and recognizes himself, albeit in an unlikely role, then a
solicitor's letter will surely follow.

Names, too, can be a trap for the unwary. If a novel features a corrupt
Member of Parliament, a financier who fiddles his tax or a vicar with an
obsessive interest in choirboys, it is as well to check that the names given
to these characters do not correspond to flesh and blood people. Often,
the more unlikely the name, the greater the risk. You may think you are
on safe ground when you relate the dubious practices of the Reverend

Harbottle Tiddles Grimston, but Sod's Law dictates that as soon as the book is in the shops, a curious coincidence will be drawn to your attention. The problem is accentuated by the sure knowledge that much of what appears in novels does relate to real life, even if the writer is not immediately aware of it. It is extraordinary what can be dredged up from the subconscious. One well-known writer recalls the awful embarrassment of realizing, too late, that the name of the leading protagonist in his steaming sex saga happened to be that of his fiancée. He avoided a libel action but she sent back his engagement ring.

A precaution Mark Le Fanu of the Society of Authors urges on all fiction writers is to check with the relevant directories before picking characters' names.

> For example, if the author has invented a corrupt landlord living in Paddington he should look up the invented name in the London telephone directory and substitute a safe one, if there is someone of that name with a Paddington telephone number. If one of the characters is a bishop of doubtful sanctity, the author should look in *Crockford's* to make sure that there is no bishop of that name.

Paul Watkins has cause to regret not checking the list of Old Etonians. His novel *Stand Up Before Your God*, based on his schooldays at Eton, featured an undesirable called Wilbraham. It was a name he had picked at random from a New York telephone directory. Unfortunately, it happened also to be the name of an Eton contemporary. Neither the author nor the real Wilbraham could remember ever having met. It was an unfortunate misunderstanding which nonetheless ended with Paul Watkins and his publisher Faber paying damages in the region of £15,000.

In 1956 an actress, June Sylvaine, sued the publishers of Antonia White's novel *The Sugar House* because it included a character called June Sylvaine, who was described as 'fat'. Both sides agreed that the coincidence of names was accidental, and the real Sylvaine admitted that it had done her no discernible harm. Nevertheless, she was awarded damages.

Since one cannot libel the dead, a valuable and safe source of names is *Who Was Who*.

Biographers of contemporary, or near-contemporary figures tread the narrowest line. To state a known fact about an individual, that he behaved deviously or dishonestly for example, may raise questions about his friends, associates or family which they feel bound to contest. A film star who was famous for his stories of licentious adventures, usually with the wives of other film stars, was never so much as challenged by his victims. But when he died and his biographer got to work, the writs began to fly. In such cases the best hope for the writer is the plaintiff's awareness that publicity generated by his action will cause him yet more pain. As Dr Johnson reminds us, 'Few attacks either of ridicule or invective make much noise but with the help of those they provoke.'

Where libel has been committed unintentionally or 'innocently', it is possible to alleviate the consequences by an 'offer to make amends'. This usually involves a published apology and a settlement of costs. Otherwise, unless it can be established that a statement, however defamatory, is true in substance and fact (a difficult trick to pull off), the defence against libel will probably turn on the assertion that the words complained of are fair comment on a matter of public interest. The defence will fail if the defendant is shown to have been activated by malice or if the facts on which he based the comment are shown to be untrue.

This is where the wheel turns full circle because writers, who are themselves inclined to rush to law when they feel aggrieved, often hear the 'fair comment' defence from their critics. The perimeters of 'fair comment' are wide enough to protect, in essence, the principles of free speech, so that, according to precedent, 'However wrong the opinion expressed may be in point of truth, or however prejudiced the writer, it may still be within the prescribed limit'. In other words, it is one thing to argue that a person's *views* are lunatic but quite another to assert that *he* is a lunatic.

The scope of 'fair comment' was defined recently when a libel action against a reviewer in the *Sunday Telegraph* was withdrawn after the complainant who felt that the 'severe criticisms of his works were quite unreasonable, was persuaded that his castigator was 'doing no more than expressing his honest opinion, which he has a right to do'.

Since there is no legal aid for libel action – reflecting, as one lawyer puts it, 'an unspoken feeling that reputation matters more to those who are important or among the better off in society' – the headline cases are reserved for the very rich or the very determined, while a plaintiff of modest means is generally urged to try for an out-of-court settlement. This way he will at least save time (a full-blooded libel case can take up to three years to get to court) and avoid risking his life's savings.

Every writer is responsible for his own work. But this should not mean that when he makes mistakes he alone carries the can. Journalists are usually covered by their employers, who take on the whole cost of a libel action. Authors, on the other hand, are more exposed to the rigours of legal censorship. A typical publishing contract includes a warranty clause which entitles the publisher to be indemnified by the author against damages and costs if any part of the work turns out to be libellous.

Publishers excuse their weakness of backbone by arguing that only the author is in a position to know whether or not a work is libellous and that the onus should be on the author to check facts before they are published. But why, asks Mark Le Fanu of the Society of Authors, should the risk be borne by the author alone when a publisher deliberately gambles on making money out of a book?

> While it is true that a writer of fiction is much more likely than the publisher to know whether or not a person has been defamed (whether intentionally or unintentionally), the issue is much less clear-cut with non-fiction. Authors are not experts in the arcane mysteries of the 'fair comment' defence to a libel claim. Publishers are well aware that certain sorts of books (e.g. biographies of the living, business exposés, etc.) inevitably carry a libel risk.

In fairness, it must be said that the indemnity is rarely invoked unless a publisher feels he has been deceived or misled. But, at the very least, the author should insist that his publisher has the manuscript read for libel and that his contract does not specify unlimited liability.

In 1972 David Irving, whose book *The Destruction of Convoy PQ17* had been the subject of a successful libel action, was in turn sued by his publishers, Cassell, who sought to recover the libel damages and costs they had paid out. The claim was for £100,000. But fortunately for Irving he had taken the advice of the Society of Authors and amended his contract. He was liable only for breaches of his warranty that the book was free of libel unknown to the publisher. Irving argued that Cassell knew all the relevant facts before an action was brought. In the end, Cassell did not proceed with the claim.

Libel insurance offers some sort of safeguard and a publisher who is insured is clearly preferable to one who is not. But most insurance policies carry severe limitations, not least a ceiling on the payout of damages. Also, reading for libel can be expensive for a book that is in any way controversial. As Richard West discovered when he wrote an investigative volume, 'the lawyer who read it for libel got £1000. The lawyer who wrote in to the publisher to complain on behalf of his client was probably paid about £5000'.

Since West himself earned about £500 for his efforts he concluded, not unreasonably, that authorship was a mug's game.

There are many cases where a cost-conscious publisher has played safe by amending a text to a point where it loses its cutting edge and thus its sales appeal. It is not unknown for an entire book to be jettisoned to save on lawyers' bills.

Another limitation on libel insurance is that few policies extend to the US market, where claims and awards can take off like Concorde. There, a thriving libel industry has been made yet more prosperous by enterprising lawyers who assess fees as a percentage of whatever they can persuade juries to award. The consolation for defendants is that while the law of libel in the States is similar to the law here, in practical terms it is more favourable to the authors, in that the reputations of public figures are thought to be in less need of protection. A politician, say, who sues for libel is ridiculed as a bad sport. Whoever puts his head above the parapet, goes the argument, should expect to be shot at. Judges are more understanding of ordinary citizens, particularly when there is an invasion-of-privacy claim, but as a general rule, for libel damages to be awarded in an American court, someone must publish untruths knowing them to be untrue. Even then, there is plenty of leeway.

Early in 1988 a conservative-led Supreme Court allowed an appeal to overturn $200,000 damages awarded to Jerry Falwell against Larry Flynt. The peculiar fascination of the case comes from knowing the identity of the contenders. Falwell is the Reverend Jerry Falwell, founder of the Moral Majority, while Flynt is the supremo of soft-porn magazines. The action arose when Falwell was parodied in a cartoon which suggested that he had gained his first sexual experience with his mother. He sued for libel, invasion of privacy and emotional distress. In striking down the decision of a lower court to declare in favour of the Baptist minister, Chief Justice William Rehnquist argued that even when cartoons are 'harsh, indecent or indecorous', they are within the bounds of America's 'robust political and social satire'.

There is a consequent danger, as Lord Goodman argued, of individuals suffering persecution by rumour, but can this be worse than the state of affairs in Britain where a statement which is genuinely believed to be true and, indeed, *is* true in part, may still be libellous? It is for this reason that impure reputations, such as that of the late Robert Maxwell, survive public scrutiny.

Peter Marsh offers these tips for writers about to embark on a controversial project.

> If the subject or subjects of critical comment are still alive, beware; if you are writing a book about real life incidents but have changed names to avoid identification, take extreme care in the choice of names for your characters; remember that damage to a person's reputation can be caused by innuendo. For example, to write of someone that most people thought he was taking advantage of the Inland Revenue may suggest some improper and unethical practice. If a living person is going to be the subject of comment which is expressly or implicitly derogatory, make absolutely sure your facts are correct and can be substantiated. Otherwise, your publisher is going to be propelled into the courtroom naked of a defence.

In one important respect, authors and publishers suffer more than anyone from the application of the libel laws. At the root of the problem is the ease with which determined plaintiffs can get a book withdrawn from circulation, on the grounds that if it continues to be sold it may, just may, aggravate a libel as yet unproved. The process, successfully used by Goldsmith in his litigation against *Private Eye*, was given a shot in the arm by Maxwell in his tussles with Tom Bower over a biography of which Maxwell did not approve. David Hooper, author of *Public Scandal, Odium and Contempt* points out that the position of distributors in such situations is extremely perilous: 'They have no means of knowing whether the book is in fact libellous. All they know is that any profit they might have made – and more – will find its way smartly into the hands of their lawyers.' The remedy, says David Hooper, is for anyone seeking to get a book withdrawn to be required to undertake to pay damages if their claims turn out to be without substance.

Is there anything to be said for those who bring libel actions? There is no better summary of the risks and tribulations for all but the excessively rich than that which appears in Adam Raphael's absorbing indictment *Grotesque Libels*.

> The problems of a libel action can be stated quite simply. The law is highly technical and the pleadings so complex that even its skilled practitioners often differ on the most basic questions. The costs of the lawyers involved are so high that they make the fees charged by any other profession appear to be a mere bagatelle. The opportunities for obstruction and delay are such that it can take as long as five years to bring a libel action to court. When it eventually does reach the court, the damages left to the whim of a jury are so uncertain that the result is often no sounder than a dodgy fruit machine. A libel action has in fact more in common with a roulette wheel than justice. The net result for both plaintiffs and defendants is that such actions are a nightmare with only the lawyers able to sleep soundly.

No wonder Bernard Levin asserts, 'If I were libelled (I have frequently been) and were given the choice of suing or having all my toenails pulled out with red-hot pincers while listening to *Pelléas et Mélisande*, I think it would be a close run thing.'

As for those who are unable to keep out of the courts, the best advice comes from Tom Crone in his book on *Law and the Media*. The libel litigant, he says, must possess two prime qualities – 'a strong nerve and a deep pocket'.

Tax and the Writer

BY A. P. KERNON, FCA

'The avoidance of tax is the only pursuit that still carries any reward.'

John Maynard Keynes

'To produce an income tax return that has any depth to it, any feeling, one must have lived – and suffered.'

Frank Sullivan

'I have always paid income tax. I object only when it reaches a stage when I am threatened with having nothing left for my old age – which is due to start next Tuesday.'

Noël Coward

'Income tax returns are the most imaginative fiction being written today.'

Herman Wouk

INCOME TAX

What is a professional writer for tax purposes?

Writers are professionals while they are writing regularly with the intention of making a profit; or while they are gathering material researching or otherwise preparing a publication.

A professional freelance writer is taxed under Case II of Schedule D of the Income and Corporation Taxes Act 1988. The taxable income is the amount received, either directly or by an agent, on his behalf, less expenses wholly and exclusively laid out for the purposes of the profession. If expenses exceed income, the loss can either be carried forward and set against future income from writing or be set against other income which is subject to tax in the same year. If tax has been paid on that other income, a repayment can be obtained, or the sum can be offset against other tax liabilities. Special loss relief can apply in the opening years of the profession. Losses made in the first four years of assessment can be set against other income of the proceeding three years.

Where a writer receives very occasional payments for isolated articles, it may not be possible to establish that these are profits arising from carrying on a continuing profession. In such circumstances these 'isolated transactions' may be assessed under Case VI of Schedule D of the Income and Corporation Taxes Act 1988. Again, expenses may be deducted in arriving at the taxable income, but if expenses exceed income the loss can only be set against the profits from future isolated transactions, or other income assessable under Case VI.

Be warned that the Inland Revenue has a built-in prejudice against the self-employed. The reason is simple: PAYE is easier to administer, it brings in more taxes and improves the Revenue's cash flow. From the taxman's point of view, it is all a question of a master–servant relationship. This quaint anachronism means that if the Revenue can establish that you work regularly for a single employer, writing to order as it were, then a determined effort will be made to tax you at source. Freelance journalists are most at risk, though even scriptwriters on long-running series have had their problems. A writer who sets up a company and becomes a director will become an employee and lose many of the benefits a self-employed author enjoys. The copyrights would have to become the property of the company and if it was decided not to continue the writer might have to buy back the copyrights from the company. Companies are expensive to run but in certain circumstances may be advantageous from a tax point of view. Professional advice should be sought, however.

Expenses

A writer can normally claim the following expenses:

(a) Secretarial, typing, proofreading, research. Where payment for these is made to the author's wife or husband, it should be recorded and entered in the spouse's tax return as earned income which is subject to the usual personal allowances. If payments reach taxable levels, PAYE should be operated and National Insurance could then become payable.

(b) Telephone, telegrams, postage, stationery, printing, maintenance, insurance of equipment, dictation tapes, batteries, any office requisites used for the profession.

(c) Periodicals, books (including presentation copies and reference books) and other publications necessary for the profession, but amounts received from the sale of books should be deducted. Some inspectors allow only capital allowances on books [see (l) below].

(d) Hotels, fares, car-running expenses (including repairs, petrol, oil, garaging, parking, cleaning, insurance, road fund tax, depreciation), hire of cars or taxis in connection with:

    (i)   business discussions with agents, publishers, co-authors, collaborators, researchers, illustrators, etc.

    (ii) travel at home and abroad to collect background material.

(e) Publishing and advertising expenses, including the costs of proof corrections, indexing, photographs, etc.

(f) Subscriptions to societies and associations, press-cutting agencies, libraries, etc., incurred wholly for the purpose of the profession.

(g) Premiums to pension schemes such as the Society of Authors Retirement Benefits Scheme. Depending on age, up to 40 per cent of net earned income can be paid into a personal pension plan.

(h) Rent, council tax and water rates, etc., the proportion being determined by the ratio which the number of rooms used exclusively for the profession bears to the total number of rooms in the residence. But see note on *Capital Gains Tax*.

(i) Lighting, heating and cleaning. A carefully estimated figure of the business use of these costs can be claimed as a proportion of the total.

(j) Accountancy charges and legal charges incurred wholly in the course of the profession, including cost of defending libel actions, damages in so far as they are not covered by insurance and libel insurance premiums. However, where in a libel case damages are awarded to punish the author for having acted maliciously the action becomes quasi-criminal and costs and damages may not be allowed.

(k) TV and video rental (which may be apportioned for private use), and cinema or theatre tickets if wholly for the purpose of the profession, e.g. playwriting.

(l) Capital allowances for equipment, e.g. car, TV, radio, hi-fi sets, tape and video recorders, dictaphone, typewriters, desks, bookshelves, filing cabinets, photographic equipment, mobile telephones, computers and word-processors. Allowances vary in the Finance Acts depending upon political economic views prevailing. At present they are set at 25 per cent. On motor cars the allowance is 25 per cent in the first year and 25 per cent of the reduced balance in each successive year. In the case of motor cars bought after 11 March 1992 the limit is £3000 each year (previously £2000 each year). The total allowances in the case of all assets must not exceed the difference between cost and eventual sale price. Allowances will be reduced to exclude personal (non-professional) use where necessary.

(m) Lease rent. The cost of lease rent of equipment is allowable; also on cars, subject to restrictions for private use and for expensive cars.

(n) Tax relief is available for three-year (minimum) covenants to charities. With effect from 1 October 1990 individuals can obtain tax relief on one-off charitable gifts subject to certain generous limits.

NB It is essential to keep detailed records. Under the new self-assessment rules failure to do so would involve an immediate penalty if the Inland Revenue became aware. Diary entries of appointments, notes of fares and receipted bills are much more convincing to the Inland Revenue than round-figure estimates.

It has recently been announced that there is a fundamental change in the method of assessment of income of the self-employed to the 'current year' basis. At present, the self-employed generally pay tax in one tax year based on their accounts for the previous tax year – for example, the 1993/4 assessment might be based on accounts for the year ended 30 April 1992, 30 December 1992 or 5 April 1993. Under the new rules, the assessment will be based on the accounts for the year ended in the *same* tax year. These new rules are applicable for 1997/8 onwards, but there are some transitional provisions for 1996/7, when assessments will be based on a proportion of the two consecutive accounting periods ended in that year. Anyone who is just starting to write for profit should take professional advice as regards the date to choose for their accounting year end and those already writing should take advice concerning the changes in Inland Revenue practice as a result of the introduction of self-assessment.

Capital Gains Tax

The exemption from Capital Gains Tax which applies to an individual's main residence does not apply to any part of that residence which is used exclusively for business purposes. The effect of this is that the appropriate proportion of any increase in value of the residence since 31 March 1982 can be taxed, when the residence is sold, at the maximum rate of 40 per cent (at present). Conversely, if the residence is sold at a loss there can be a proportionate set-off against other Capital Gains.

Writers who own their houses should bear this in mind before claiming expenses for the use of a room for writing purposes. Arguments in favour of making such claims are that they afford some relief now, while Capital Gains Tax in its present form may not stay for ever. Also, where a new house is bought in place of an old one, the gain made on the sale of the first study may be set off against the cost of the study in the new house, thus postponing the tax payment until the final sale. For this relief to apply, each house must have a study, and the author must continue his profession throughout. On death there is an exemption of the total Capital Gains of the estate. Some relief from tax will be given on Council Tax.

NB Writers can claim that their use is non-exclusive and restrict their claim to the cost of extra lighting, heating and cleaning to avoid Capital Gains Tax liability.

Can a writer average out his income over a number of years for tax purposes?

Under Section 534 of the Income and Corporation Taxes Act 1988, a writer may in certain circumstances spread over two or three fiscal years lump sum payments, whenever received, and royalties received during two years from the date of first publication or performance of work. Points to note are:

(a) The relief can only be claimed if the writer has been engaged in preparing and collecting material and writing the book for more than twelve months.

(b) If the period of preparing and writing the work exceeds twelve months but does not exceed twenty-four months, one-half of the advances and/or royalties will be regarded as income from the year preceding that of receipt. If the period of preparing and writing exceeds twenty-four months, one-third of the amount received would be regarded as income from each of the two years preceding that of receipt.

(c) For writers on a very large income who otherwise fulfil the conditions required, a claim under these sections could result in a tax saving. If their income is not large they should consider the implication, in the various fiscal years concerned, of possible loss of benefit from personal and other allowances and changes in the standard rate of income tax.

It is also possible to average out income within the terms of publishers' contracts, but professional advice should be taken before signature. Where a husband and wife collaborate as writers, advice should be taken as to whether a formal partnership agreement should be made or whether the publishing agreement should be in joint names.

Is a lump sum paid for an outright sale of the copyright or part of the copyright exempt from tax?

Section 535 of the Income and Corporation Taxes Act 1988 gives relief where not less than ten years after the first publication of the work the author of a literary, dramatic, musical or artistic work assigns the copyright therein wholly or partially, or grants any interest in the copyright by licence, and:

(a) the consideration for the assignment or grant consists wholly or partially of a lump sum payment, the whole amount of which would, but for this section, be included in computing the amount of his/her profits or gains for a single year of assessment, and

(b) the copyright or interest is not assigned or granted for a period of less than two years.

In such cases, the amount received may be spread forward in equal yearly instalments for a maximum of six years, or, where the copyright or interest is assigned or granted for a period of less than six years, for the number of whole years in that period. A 'lump sum payment' is defined to include a non-returnable advance on account of royalties.

It should be noted that a claim may not be made under this section in respect of a payment if a prior claim has been made under Section 534 of the Income and Corporation Taxes Act 1988 (see section on spreading lump sum payments over two or three years) or vice versa.

Are royalties payable on publication of a book abroad subject to both foreign tax as well as UK tax?

Where there is a Double Taxation Agreement between the country concerned and the UK, then, on the completion of certain formalities, no tax is deductible at source by the foreign payer, but such income is taxable in the UK in the ordinary way. When there is no Double Taxation agreement, credit will be given against UK tax for overseas tax paid. A complete list of countries with which the UK has conventions for the avoidance of double taxation may be obtained from the Inspector of Foreign Dividends, Fitzroy House, P.O. Box 46, Nottingham, NG2 1BD, or the local tax office.

Residence abroad

Writers residing abroad will, of course, be subject to the tax laws ruling in their country of residence, and as a general rule royalty income paid from the United Kingdom can be exempted from deduction of UK tax at source, providing the author is carrying on his profession abroad. A writer who is intending to live abroad should make early application for future royalties to be paid without deduction of tax to HM Inspector of Taxes, Foreign Division, Prudential Building, 72 Maid Marian, Nottingham NG1 6AS. In certain circumstances, writers resident in the Irish Republic are exempt from Irish Income Tax on their authorship earnings.

Are grants or prizes taxable?

The law is uncertain. Some Arts Council grants are now deemed to be taxable, whereas most prizes and awards are not, though it depends on the conditions in each case. When submitting a statement of income and expenses, such items should be excluded, but reference made to them in a covering letter to the Inspector of Taxes.

What if I disagree with a tax assessment?

Income Tax law requires the Inspector of Taxes to make an assessment each year calculating the amounts of income tax payable on the 'profits' of the profession. Even though accounts may already have been submitted the assessment can quite possibly be estimated and overstated.

The taxpayer has the right of appeal within thirty days of receipt of the assessment and can request that the tax payable should be reduced to the correct liability, which he must estimate as accurately as possible. However, if he underestimates the amount, interest can become payable on the amount by which he underpays when the correct liability is known.

What is the item 'Class 4 N.I.C.' which appears on my tax assessment?

All taxpayers who are self-employed pay an additional national insurance contribution if their earned income exceeds a figure which is varied each year. This contribution is described as Class 4 and is calculated in the tax assessment. It is additional to the self-employed Class 2 (stamp) contributions but confers no additional benefits and is a form of levy. It applies to men aged under sixty-five and women under sixty. Tax relief is given on half the Class 4 contributions.

One of the curiosities for writers of the national insurance system is that while the Government is keen to take money off us, it is not overready to hand out benefits. When actors are unemployed they sign on for unemployment benefit. Writers cannot do this because while they are writing, even if their efforts are unpublished and unpaid, they are deemed to be employed. This rule has given rise to some dotty cases, the latest being that of Joy Peach, who was denied income support on the grounds that her writing was remunerative work. The fact that she had never had a single word published made no difference. To qualify for support, she was told, she had to give up writing.

Pensions

Writers can obtain relief on payments made into a pension fund so as to provide an income later in life. They would be well advised to make enquiries from reputable insurance companies for further information.

VALUE ADDED TAX

Value Added Tax (VAT) is a tax currently levied at 17½ per cent on:

(a) the total value of taxable goods and services supplied to consumers

(b) the importation of goods into the UK

(c) certain services from abroad if a taxable person receives them in the UK for the purpose of their business

Who is taxable?

A writer resident in the UK whose turnover from writing and any other business, craft or art on a self-employed basis is greater than £47,000 annually, before deducting agent's commission, must register with HM Customs & Excise as a taxable person. A business is required to register:

(a) at the end of any month if the value of taxable supplies in the past twelve months has exceeded the annual threshold; or

(b) if there are reasonable grounds for believing that the value of taxable supplies in the next twelve months will exceed the annual threshold.

Penalties will be claimed in the case of late registration. A writer whose turnover is below these limits is exempt from the requirements to register for VAT, but may apply for voluntary registration, and this will be allowed at the discretion of HM Customs & Excise.

A taxable person collects VAT on outputs (turnover) and deducts VAT paid on inputs (taxable expenses), and where VAT collected exceeds VAT paid, must remit the difference to HM Customs & Excise. In the event that input exceeds output, the difference will be repaid by HM Customs & Excise.

Outputs (Turnover)

A writer's outputs are taxable services supplied to publishers, broadcasting organizations, theatre managements, film companies, educational institutions, etc. A taxable writer must invoice, i.e. collect from, all the persons (either individuals or organizations) in the UK for whom supplies have been made, for fees, royalties or other considerations plus VAT. An unregistered writer cannot and must not invoice for VAT. A taxable writer is not obliged to collect VAT on royalties or other fees paid by publishers or others overseas. In practice, agents usually collect VAT for the registered author.

Remit to Customs

The taxable writer adds up the VAT which has been paid on taxable inputs, deducts it from the VAT received and remits the balance to Customs. Business with HM Customs is conducted through the local VAT Offices of HM Customs, which are listed in local telephone directories, except for tax returns which are sent direct to the Customs and Excise VAT Central Unit, Alexander House, 21 Victoria Avenue, Southend on Sea, Essex ss99 1AA.

Taxable at the standard rate

Rent of certain commercial premises

Advertisements in newspapers, magazines, journals and periodicals

Agent's commission (including commission relating to monies from non-EEC countries; monies from other EEC countries are zero-rated)

Accountant's fees

Solicitor's fees re. business matters

Agency services (typing, copying, etc.)

Word processors, typewriters and stationery

Artists' materials

Photographic equipment

Tape recorders and tapes

Hotel accommodation

Motor-car expenses

Telephone

Theatres and concerts

Taxable at the zero or special rate

Books (zero)

Periodicals (zero)

Coach rail and air travel (zero)

From 1 April 1994 electricity (8%)

Gas (8%)

Other fuel (8%)

Exempt

Rent of non-commercial premises

Council Tax

Postage

Services supplied by unregistered persons

Subscriptions to the Society of Authors, PEN, NUJ, etc.

Wages and salaries

Insurance

Taxicab fares

Outside the scope of VAT
PLR (Public Lending Right)
Profit shares
Investment income

NB This list is not exhaustive

Separate rules apply for motor fuel. You can reclaim all the VAT paid on fuel, but must add into your sales an agreed scale charge based on the engine capacity of the car. It is worth noting in passing that you can sometimes be better off leaving fuel out of the equation completely, reclaiming no VAT at all. VAT cannot be reclaimed on the purchase of cars (unless you run a driving school or taxi business as a day job). Vans are a different proposition. Customs and Excise define a van according to the size of its rear window.

Accounting

A taxable writer is obliged to account to HM Customs & Excise at quarterly intervals. Returns must be completed and sent to VAT Central Unit by the dates shown on the return. Penalties can be charged if the returns are late.

It is possible to account for the VAT liability under the Cash Accounting Scheme (Note 731), whereby the author accounts for the output tax when the invoice is paid or royalties etc. are received. The same applies to the input tax, but as most purchases are probably on a 'cash basis', this will not make a considerable difference to the author's input tax. This scheme is only applicable to those with a taxable turnover of less than £350,000 and therefore is available to the majority of authors. The advantage of this scheme is that the author does not have to account for VAT before receiving payment, thereby relieving the author of a cashflow problem.

It is also possible to pay VAT by nine estimated direct debits, with a final balance at the end of the year.

Registration

A writer will be given a VAT registration number which must be quoted on all VAT correspondence. It is the responsibility of those registered to inform those to whom they make supplies of their registration number. The taxable turnover limit which determines whether a person who is registered for VAT may apply for cancellation of registration is at present £44,000.

Voluntary Registration

A writer whose turnover is below the limits may apply to register. If the writer is paying a relatively large amount of VAT on taxable inputs – agent's commissions, accountant's fees, equipment, materials, or agency services, etc. – it may make a significant improvement in the net income to be able to offset the VAT on these inputs. An author who pays relatively little VAT may find it easier, and no more expensive, to remain unregistered.

Fees and Royalties

A taxable writer must notify those to whom he makes supplies of the Tax Registration Number at the first opportunity. One method of accounting for and paying VAT on fees and royalties is the use of multiple stationery for 'self-billing', one copy of the royalty statement being used by the author as the VAT invoice. A second method is for the recipient of taxable outputs to pay fees, including authors' royalties, without VAT. The taxable author then renders a tax invoice for the VAT element and a second payment, of the VAT element, will be made. This scheme is cumbersome but will involve only taxable authors. Fees and royalties from abroad will count as payments for exported services and will accordingly be zero-rated.

Agents and Accountants

A writer is responsible to HM Customs for making VAT returns and payments. Neither an agent nor an accountant nor a solicitor can remove the responsibility, although they can be helpful in preparing and keeping VAT returns and accounts. Their professional fees or commission will, except in rare cases where the adviser or agent is himself unregistered, be taxable at the standard rate and will represent some of a writer's taxable inputs. They will also be allowed as an expense for income tax purposes.

Self-billing

If your publisher operates a self-billing scheme for VAT you should not raise a VAT invoice. Remember to include the VAT you receive as output tax.

Sale of Business Assets

If you have sold business fittings, equipment or vehicles (but not private cars) during the quarter, check that you have charged VAT on the disposal. The sum you end up with should be split between you and Customs & Excise, which gets 7/47 of the price; you keep the rest. The Customs & Excise share should be added to your output tax for the quarter.

Entertainment

The basic rule is that business entertainment is not allowable.

Income Tax – Schedule D

An unregistered writer can claim some of the VAT paid on taxable inputs as a business expense allowable against income tax. However, certain taxable inputs fall into categories which cannot be claimed under the income tax regulations. A taxable writer who has already offset VAT on inputs cannot charge it as a business expense for the purposes of income tax.

Certain Services From Abroad

A taxable author who resides in the United Kingdom and who receives certain services from abroad must account for VAT on those services at the appropriate tax rate on the sum paid for them. Examples of the type of services concerned include: services of lawyers, accountants, consultants, provisions of information and copyright permissions.

INHERITANCE TAX

Inheritance Tax was introduced in 1984 to replace Capital Transfer Tax, which had in turn replaced Estate Duty, the first of the death taxes of recent times. Paradoxically, Inheritance Tax has reintroduced a number of principles present under the old Estate Duty.

The general principle now is that all legacies on death are chargeable to tax (currently at 40 per cent), except for legacies between spouses, which are exempt, as is the first £200,000 of legacies to others. Gifts made more than seven years before death are exempt, but those made within this period are taxed on a sliding scale. No tax is payable at the time of making the gift. In addition, each individual may currently make gifts of up to £3000 in any year and these will be considered to be exempt. A further exemption covers any number of annual gifts not exceeding £250 to any one person. If the £3000 is not utilized in one year it, or the unused balance, can be given in the following year (but no later), plus that year's exemptions. Gifts out of income, which means those which do not reduce one's capital or one's living standards, are also exempt if they are part of one's normal expenditure.

At death all assets are valued: they will include any property, investments, life policies, furniture and personal possessions, bank balances and, in the case of authors, the value of their copyrights. All, with the sole exception of copyrights, are capable (as assets) of accurate valuation, and, if necessary, can be turned into cash. The valuation of copyright is, of course, complicated, and frequently gives rise to difficulty. Except where it is bequeathed to the owner's husband or wife, very real problems can be left behind by the author.

Experience has shown that a figure based on two to three years' past royalties may be proposed by the Inland Revenue in their valuation of copyright. However, it all depends. If a book is running out of print or if, as in the case of educational books, it may need revision at the next reprint, these factors must be taken into account. In many cases the fact that the author is no longer alive and able to make personal appearances, or provide publicity or write further works will result in lower or slower sales. Obviously this is an area in which help can be given by the publishers, and in particular one needs to know what their future intentions are, what stocks of the books remain, and what likelihood there will be of reprinting.

There is a further relief available to authors who have established that they have been carrying on a business, normally assessable under Case II of Schedule D, for at least two years prior to death. It has been possible to establish that copyrights are treated as business property and, in these circumstances, 'business property relief' is available. This relief at present is at 100 per cent on business assets including copyrights, so that the tax saving can be quite substantial. The Inland Revenue may wish to be assured that the business is continuing and consideration should therefore be given to the appointment, in the author's will, of a literary executor, who should be a qualified business person, or, in certain circumstances, the formation of a partnership between the author and his or her spouse, or other relative, to ensure that it is established that the business is continuing after the author's death.

If the author has sufficient income, consideration should be given to building up a fund to cover future liabilities. One of a number of ways would be to take out a whole life assurance policy which is assigned to the children, or other beneficiaries, the premiums on which are within the annual exemption of £3000. The capital sum payable on the death of the assured is exempt from inheritance tax.

A Literary Executor?

The role of an executor is to collect in a deceased person's assets, meet any outstanding liabilities and then retain or distribute the balance as directed by the will. The term 'literary executor' has no precise meaning in law but it is generally understood to mean an executor whose responsibilities are limited to the literary assets of the deceased's estate and it would follow, therefore, that his duties end once those assets have been distributed.

However, many authors intend that their 'literary executor' should, in effect, act as a trustee of their literary assets, including manuscripts and copyrights, and manage them for an indefinite period for the beneficiaries. This may be either because the beneficiaries are too numerous or too young to fulfil this role themselves or because, despite the competence of the beneficiaries, the person chosen has particular experience of publishing. Where this is your intention you should bequeath all manuscripts, whether published or not, and any copyrights not previously assigned to others to the 'literary executor' in trust for named beneficiaries, with or without a time limit on the duration of the trust.

Anyone wondering how best to order his affairs for tax purposes should consult an accountant with specialized knowledge in this field. Experience shows that a good accountant is well worth his fee, which, incidentally, so far as it relates to matters other than personal tax work, is an allowable expense.

———

Queries on taxation may be addressed to A. P. Kernon, c/o The Writer's Companion, 45 Islington Park Street, London N1 1QB.

Proofreading

THE ULTIMATE RESPONSIBILITY for checking proofs rests with the author.

Make an absolute minimum of alterations, as distinct from correcting misprints. Making alterations at proof stage is wasteful in time and effort, and is very expensive. An author is liable to be charged for all corrections in excess of the allowance agreed in his contract. (Remember this allowance is a proportion of the typesetting cost and not a proportion of the length of the book.) Alterations may cause delay and can result in new errors being introduced. They can also have knock-on effects throughout the book on cross-references and an index.

The author normally receives page proofs – that is, the type matter will already have been divided into numbered pages. The proofs will not reflect the quality of the finished book, especially if, as is often the case, they take the form of photocopies.

It is a great help in working out the cost of the corrections if you mark the proofs with red ink for printer's errors (that is, any deviation from the typescript as it was sent to him); and blue or black ink for your alterations or additions.

The following paragraph shows the most common correction marks and how they can be employed. Where more than one correction is required on the same line, marginal marks can be divided between left and right margin space logically and as appropriate. All corrections (margin marks) should be followed by a diagonal line (/) to indicate that the correction is finished.

INTRODUCTION

Straddling the top of Europe, the Nordic races have been for much of their history culturally sheltered on the south and west by the sea and on the east by the forest and swamps which separated Finland from the inhabited areas of Russia. Naturally, they tended to look inwards and, irrespective of political differences to develop a common set of values. Down the centuries, the achievements of one country – from the Icelandic sagas to the Swedish invention of the ball-bearing – were adopted by the others as part of the Nordic creative genius. So, today, a Swede will take pride in a Finn's design, a Norwegian looks to Swedish technology to multiply wealth from North Sea oil and a Dane acknowledges the mid night sun as part of his heritage, even though geographically he is ill suited ever to see it.

Text Marks	Function	Margin Marks
¢label	Delete character(s), word(s) or line	
⋏	Insert character(s), word(s)	
⋏	Insert space	
⋏	Insert comma	
⋏	Insert full stop	
⋏	Insert colon	
⋏	Insert semicolon	
⋏	Insert apostrophe, quotation marks	
mid night	Close up space	
Naturally	Delete character(s), punctuation, words, etc., and close up	

text	Retain character(s), word(s), punctuation which have been marked for deletion	(stet)/
INTRODucTION	Change lower case (lc) character(s) to upper case (caps)	(caps) or ≡/
EUrope	Change to lower case, not caps	(l.c.)
FOUNDED	Set in small caps	(s.c.) or =/
Russia	Wrong face/typesize	(w.f.)
sagas	Set in italics	(itals) or ⊔⊔/
INTRODUCTION	Set in bold	(bold) or ⌣⌣/
text	Set in bold italics	(bold itals) or ≈/
text	Set in roman, not itals	(roms) or ⌐/
⌐——⌐	Run on text (no new line or para.)	(R/o)
∽	Transpose characters or words	(trs) or ∽/
3 2 4 1 (over words numbering them in order)	Transpose words (when above method not easy to use)	1 2 3 4 (listings new order required)
⌐text	Take over to next line	(t/o)/
text⌐	Take back to previous line (commonly used to correct widows)	(t/b)/
text⌐text	Take over to start new para.	(N.P.)/
	or commonly in front of text	
⌐text	Indent	⌐/
←⌐text	Cancel indent	⌐/
text	Correct horizontal alignment	=/
‖text	Correct vertical alignment	‖/

Books for Writers

REFERENCES:

Bartletts Quotations (Macmillan)
The Routledge Dictionary of Quotations, Robert Andrews
The Penguin Dictionary of Modern Humorous Quotations, compiled by Fred
  Metcalf
The Writer's Handbook, ed. Barry Turner (Macmillan)
The Good English Guide – English Usage in the 1990s, Godfrey Howard
  (Macmillan)
The Oxford Dictionary for Writers and Editors
The Oxford Dictionary of Quotations
The Times English Styles and Usage (Times Books)
Writers' & Artists' Yearbook (A. & C. Black)

LITERARY GUIDES:

Mother Tongue – The English Language, Bill Bryson (Penguin)
The Cambridge Encyclopedia of the English Language, David Crystal
The English Language, David Crystal (Penguin)
Oxford Companion To English Literature, ed. Margaret Drabble
The Complete Plain Words, Sir Ernest Gowers (HMSO)
The Story of English, Robert McCrum, William Cran and Robert
  MacNeil (Faber)
The State of the Language, Christopher Ricks and Leonard Michaels
  (Faber)
Macmillan Guide To Modern World Literature, ed. Martin Seymour Smith

The Joy of Words, Fritz Spiegel (Elm Tree Books)
Best Sellers, John Sutherland (RKP)
Victorian Fiction, John Sutherland (Macmillan)
The Cambridge Guide to Literature in English
Oxford Companion To Classical Literature

PUBLISHING:

The Book Book, Anthony Blond (Cape)
Publishing Agreements, Charles Clark (Butterworths)
A History of British Publishing, John Feather (Routledge)
An Author's Guide to Publishing, Michael Legat (Robert Hale)
Understanding Publishing Contracts, Michael Legat (Robert Hale)
Publishing – The Future, ed. Peter Owen (Peter Owen)
Publishing Now, ed. Peter Owen (Peter Owen)
Cassell & Publishers Association – Directory of Publishing

THEORY AND PRACTICE OF WRITING:

The Way to Write Short Stories, Michael Baldwin (Elm Tree Books)
Writing with Precision, Jefferson D. Bates (Acropolis Books)
How to Write and Illustrate Children's Books and Get Them Published,
   by Bicknell and Trotman (Macdonald Orbis)
Word Power – A Guide to Creative Writing, Julian Birkett (A. & C. Black)
The Author's Handbook, David Bolt (Piatkus)
Writing a Novel, John Braine (Methuen)
Becoming a Writer, Dorothea Brande (Macmillan)
Breaking into Print: A Practical Guide for Would-be Authors, Denis Brinig
   and Jan Woudhuysen (Wildwood House)
Authors by Profession, Vols I and II, by Victor Bonham Carter
Writing for Children, Margaret Clark (A. & C. Black)
Writing About Travel, Morag Campbell (A. & C. Black)
Writing for the Teenage Market, Ann de Gale (A. & C. Black)
Saroyan Memoirs, ed. Brian Darwent (Minerva)
The Craft of Novel Writing, Dianne Doubtfire (Allison & Busby)
The Way to Write (Basic Manual), John Fairfax and John Moat (Elm Tree
   Books)

Author! Author! (anthology of the *Author*), ed. Richard Findlater (Faber)
How to Write a Damn Good Novel, James N. Frey (Papermac)
30 Ways to Make Money in Writing, Jennie Hawthorne (Rosters)
Writing Crime Fiction, H. R. F. Keating (A. & C. Black)
The Way to Write Novels, Paddy Kitchen (Elm Tree Books)
The Way to Write for Children, Tessa Krailing (Allison & Busby)
How to Write Crime Novels, Isobel Lambot (A & B Writers Guide)
How to Write Historical Novels, Michael Legat (Allison & Busby)
The Nuts and Bolts of Writing, Michael Legat (Robert Hale)
Plotting the Novel, Michael Legat (Robert Hale)
Non-fiction Books: A Writer's Guide, Michael Legat (Robert Hale)
Writing for Pleasure and Profit, Michael Legat (Robert Hale)
Creative Editing, Mary Mackie (Victor Gollancz)
How to Write Articles for Profit and PR, Mel Lewis (Kogan Page)
Writing for a Living, Ian Linton (Kogan Page)
How to Write for Publication, Chriss McCallum (How To Books)
A Practical Guide to Writing for Children in Australia and New Zealand, Sally
    Farrell Odgers (Kangaroo Press, Australia)
Writing Erotic Fiction, Derek Parker (A. & C. Black)
The Way to Write Crime, Lisanne Radice (Elm Tree Books)
Writing Popular Fiction, Rona Randall (A. & C. Black)
The Whole Voyald and Other Stories, William Saroyan (Faber & Faber)
The Assyrian and Other Stories, William Saroyan (pp. 18–39, 'The Writer
    on Writing') (Faber & Faber)
I Used to Believe I Had Forever Now I'm Not so Sure, William Saroyan
    (Cassell)
The Craft of Writing Romance, Jean Saunders (Allison & Busby)
Successful Writing, George Ryley Scott (Lloyd Cole)
How to Write for Teenagers, David Silwyn (Allison & Busby)
Write a Successful Novel, Frederick E. Smith & Moe Sherrard-Smith
    (Escreet Publications)
The Fiction Writers' Handbook, Nancy Smith (Piatkus)
Writing Your Life Story, Nancy Smith (Piatkus)
How to Make Money out of Writing, G. Stevenson (Wildwood House)
The Book Writers' Handbook, Gordon Wells (Allison & Busby)
Writers' Questions Answered, Gordon Wells (Allison & Busby)

Writing, the Hobby that Pays, Gordon Wells (EPB Publishers)
How to Write Tales of Horror, Science Fiction & Fantasy, ed. J. N.
  Williamson (Robinson Books)
Writing the Blockbuster Novel, Albert Zuckerman (Little Brown)

PUBLIC LENDING RIGHT:

A Guide to Public Lending Right, Brigid Brophy (Gower)
PLR Loans: A Statistical Exploration – Part 2, Anne Hasted, Roger Mead,
  Eleanor Allan and Laura New (available from PLR Office)
PLR in Practice, John Sumsion (available from PLR Office)

WORD PROCESSORS/DESKTOP PUBLISHING:

Word Processing Secrets for Writers, Michael A. Banks and Ansen Dibell
  (Writer's Digest)
Writing on Disk, Jane Dorner (John Taylor Book Ventures)
The Writer and the Word Processor, Ray Hammond (Coronet)
The Desktop Publishing Companion, Graham Jones (Sigma Press)
The Writer's Guide to Desktop Publishing, Kath Lang (Academic Press)
Into Print, Susan Quilliam and Ian Grove-Stephenson (BBC)
Editing for Desktop Publishing, John Taylor and Shirley Hale (John Taylor
  Book Ventures)
Desktop Publishing, Kirsty Wilson-Davies, Joseph St John Bate and
  Michael Barnard (Blueprint)

SELF-PUBLISHING:

The Writer's Guide to Self-Publication, Charlie Bell (Dragonfly Press)
So You Want to be Published, Roísín Conroy (Attic Press)
How to Publish Your Poetry, Peter Finch (Allison & Busby)
How to Publish Yourself, Peter Finch (Allison & Busby)
How to Publish a Newsletter, Graham Jones (How To Books)
Brief Guide to Self-Publishing, Ann Kritzinger (Scriptmate Editions)
Marketing for Small Publishers, Keith Smith (Inter-Action Inprint)
How to Publish a Book, Robert Spicer (How To Books)
Publishing Your Own Books, John Wynne-Tyson (Centaur Pres)

MULTIMEDIA:

Being Digital, Nicholas Negroponte (Hodder & Stoughton)

JOURNALISM:

How to Write Stories for Magazines, Donna Baker (Allison & Busby)
Handbook of Magazine Article Writing, ed. Jean M. Fredette (Writer's Digest)
The Way to Write Magazine Articles, John Hines (Hamish Hamilton)
1,000 Markets for Freelance Writers, Robert Palmer (Piatkus)
The Craft of Writing Articles, Gordon Wells (Allison & Busby)
The Magazine Writer's Handbook, Gordon Wells (Allison & Busby)

POETRY:

The Way to Write Poetry, Michael Baldwin (Hamish Hamilton)
The Poetry Business, Peter Finch (Seren Books)

FILM:

Films, Books and Plays, A. G. S. Enser (André Deutsch)
Adventures in the Screen Trade, William Goldman (Warner Books)
Macmillan International Film Encyclopedia, Ephraim Katz
The Story of Cinema, Vols I and II, David Shipman (Hodder & Stoughton)
Biographical Dictionary of Film, David Thomson (André Deutsch)

THEATRE:

Cambridge Guide to Theatre, ed. Martin Banham
Cambridge Illustrated History of British Theatre, Simon Trussler
Oxford Illustrated History of the Theatre, John Russell Brown
The Theatre, A Concise History, Phyllis Hartnoll

PRIZES AND AWARDS:

Guide to Literary Prizes, Grants and Awards (Society of Authors/Book Trust)

TV AND RADIO:

How to Make it in Films & TV, Robert Angell (How To Books)
The Way to Write Radio Drama, William Ash (Elm Tree Books)
Writing for Radio, Colin Haydn Evans (Allison & Busby)
Debut on Two – A Guide to Writing for Television, Phillipa Giles and Vicky
   Licorish (BBC)
The Craft of TV Copywriting, John Harding (Allison & Busby)
Writing for Radio, Rosemary Horstmann (A. & C. Black)
How to Make Money Scriptwriting, Julian Friedmann (Boxtree)
Writing for Television, Gerald Kelsey (A. & C. Black)
Writing for the BBC, Norman Longmate (BBC)
The Way to Write for Television, Eric Paice (Elm Tree Books)
The Craft of Writing TV Comedy, Lew Schwarz (Allison & Busby)
Television Drama – An Introduction, David Self (Macmillan)
How to Write for Television, William Smethurst (How To Books)
Notes on Radio Drama (available from: Script Editor, BBC Radio Drama,
   Broadcasting House, London WIA IAA)

CONTRACTS AND COPYRIGHT:

A Handbook of Copyright in British Publishing Practice, J.M. Cavendish and
   Kate Pool (Cassell)
Publishing Agreements, A Book of Precedents, Charles Clark (Butterworths)
Media Law, Geoffrey Robertson, QC, and Andrew Nicol (Penguin)
Authors and Owners: The Invention of Copyright, Mark Rose (Harvard)
The Law of Copyright and Rights in Performances, (leaflet available from The
   British Copyright Council, Copyright House, 29–33 Berners Street,
   London WIP 4AA)

LIBEL:

Law and the Media, Tom Crone (Heinemann)
Public Scandal, Odium and Contempt, David Hooper (Coronet)
Grotesque Libels, Adam Raphael (Corgi)

MAGAZINES:

The Author (Society of Authors)
Chapmans
The Electronic Author (Society of Authors)
Metropolitan
Quartos
Small Press Listings
Writers' News (Writers' Guild)
Writers' Monthly

Index

H

Hampstead Theatre 132,
    143, 145, 147
Haran, Maeve 27
Hare, David 131
Harlequin Mills & Boon
    30–32, 34, 35,
    39–40, 256
HarperCollins 9, 10, 15,
    35, 229
Harvey, Jonathan 132
Harvill Press 200
Hat Trick 103, 188
Hawking, Stephen 27
Heggie, Iain 132
Heinemann 229, 257
Hemingway, Ernest 60
HMB *see* Harlequin Mills
    & Boon
Ho, Ming 172, 179–180
Hodder Headline 9, 15,
    35, 37
Hodge, John 161
Hooper, David (author
    of *Public Scandal,
    Odium and Contempt*)
    267
Hopkins, Adam 65, 66
HTV 174
Hull Truck 131, 141
Hunter, David 100
Hurley, Elizabeth 159
Hutchinson 200

I

ICM 155, 156
IMPACT 159
Imrie, Marilyn 99, 100
*I'm Sorry I Haven't A
    Clue* 102

Independent Producers
    see BBC Radio
Independent Radio
    Drama Producers 93
Indexing 8, 15, 210–221
Information Retrieval 13
Informed Disputes
    Settlement 24
Intellectual Property
    Policy Directorate,
    British Copyright
    queries 255
International Federation
    of Reprographic
    Rights Organisations
    206
International Standard
    Book Number 206
International Standards
    Organisation 207
Iota 199
Irving, David 265
ISBN *see* International
    Standard Book
    Number
ITV 168, 169, 177, 183,
    189
    Network Centre 170,
    171
    Network Centre,
    Controller of Drama
    and Entertainment
    188
    Networking
    Committee 187
    Schools' Programmes
    175

J

James, P. D. 54
James-Moore, Jonathan
    102

Jameson, Derek 257
Jennings, Paul 42
J. F. Sports 82
John, Elton 258
Johnson, Catherine
    174–175
Johnson, Terry 132, 136
Joseph, Michael 201
Joseph, Stephen, Theatre
    131
Joyce, Linda 260–261

K

Karr, Jillian 37
Kenny, Mary 55

L

Ladbroke 103
Langridge, Richard 175
Lawrence, Vernon 188
Lear, Edward 42
Le Carré, John 29
Le Fanu, Mark 14, 263,
    265
Le Frenais, Ian 189
Legal Aid Board 251
Leonard, Hugh 63
Levin, Bernard 268
Lewis, Roger 3
Lewis, Sinclair 51
Libel 18, 256–268
    Faulkes Committee on
    Defamation 262
Liddiment, David 188
Lister, Robin 156
Literary Review, The 89
Little Brown 37
Littlewood Arc 201
Live Theatre, Newcastle
    131, 132
Lloyd, Phyllida 132